*The History and Origin
of Language*

THE
HISTORY AND ORIGIN
OF LANGUAGE

A. S. DIAMOND, LL.D.

PHILOSOPHICAL SOCIETY

NEW YORK

First published in 1959
© *by A. S. Diamond* 1959

Printed in Great Britain

Contents

	Synopsis	page 6
1.	Introductory	9
2.	The Sentence	16
3.	The Vocabulary and the Parts of Speech in English	23
4.	The Vocabulary and the Parts of Speech in the different Languages	39
5.	The Origin of the Nouns, Adjectives and Adverbs in English	59
6.	The Origin of the Nouns, Adjectives and Adverbs in the Classical Languages	66
7.	The Origin of the Nouns, Adjectives and Adverbs in the Languages of the Simpler Communities—the Pronouns	78
8.	Grammar	93
9.	The Request for Action	111
10.	The Infinitive	123
11.	The Third Person Singular of the Aorist Indicative	130
12.	Animal Behaviour	142
13.	The History of Meaning	162
14.	The History of Meaning (continued)	173
15.	The Earliest Words	186
16.	The Earliest Words of Children	201
17.	The Larynx	209
18.	The Origin of Language as displayed in Semitic and Bantu	218
19.	The Origin of Language as displayed in Semitic and Bantu (continued)	240
20.	Theories of the Origin of Language	259
	List of Abbreviated References	276
	Index	278

Synopsis

Chapter 1. Introductory.

Chapter 2. The complete communication in language is a sentence; and there are 3 types of sentence:
 1. The request for action (or command) – e.g. 'Look!'
 2. The statement – e.g. 'George runs'.
 3. The description-statement – e.g. 'George is fast'.

The first is the simplest and most primitive, the third the most complex and advanced, judged by all standards, including that of mental development; and linguistically, comparing the first with the second, and the second with the third, we see a process of decrease in the proportion of verbs, and, firstly, increase in the proportion of nouns, and, secondly, increase in the proportion of adjectives. Furthermore, as each sentence is developed to become more precise, it is again by the addition of nouns and adjectives.

Chapter 3. If we look at the vocabulary of an Englishman (for example, Shakespeare) we see phenomena that reflect the same situation: among the commonest and most familiar words the proportion of verbs is greatest, among the less common there is an increase in the proportion of nouns and among the least used words an increase in the proportion of adjectives. And if we examine the English language from Anglo-Saxon times down to the present century, we see the same development in point of time: namely, while the vocabulary increases, there is a slow increase in the proportion of nouns and a later and more rapid increase in the proportion of adjectives and a decrease in the proportion of verbs. Adverbs are less important, and words of the other parts of speech are few. Accordingly, the increase in vocabulary is, by and large, an addition to it of nouns and their adjectives. And if we look at vocabularies of individual writers throughout the successive centuries in the history of English literature, there is again an increase in the total vocabulary of each, represented by an addition of nouns and still more of adjectives, and a corresponding reduction in the proportion of verbs.

Chapter 4. If we turn to the other languages of the world, past and present, we see the same phenomenon: as between the languages of the most backward and primitive peoples known to us, down to European languages of the present day, there is the same process of change – so that among peoples at the close of the Palaeolithic Age the verbs are approximately 50 per cent of the language, whereas in modern English they represent under 10 per cent.

Chapter 5. This process is exemplified, and its existence corroborated, by an examination of the nouns, adjectives and adverbs in the various languages, in order to see from what origin they come. In English, for example, nouns are generally formed from verbs, adjectives overwhelmingly from nouns, and adverbs almost always from adjectives.

Chapters 6 and 7. The same is true of the classical Indo-European and Semitic languages, and the languages of primitive peoples. The 'roots' are verbs. It is also very noticeable that the roots are almost everywhere of the same form, namely CVC or CVCV and sometimes CV, where C is a consonant, and V a vowel, usually short and predominantly A. Accordingly the roots, as far as we can trace them, are not merely of the same function (namely verbs) but also of the same general form. Looking down the vista of the millennia we get a glimpse of languages receding to a smaller and smaller vocabulary, where the earliest words that we can envisage are a few verbs, all of the form CVC(V).

Chapters 8 and 9. Grammar presents such unlimited variety between one language and another that it seems idle to look here for common or universal features of language – and yet there is one common and universal feature: the form of the verb signifying a command or request for action is entirely devoid of grammatical apparatus. Substantially everywhere the plain root of the verb signifies a request for action addressed to one (male) person.

Chapter 10. Only a little less common is the phenomenon that the plain root of the verb signifies the infinitive (or verbal noun) and also

Chapter 11. the 3rd person singular (masculine) of the aorist indicative of the verb.

Resuming what we have said, we see that our most primitive sentence (the request for action of one term – e.g. 'Look!') is also the origin of the vocabulary and the origin of language. As we add nouns and their adjectives to form the sentences of Type 2 and Type 3, and the more complex forms of all three, we are also witnessing the course of history of language, during which the proportion of verbs steadily diminishes and through the development of verbal nouns from requests for action, and 3rd person singular aorists from verbal nouns, the proportion of nouns and their adjectives steadily increases.

Chapter 12. All this indicates that language emerged out of requests for assistance addressed by one (male) person to another in these small local semi-nomadic groups out of which human society seems to have developed. If so, can we hazard a guess, what were the earliest meanings of these requests? It is suggested that they were requests for assistance to do what a man could not do for himself – requests for action requiring the maximum of bodily effort – requests to break, cut, smash, kill, destroy. If we now look at language from the farther end, and study the developing, pre-human animal behaviour, we notice the overwhelming importance of movement to the mind: how movement attracts the attention. This is one psychological foundation of the origin of language in verbs. And the most important movements and sounds to an animal are the movements and sounds made by its fellows. We also see plainly among the apes requests for assistance; and also their propensity for smashing and breaking to pieces. And in so far as their activity consists in *making*, it is making by breaking – e.g. making tools by breaking or cutting materials naturally to hand.

Chapters 13 *and* 14. Another way to trace the original meanings of language is through semantic history – through the history of the changes of meaning in words. The chief processes of change of meaning, it is submitted, lead us back to the same origin, that is, to meanings of vaguer but more emotive content, signifying maximum human effort.

Chapter 15. The solution of the problem, what were the forms of the earliest words, is assisted by the physiological study of speech-sounds. Various tests suggest that the easiest and earliest speech-sounds were syllables consisting of a consonant followed by the vowel A, and that that consonant was usually either a plosive or a nasal (e.g. bă, dă, mă, etc.).

Chapter 16. The earliest words of children are still of the same form – single plosive or nasal consonants, usually followed by the vowel A, often reduplicated to form dădă, mămă, păpă, etc. These facts corroborate the view that for early man these were the easiest speech-sounds to pronounce, and for the same reason probably the earliest. Such records as have been made of the vocal sounds of chimpanzees give general support to these conclusions.

Chapter 17. There is another aspect of the study of the physiology of speech, namely the study of the larynx and its history, and the physiological relation between the use of the larynx and the forceful use of the arms. A forceful effort of the arms is accompanied by a closure of the glottis and consequently a temporary stoppage of vocal sound, and when the tense vocal cords are suddenly relaxed there tends to be a gasp of released breath. This suggests that, in the beginning, speech sound consisted of a gasp of released breath accompanying forceful use of the arms – or, in other words, that a gasp of released breath meant a forceful use of the arms. This consideration corroborates the view that, in the earliest language, a loud bă, dă, mă, pă, etc., meant maximum human effort.

Chapters 18 *and* 19. It remains to consider whether there are any languages known to us which still retain traces of an origin in verbs of the form CVCV, the vowel being A, and the consonants plosives or nasals, signifying *break, cut* and the like. It might have been thought impossible to find such. If there is one group of languages that would be more likely than any other to show its origin, it would be the Semitic; for, at least in historical times – that is, during the last four millennia – they have changed far less than any other. And indeed the Semitic languages do contain unmistakable traces of this same origin. The Bantu languages also, it is suggested, contain such traces.

Chapter 20. We end by reviewing the best-known theories of the origin of language. If the view adduced in this book is correct, there is part of the truth in most of them.

CHAPTER ONE

Introductory

Speech is a possession of mankind. No animals have it, and there are no human societies, of which we have knowledge in the past or present, so simple or primitive that they have not evolved a language elaborate and complex. Speech is the communication between individuals by means of sounds produced by the vibration of a column of air, passing between the larynx and the mouth and nostrils and coming into contact with the neighbouring parts of the throat, palate, tongue, cheeks, teeth and lips. Man's capacity to make such sounds, and to recognize and imitate them when made by others, is the raw material out of which language has been forged. His practice or habit to use this means of communication is usually termed 'speech' (French *parole*) in contradistinction to a 'language' (French *langue*) which is the sum of the speech-sounds employed in a community, together with the meanings attributed to them in that community. A community which uses a common language is known as a 'speech-community', and a language (as distinct from a dialect) is unintelligible to the members of a different speech-community as such. The sum of all languages is 'language' in its abstract sense (French *langage*).

The meaning of a group of speech-sounds is that which is communicated to the mind of the hearer through, firstly, the vibrations of sound so produced and heard, and, secondly, the context in which those sounds have been uttered by the members of that community on past occasions, and are uttered by the speaker on the particular occasion. Accordingly, though the speaker may choose to employ those sounds with a view to produce a particular meaning, the effective meaning of those sounds is in the mind of the hearer rather than the speaker.

The smallest separate unit of speech which has meaning is called a 'word'. This may consist of only one sound, but generally of a group of sounds. The minimum complete communication is a 'sentence'. For example, the three sounds making up the group of sounds 'man' together have meaning in the language of the English speech-community, and therefore constitute an English word; though by itself that word effects an incomplete communication. But the group of words 'Every man deceiveth' effects a complete communication, whether true or false, and is a sentence. All languages include both words and sentences.

Languages are commonly divided into dialects, each spoken by a section of the speech-community occupying a portion of its territory, so that in one dialect the whole set of speech-sounds of the language, and especially the vowels, may be slightly different from that in another, or different grammatical forms or different words may be employed, or the same words may have different meanings. But there are many other divisions of a speech-community besides the speakers of its dialects. For example, a social group having a common and distinct interest, such as a common trade or calling, may use words not used by the other speakers of the same language, such as the names of specialized tools, processes or conceptions, or may use and understand the same words with a special meaning; and to some extent among civilized nations, and to a larger extent among the simpler peoples, words are employed by one sex and not by the other. These and suchlike divisions have been called 'langues particulières' by French writers. Then there is the 'standard (or common) language', sometimes originating in the neighbourhood of the seat of government, to which a growing part of the population resorts from time to time, relying for favour on speaking the dialect of the mighty. This may become the accepted speech of a widening social class, like the 'standard English' of south-east England, moderating the local dialects. But there are wide differences in the vocabulary (or set of words) and the pronunciations, not only between the districts, callings, social classes and sexes, but also between the age-groups; and not only the slang but the imperfections of childhood speech in grammar and pronunciation may be perpetuated in a rising generation. Indeed no two persons use wholly the same words or the same pronunciation.

The rise of literature – written speech – has created or stressed some features of language. At first, writing recorded for the most part what was already being spoken. It chiefly contained laws and other public records, in the language of the day. So, written records in Anglo-Saxon England begin with the Laws of Aethelberht, King of Kent, written in the language of their day. But poetry (that is to say, song) was also recorded in writing, and there had long been an oral language of song. Indeed an oral language of song is to be found among some of the most primitive peoples of all mankind: even some aboriginal tribes of Australia have nouns and adjectives only used in song.[1] Speech early becomes an art as well as a means of social activity, and it is not from yesterday that the artistic soul of man finds beauty in words as well as in music and dance, and the speaker loves to show in words the skill that others have in the making of weapons and the hunt. So, when the grand tradition of written English poetry opens with Beowulf, and the poetry of the ancient Greeks with Homer, the language of both is seen to be a long-developed language of song, containing much of traditional nouns and adjectives and other literary usages, which had never formed part of the speech of every day. As the use of writing spreads and develops, it records in prose, as in verse, language that is never wholly the speech of every day. In an extreme case a spoken language may never be recorded in literature, as, for example, till the last century literature scorned the Finnish tongue. Conversely, a literary language may cease to be spoken, and in modern Greece and Southern India the conservatism of a literary tradition may retain and separate the written from the spoken tongue. Religion is the greatest of conservative forces, and may long retain language-forms whose meaning is lost.[2] In Christian Abyssinia the priest can read Ge'ez, the dead classical Semitic language of the sacred scriptures and liturgy, but he cannot understand it; and in China the Buddhist priest does not understand the Pali of the Buddhist canon. Vast numbers of Roman Catholics and Jews do not understand the Latin and Hebrew of their prayers.

But these are extreme instances of the differences between written and spoken language. It is more important to notice the common differences. Written speech is more artistic and more precise; it excludes the fragments of sentences, the slang, the not-yet accepted words, grammatical forms, syntax and meanings of today that may become the accepted language of tomorrow. It is the more important to make allowances for the differences between speech and literature because we must learn from the latter the languages of the past. Even the languages of the simpler peoples around us must be learned by

[1] For an example, see *J.R.A.I.*, vol. lxxvii, part ii (1947), p. 133.
[2] A phenomenon not, however, limited to literate peoples. African tribes often use for religious purposes words whose meaning has been lost. And the Arabic-speaking Jew of Morocco orally translates the Hebrew Pentateuch into an Arabic whose words are often obsolete and unknown.

most of us from dictionaries, grammars and texts that others have left behind. And even the spoken language of our own country and time is best learned from the generous, undoubted texts of contemporary literature, once we have satisfied ourselves of the relations between written and spoken language.

But the vast bulk of the world's population was, at least until the beginning of the present century, everywhere and at all times wholly illiterate, and we seek the nature and origin of language in the days before man had evolved a written record. It is therefore necessary to notice that the common notions of the nature of language are derived from literature, and not from speech. Most kinds of advanced literature – especially didactic literature – are unilateral speech: the one, the writer, is always the speaker, and the other, the reader, is always the listener. From this situation derive the familiar definitions of language as 'the means of expression of human thought'[1]; 'the expression of thought by means of speech sounds'[2]; 'outward manifestations of inward workings of the mind'[3]; 'significant sound, the outward embodiment and expression, however imperfect, of thought'.[4]

These phrases fail to express the chief facets and functions of language. Speech is a bodily habit. In the words of Plato in the *Cratylus*, 'Speech is an action, is it not? A kind of action concerned with things.' It is no unilateral process but a play between two persons, now from the one side and now from the other. The meaning, as we have said, is in the mind of the hearer, rather than the speaker. The meaning of the spoken word is to be derived partly from the physical context in which it is spoken on the particular occasion. Speech is not so much the instrument by which the inward workings of the mind are manifested: rather it is 'the instrument by which human behaviour in society is initiated and fostered'.[5] It is 'the necessary means of communion; it is the one indispensable instrument for creating the ties of the moment, without which unified social action is impossible'.[6] Man speaks to make an impression upon his fellows, and language is the means whereby he enlists the aid of his fellows for the purpose of controlling his environment.

[1] Whitney, L. G. (1896), p. 1.
[2] Sweet, *History of Language*.
[3] Tylor.
[4] Sayce, vol. 1, p. 132. See a number of other definitions collected in De Laguna, *Speech, Its Function and Development* (1927), pp. 12 *et seq.*
[5] See Dewey, 'Psychology of Infant Language', *Psych. Rev.*, i (1894); *Context and Thought* (Univ. of California Publications in Philosophy, xii, 3 (1931)).
[6] Malinowski in *The Meaning of Meaning*, p. 310.

Indeed the definition of language as 'the means of expression of human thought' is but a pale reflection even of the function of language in regard to the workings of the mind. Many have doubted whether thought is even possible without language, and have urged that thought is but silent speech. It is at least clear that a new idea or concept, though it may be achieved in some measure before it is expressed in language, could never be retained, much less handed down to others or furthered, except by its means. Language, therefore, must be in some sense the embodiment of all the advances in thought of all our human ancestors – a diary of their day-to-day thoughts.

But for the purpose of an approach to the subject of this enquiry, there are perhaps three aspects of language more necessary to appreciate than any others. The first is that language is no physical entity with an independent existence of its own, but consists merely of types of sounds, uttered and heard by men, which take their meaning from circumstances outside itself. The second is that language is forever changing. The third is its communally organic character.

The first two of these aspects are self-evident, but we least remember them. Everywhere, in all languages, we find change. The grammar changes, the form of the word, the meaning changes: ultimately all change. Yet we are conscious of the smallest minutiae of the common language of our day. Language is the greatest social accomplishment and asset of each of us. We speak mainly to impress and enlist the aid of others. We know the importance and necessity of producing the fit word for each purpose and occasion. The shade of difference of meaning between one word or phrase and another is often so delicate as hardly to be capable of definition in speech, and only to be sensed by a native member of the same speech-community with a similar cultural background. The fit word may open any door: the wrong word may stamp the speaker as an ignoramus or impostor and 'not one of us'. We rightly attribute to the use of unfit speech our failure to obtain our ends on a particular occasion. It is not for nothing that, in the days of magic, the success or failure of any act, where success is a matter of chance, is put down to the use of the fit or unfit word, and ceremonial phrases are handed down from generation to generation. It is not for nothing that in the early days of religion the devotee prays 'Teach me what words to use to gain Thy forgiveness', and thinks it vital to know the name of a God, or, on the other hand, deadly to speak it; or that the language of religious ritual remains long after the meaning is lost. It is not for nothing that in the early days of philosophy there is confusion between distinctions of language and distinctions in the things that language represents, so that in Plato and even in Aristotle and even today notions of the nature of objects in the physical world are often shaped by notions of the nature of the words used to express them. But these views of language, necessary for practical affairs, are remote from its true nature. The only physical entities involved are man and his environment.

If this is so, and if all is change, what is the use of searching for the origins of language? Our chief hope lies in the third aspect of language – that it is communally organic. To help us to understand what this means, let us use the analogy of the law. Law is above all things communally organic. It is, within its sphere, the instrument by which a whole community is organized and works; it is also the expression of that working organization. The law and its rules must suit the needs and have the approval of the whole community if it is to be observed; and every facet of the communal life determines that approval and shapes that law. So with language: language, within its sphere, is the instrument by which a whole community is organized and works, and it is also the expression of that working organization. We can speak of the law of England, and the language of England, in a sense in which we cannot, for example, speak of the music or painting of England or the religion of England. Each of us, in order to be understood, must speak in the language of our speech-community. We may from time to time dare to use a word or phrase which appears to us new and attractive, but it must be, as it were, within the field of the language, if it is to be understood. We must use familiar words with their familiar meanings, or words of a form accepted and familiar and approved, sounding well in the ear of the community, and sufficiently resembling other words to suggest readily their intended meaning. But the approval of a community is not obtained by chance: it is determined by innumerable circumstances common to the community—not only the sounds of its language but also the common physical surrounding circumstances that afford the context, and the common circumstances of the past. And because, over the millennia, we know the broad stages of change in man's environment and in the economics of society and man's needs, and because men speak to gain the assistance of their fellows, we may believe that the changes in language, like the changes in law, may be related to these known changes in society and environment. Hence, while language is forever changing, we may hope that it changes according to laws that can be extracted. And if it does, what rewards at the end of the search! We shall not find the history of the succession of sounds and meanings unless at the same time we find the history of the succession of the ideas represented by them. We shall not trace the advances in human language without tracing at the same time the successive advances of the human mind.

CHAPTER TWO

The Sentence

One main feature of language only comes to light when we compare it with animal cries. Like human beings, many of the higher animals utter audible sounds, and by this means are capable of communicating with their fellows and, in some measure, of doing so intentionally. But animal cries, so far as is known, always express an appeal or some other feeling. These are also among the uses of language, but language is also used to communicate facts and does so by the use of phonetic units each of which expresses a purely intellectual element. Meillet expresses this truth as follows:

'Many animals emit various sounds to various ends. Cats miaow in very different fashion according as they appeal or complain, show anger or desire. . . . But whatever be their precision and variety, these different miaowings never express anything but a desire or an appeal. They seem never to serve to communicate a fact. Human language, which uses a number of sounds nicely differentiated from each other, and to a far greater extent than any "animal-language", is distinguished from the latter by one essential characteristic – the phonetic groups that it employs do not directly serve to communicate an affective state or an appeal. Where they indirectly serve this end – and it often occurs – they do so by the use of *words*. To each notion is attached a phonetic unit, called a word, giving body to this notion in the mind of the speaker and awakening the like notion in the mind of his opposite number. However important be the part played in human language by *affective* or *active* elements,[1] the essential element in it is the intellectual, and it is by intellectual elements that feelings, appeals and commands are expressed.'[2]

Accordingly, though Darwin was right in recognizing the psychological continuity underlying the use of animal cries and some of the uses of language, he was wrong in seeing a continuity between animal

[1] That is to say, by elements expressing a state of feeling or appealing for some action.
[2] Meillet, Tom ii, p. 1.

sounds and the phonetic elements of language. Man is using a different implement derived from a different use. There is the difference in the form, for language alone has consonants; there is also the difference in the kind of meaning, derived from use for a different kind of purpose. We should add, to complete the contrast, that man, and especially the child, has also his inarticulate cries, which are distinct from his language, and resemble animal cries in their form and use.

There is another characteristic of language which indeed it shares with animal cries. Since meaning is in the mind of the hearer, who can at the same time hear other sounds besides the cry or word, and see other sights besides the caller or speaker, meaning is derived partly from the cry or word and partly from the physical context. The task, therefore, of the speaker of language is eased: he is able to rely in part on the context to convey the intended meaning. So, according to the context, 'Fire!' may mean 'the house is on fire', or 'Don't let the fire go out', or 'Shoot at the three men coming through the gate'. And yet each of these snatches of words is, in the mind of the hearer, a complete communication – that is, a sentence, which he readily expresses, if necessary, in the form of one of the sentences just mentioned. Perhaps – we shall see – that is because his mind has been built up by language, which consists of communications – that is, sentences.

Looking at these sentences, we notice one outstanding characteristic, namely that they always include a verb. This is a universal character of all sentences, the first of the fundamental characters that we meet in language.

The words composing the sentence are normally divided among a number of 'parts of speech' according to the functions which they perform in the sentence. In all languages the function of a word is partly to be recognized by the sense; in some (as in English) also by the position and form of the word; in others (as in Latin) by form rather than position. Let us construct for ourselves an English sentence by way of illustration.

Let us start with the word 'struck' – a 'verb', because it signifies action or movement. The kind of action or movement is very vague – it might be a collision, or the striking of camp or of the hour or a mere stoppage of work. The time, manner and place of the striking are unknown, though from the vowel it seems likely that it happened in the past. If we now add a 'noun'[1] or 'pronoun' and say 'George struck', or

[1] The word 'noun' is used in this book in the usual English sense as equivalent to 'substantive' and not including 'adjective'.

'he struck'. the meaning is less vague. We have made the verb more precise: the striking definitely happened in the past, and it was George (or some other male) striking, and not being struck, as we recognize from the word-order and also the form of the pronoun. Also the striking is quite different from what it would be if 'Georgina', or 'she' struck. If we expand to add another noun and a 'definite article' and say 'George struck the iron', the striking is further defined: the iron is the object of the striking, as we can tell from its order in the sentence, and it is quite a different striking from striking camp or striking work. If we now expand further by the addition of an 'adverb', and says 'George struck the iron hard' – and we can tell it is an adverb, not an adjective, because of its position – the striking is more precise, and still more precise if we add a 'preposition', indefinite article and noun, and say 'George struck the iron hard with a hammer'. It is quite a different action from striking it with a tuning-fork; and if we add an 'adjective' to 'hammer' and say 'George struck the iron hard with a heavy hammer', again the striking is more precise. It is quite a different action from striking with a light hammer. Though, therefore, the adjective 'heavy' makes more precise the kind of hammer used, like all the other words in the sentence it defines the kind of striking to which we refer.

As the sentence grows larger, and the proportion of verbs to other parts of speech progressively diminishes, the meaning of the sentence and the verb becomes progressively more precise.

But it may be said that the above analysis of the sentence results from keeping our eyes fixed throughout upon the verb, and that we might equally well, like some grammarians, have regarded the sentence from the point of view of the subject 'George'; and that, if we had, we would have seen a predicate, or message, relating to him, containing a growing amount of information, if not a growing precision. But this is not so, and such an analysis is impossible. An important type of sentence, the simplest of all, has no subject.

There are in language three types of sentence, and when reduced to their simplest form they may be exemplified in English as follows:

1. Look!
2. George runs.
3. George is fast.

The first type of sentence, in its simplest form, consists of one word, a verb alone, in what is called the second person singular of the imperative mood. But the word 'imperative' is not apt: it indicates a command, and the sentence may be a command, or an appeal or anything intermediate. The command is an infrequent use of the 'imperative'. When Mark Antony says

Friends, Romans, countrymen, lend me your ears

is he expressing a command or an appeal or something between? Certainly not a command, rather an appeal, but we cannot be sure. When a person says 'Love me, love my dog', the imperative or affective element is so deficient that we cannot call it command or entreaty, and it has almost the colourless quality of an infinitive. Let us content ourselves by describing this first type of sentence, in the most general and non-committal terms we can find, as a 'suggestion of (or request for) action'. Now it is important to notice that a suggestion of action, like a statement, is addressed to a hearer, but whereas the suggestion is of action by the hearer, the statement is, typically, a statement of action by a third person (for every person or thing in the world is a third person for this purpose, save only the speaker and hearer). Accordingly the former is the simpler of the two types of sentence: the minimum of the first type is a mere suggestion of action; the minimum of the second type is action plus the name of a third person or thing acting. Accordingly the simplest form of the first type contains only one term – action (a verb): the simplest form of the statement contains two terms – action (a verb) plus a subject noun (or pronoun). This is so in all language. The third type of sentence is the description-statement. The minimum form of this type is even less simple. It contains three terms, a noun and a verb, as before, but now an adjective also. This, then, is the first fundamental difference between these three minimum types of sentence, that the first contains verb alone; the second, verb plus noun; and the third, verb plus noun plus adjective.

The second fundamental difference which we notice between the three types of sentence is that the first alone performs directly the basic function of all language – namely, that by it man in society, through the person addressed, wields and gains control over his environment. In the statement, and still more in the description, the exercise of this function is indirect.

Thirdly, the request for action is the simplest form of mental process. It is the expression of a desire: the nearest thing in language to the interjection or call produced by an animal – to Meillet's 'désir ou appel'. It is the nearest thing in language to the operation of instinct.

The minimum features of instinctive action are a *feeling* (the affective element), a striving (the conative element) and the resulting action. In the request for action there is the affective element, which we often record, as here, by an exclamation mark, and the conative element; but now, instead of a direct striving, the speaker seeks by his *word* to bring about the action of another – Look! Hit! Kill! Run! By tools man has extended his power of action, of influencing his environment. By the social tool of speech he seeks to bring about the action of his fellow. If the request for action is completed, it is completed by the action of the hearer, which it procures. The affective element communicates itself to the hearer and renders the words appealing and persuasive and helps to bring about the action of the hearer.

On the other hand, the third type, 'George is fast', is a *thought* in the mind of the speaker – the expression of an intellectual activity. It involves observation of the event of George running, and an analysis of that event and a comparison with similar events, the running of other persons, probably at other times and places. The second type, 'George runs', may perhaps also be described as a thought. But it is certainly a very simple thought; it is a mere mental reflection of the physical event of George running at that time and place. But Type 1, 'Look', is not a thought at all in any intelligible use of that word. I may see George running and think that 'George is fast'. I may perhaps think that 'George runs'. I cannot think that 'Look!' This first type is not the expression of a thought but of a desire.

We may express the difference in another way again by saying that in the third type of sentence there is a subject (George) and a predicate – something stated of him, namely that he is fast. The second type of sentence may be regarded as containing a subject ('George') and a predicate ('runs'), though the construction seems somewhat pointless, artificial and unhelpful. It might equally be said that there is a verb or action, rendered more precise by the addition of a doer. But in the first type of sentence there is no subject and no trace of a subject.

In other words, the request for action is typically related to the environment. It is true that the request may be for action in another place or time – a request which we readily recognize as not being the simplest case. So, too, the statement may be of action in another time or place, and the description is never simply related to the environment: it always involves some intellectual analysis and a synthesis with other persons, objects or events. But the request for action is typically related to the environment. This, however, does not mean that when the request is interpreted in the light of the environment more elements are incorporated into it, so that it is no simpler than the statement. If I say to a man 'Go' or 'run', that is the whole meaning of the request, and nothing further is necessarily incorporated. This is especially true of the intransitive verbs.

As the request for action is typically related to the environment, it is typically not to be found in literature – not in history or philosophy, for example, but in speech and to a lesser degree in drama that mirrors speech. The statement is the commonest type of all, and found throughout speech and literature. The description-statement is typical of literature, and especially of advanced forms of literature, such as the novel and philosophy. We are speaking not merely of the form of the description-statement but of its substance, description.

We noticed earlier that the thought embodied in a statement became progressively less vague and more precise by the addition of non-verbs, so that the proportion of verbs to the total of words diminished. We see the same relation between the request for action, the statement and the description-statement. The minimum form of the request for action contains a greater proportion of verbs even than the minimum statement, and the latter than the description-statement. The first, in its simplest form, consists wholly of verb: the second is half verb, and the third one-third verb. We may put the matter in another way by saying that as the thought embodied in a statement becomes less vague and more precise, the sentence increases in length. In the minimum request for action we see the sentence at its simplest, and indeed in nuclear form. All language, we said, consists of both words and sentences. The minimum request for action consists of a word which is also a sentence. Yet as the thought contained in the statement can be made progressively more precise by the addition of non-verbs, so can the description, and so can the request for action – 'Strike!' 'Strike the iron!' 'Strike the iron hard!' and so forth.

The request for action retains, in practice, a certain simplicity and brevity. The statement, as it develops, becomes more varied and complex. In the more modern languages two of these sentences are often connected together by conjunctions, adverbs or relative pronouns. One form of the statement is the question, in most languages indistinguishable in form from any other statement, except perhaps by a difference in tone or word-order or an added particle or negative, or (as in Indo-European, Semitic, Polynesian and other languages) by all these.

The description-statement becomes even more varied, lengthy and complex. As we shall see, it develops out of the statement, and that is why we have given it this name. In the description-statement not only is the proportion of verbs, as we have seen, smaller than in the two former types, but in addition the verb itself has lost its force and, in its present form, namely the verb 'to be' ('George is fast') contains a minimum of action or movement. The process that has brought about this change in the verb is world-wide, and part of the fundamental process of change in language. We shall later see how and why it occurs.

These, then, are the three types of sentence and the three types of communication, and these analyses apply not merely in the English language but in language generally, and in thought generally.

CHAPTER THREE

The Vocabulary and the Parts of Speech in English

Let us now turn from the sentence to the language that it creates, and see how the characteristics of the sentence are reflected in the language.

For the sake of precision we should wish to make our test upon a language as it exists at one point of time. Language is forever changing, and the truth will be clouded for us if, for example, we take as representative of modern English the Oxford Dictionary, which exhibits much of the vocabulary of English in use at any time over the last millennium. How great must have been the changes wrought during those centuries! and how the pace of change must have quickened since, for example, the beginning of the Industrial Revolution! We can make shift to follow most of the meaning of Shakespeare, but a vast number of new words, phrases, meanings and usages have entered the language since his day, and he would have had far greater difficulty in understanding us.

We could, of course, follow a contemporary Englishman about for a number of years and record his vocabulary. Having surmounted the difficulty of accurately embodying in his utterances the references to the physical context, we would still find it necessary to test our results by the vocabulary of others so as to trace idiosyncrasies in his speech. Such a scheme is not practicable. The only alternative is to examine the vocabulary of a past English writer as we find it in the total of his works. It is plain from what has been said that, subject to certain safeguards, literature will serve our purpose as well as speech. In literature the complete sentences, almost the complete thoughts are expressed, and the immediate environment is insignificant. But there are several potential dangers. First, there may be the comparative smallness of one man's vocabulary, at least as exhibited in his written works. Secondly, we must avoid the writer who has a vocabulary partly of his own, or, as in the case of Edmund Spenser, a vocabulary containing much that is archaic and obsolete.

Let us take the vocabulary of the chief glory of our literature, Shakespeare. It is for several reasons the most suitable for our purpose. First, the vocabulary of his total works is large – approximately 14,440[1] words excluding (as we shall exclude throughout this book) all proper names. We can appreciate its size when we compare it with that of the Homeric poems (about 6,750 words),[2] of Dante's *Divina Commedia* (about 7,000),[3] of Milton's, Spenser's or Chaucer's poetical works (all about 8,000)[4] and a vocabulary of about 6,000 words in the whole of the Hebrew Old Testament.[5] Secondly, in spite of the common notion that Shakespeare did much to create modern English, it is well established that he wrote in the language of his day. Such genius has no need of solecism or archaism to express itself, and one must search for the magic beyond the form of the individual word and its immediate meaning. They are but the same as are found among his contemporaries. Nor is poetry any less suitable for our purpose than prose, for if it is to move the heart of the reader it must speak from the heart of the language. A reason no less important why Shakespeare's language serves our purpose so well is that we have at our disposal Dr Alexander Schmidt's magnificent *Shakespeare Lexicon*, which gives us, except in regard to the commonest words, every reference for every word and usage.

Let us consider the proportion between the different parts of speech in his vocabulary. This is a task somewhat different from that which we undertook when, in the previous chapter, we were considering the different types of sentence. We were then comparing the relative frequency of the verbs and the other parts of speech, not the relative

[1] The figures given in various places in the present book—for example, the proportions of the parts of speech in a number of dictionaries – are, unless the contrary is stated in the context, obtained by calculation from a large number of samples. I am satisfied of the substantial accuracy of the results. For example, the figures of Shakespeare's vocabulary in the present chapter were at first got out by the same method. Subsequently I verified them by counting all the words in Schmidt's Lexicon, and the results were substantially the same.

[2] My calculation of the contents of G. C. Crusius' *Greek and English Lexicon for Homer* (trans. by H. Smith, New Ed., London, 1876).

[3] My calculation of the contents of L. C. Blanc's *Vocabolario Dantesco* (Leipsic, 1852).

[4] My calculation of the contents (8,000 words) of Laura E. Lockwood's *Lexicon to the English Poetical Works of John Milton* (New York, 1907); of Osgood's *Concordance to the Poems of Edmund Spenser*, 1915 (8,500 words); and of Tatlock and Kennedy's *Concordance of Chaucer*, 1927 (8,000 words).

[5] My calculation of the vocabulary of Brown, Driver and Briggs' *Hebrew and English Lexicon of the Old Testament*. Leusden counted 5,642 Hebrew and Chaldee words in the Old Testament.

frequency of the *different* verbs and the *different* words of other parts of speech.

But first we must decide in what sense we shall use the term 'word'. In this book we shall speak of words, as we have been speaking of language, in their functional sense, and accordingly, for us, a word is a different word each time that it is used as a different part of speech; and, on the other hand, a verb is one word, whatever part of the verb is used. So the word 'that' when used as a conjunction is a different word from 'that' when used as an adjective, or as a pronoun, or (as in the phrase 'that much better') as an adverb. But 'gone', 'goes' and 'going' (present participle) are all the same word, whereas 'going', a noun, as in the phrase 'Stand not upon the order of your going',[1] is a different word. Words are so treated in Schmidt's *Shakespeare Lexicon*.[2]

Speaking of 'words' in this sense, we find 14,440[3] words in Schmidt's *Shakespeare Lexicon*, and the percentages of the parts of speech among them are:

Verbs	*Nouns*	*Adjs.*	*Advbs.*	*Prons.*	*Preps.*	*Conjs.*	*Intjs.*
25·5	48	19	6·6	·4	·5	·3	·3

But in the heart of Shakespeare's vocabulary – as in the vocabulary of everyone else – there is a small number of words which are used with great frequency; and, on the other hand, at its extremities is a large number of words which are rarely used. To count the whole without differentiation is to get a false picture of his language. Let us divide his vocabulary into three sections according to the frequency with which he uses the words – the first (Section A) consisting of words so commonly used that each is represented by an entry of at least 25 lines [4] in Dr Schmidt's Lexicon; the second (Section B) consisting of words of intermediate frequency, each of which is represented by an entry of between 4 and 24 lines in his Lexicon; and the third (Section C) consisting of the least-used words, each represented in the Lexicon by an entry of 3 lines or less. Of the 14,440 words in the

---

[1] *Macbeth*, III. iv. 118.
[2] Hyphenated words, of which there are about 2,125 in Shakespeare (such as *here-approach*, *cursed-blessed*, and *not-appearance*), are a borderline case. In some instances there is a difference of opinion as to whether there should be a hyphen at all. I have decided to discard them, remembering that their component words already appear elsewhere in the vocabulary, but we must be consistent in this respect when we come to other authors and dictionaries.
[3] I have arrived at these and the following figures by counting each word in Schmidt's Lexicon, and attributing each word, in almost all cases, to the part of speech to which he attributes it.
[4] I subsequently counted the number of mentions instead of the number of lines, and found no appreciable differences.

vocabulary, Section A is represented by a mere 1,625 words; Section B by 6,330 words[1]; and Section C by 6,485. Two-thirds of the words in Section C occur only once in his works. But the 1,625 words in Section A are so frequently used that they take up nearly two-thirds of all Shakespeare's writings, and these and the intermediate section (B) together take up more than nine-tenths of the whole.

Distributing the different words of each section among the various parts of speech, we find the percentage of each part of speech in each section to be as follows:

Section A – (each word occupying 25 lines or more)

Verbs	*Nouns*	*Adjs.*	*Advbs.*	*Prons.*	*Preps.*	*Conjs.*	*Intjs.*
36	36	16	6·4	1·5	2	1	0[2]

Section B – (intermediate frequency)

| 27 | 49 | 16 | 6·4 | 0 | ·5 | 0 | 0 |

Section C – (each word occupying 3 lines or less)

| 20 | 50 | 22 | 7 | 0 | 0 | 0 | ·5 |

These figures begin to be of great significance. We noticed, in the previous chapter, that the one necessary term of the sentence was the verb, and that as we moved from sentences of Type 1 (the request for action) to Type 2 (the statement), the proportion of verbs diminished, mainly by increase in the proportion of nouns, and from Type 2 to Type 3 (the description-statement) it further diminished, mainly by increase in the proportion of adjectives. At the same time all three types of sentence were developing by the addition of non-verbs. In these figures of the language of Shakespeare we notice that of the familiar words of commonest use (Section A) 36% are verbs, in Section B the percentage has dropped to 27, and among the rarest words (Section C) to only 20. Indeed, if we subdivided these sections we should find a continuation of this process of change. For example, of the words in Section B the commonest – those occupying 14-24 lines each – contain a higher proportion of verbs than those occupying 4-14 lines. And of the 1,625 words in Section A, 419 words (Section AA) are so commonly used that they each occupy over a column (66 lines) in Schmidt's Lexicon, and in total they take up one-third of Shakespeare's works. Here the percentage of verbs is still larger, and the process of change in the other parts of speech continues. Of these 419 words, 128 (Section

[1] Of which the words occupying 14-24 lines constitute only one-fifth of this section, and those occupying 4-14 lines four-fifths.
[2] To the nearest integer – i.e. less than ·5%.

PARTS OF SPEECH IN ENGLISH

AAA) are so common that each occupies over a page (132 lines) in Schmidt's Lexicon, and the process continues, as follows:

Section	Total Words	Verbs	Nouns	Adjs.	Advbs.	Prons.	Preps.	Conjs.	Intjs.
AAA	128	47	18	10	9	5	8	3	0
AA	419	38	31	15	7	3	4	2	0
A	1,625	36	36	16	6·4	1·5	2	1	0

In this table Section A includes the words in Section AA, and the latter includes Section AAA. If we exclude from AA the words in AAA, and from A the words in AA, the whole table is as follows[1]:

Section	Total Words	Verbs	Nouns	Adjs.	Advbs.	Prons.	Preps.	Conjs.	Intjs.
A^1	128	47	18	10	9	5	8	3	0
A^2	291	35	37	16	5·9	2	2·5	2	0
A^3	1,206	35	37·5	16	6·2	1·5	1·5	1	0
B	6,330	27	49	16	6·4	1·5	1·5	0	0
C	6,485	20	50	22	7	0	0	0	·5

We might even pursue this process one step further. Forty words in Shakespeare's vocabulary are so frequently used that each takes up more than 2 pages (264 lines) in the Lexicon. Of these, 21 words (52·5%) are verbs[2]; the nouns have dropped to 3 (7·5%); there are no adjectives (except the definite and indefinite articles), and the adverbs and prepositions (the latter themselves originally adverbs) together form 19·5% of the whole.

This fall in the proportion of the verbs between Sections A, B and C is not represented by an equal increase in each of the other parts of speech. First[3] comes an increase in the nouns (that is, in Sections A and B; there is hardly any increase from B to C). Later[4] comes an increase in the proportion of adjectives (Section A 16%, Section B 16%, Section C 22%). So that the picture is, first, of the verb losing ground to the noun (A^1, 47% verbs, 18% nouns; A^2 and A^3, 35% verbs, 37% and 37·5% nouns; in Section B the nouns are nearly double the number of verbs, and in Section C $2\frac{1}{2}$ times their number). At the extremities of the language, the adjectives gain ground upon the verb and also upon the noun. If we were to add to our table the 2,125 hyphenated words we spoke of earlier, this process would be carried still further, for practically none of these 'words' occur more than once; they consist almost entirely of nouns and adjectives, and the adjectives are more numerous than the nouns (58% adjectives, 41% nouns).

---

[1] AAA is called A^1; AA less AAA is A^2; the remainder of A is A^3.
[2] The verbs are: to be, bear, break, come, do, fall, go, have, hold, keep, lay, look, make, move, put, set, stand, take, turn; and shall and will.
[3] As we saw between sentences of Type 1 and Type 2.
[4] As we saw between Type 2 and Type 3.

The pronouns, prepositions and conjunctions, though frequently used in Shakespeare's vocabulary, and even important, are very few in number, and the interjections equally few and of no importance whatsoever.

The most curious process of change in the above tables is among the adverbs. Among the most common words (Section A[1]) they constitute 9% of the whole. In Section A[2] they drop quickly to 5·9%, and from that point slowly increase. We shall meet this curious little phenomenon again in other circumstances. The adverbs in Section A[1] are largely the oldest and most familiar of our adverbs (as, so, forth, thus, how, there, etc.). The increase in Section C is largely the modern spread of the form *adjective* + '*ly*', and includes a great many familiar modern adverbs which only occur once in Shakespeare.[1]

The words of Section C are interesting in several ways. For example if, as is plain, language is ever changing, here, among these rarely used words, is some of the raw material out of which additions to the language form themselves. Of these occasional words many will be weighed and found wanting, and not repeated: others will be accepted and approved and become permanent and common. For example, among words used only once in Shakespeare, including the hyphenated words, are expressions now commonplace in our language, such as the adverbs just mentioned and the adjectives 'tearful',[2] 'traditional',[3] 'blood-thirsty',[4] 'tear-stained',[5] 'earth-bound',[6] 'cloud-capped'[7] and many others.[8] Some few of these, Shakespeare probably evolved himself (as we have all coined words from time to time), and they have become commonplace. Most of them were words recently introduced, and used occasionally by his contemporaries also. Many, on the other hand, were merely jocular,[9] or used for momentary effect, or of intense beauty,[10] or for other reasons not suitable for general and permanent use.

The above figures, then, we may take as truly representative of a large vocabulary in the Elizabethan age, of the date of, say, 1590. We have no dictionary of Elizabethan English.

---

[1] For example, mercifully, affectionately, reasonably, seemingly, stiffly, wearily, blindly, and many others.
[2] *3 Henry VI*, v. iv. 8.   [3] *Richard III*, III. i. 45.
[4] *1 Henry VI*, II. iii. 34.   [5] *2 Henry VI*, II, iv. 16.
[6] *Macbeth*, IV. i. 96.   [7] *Tempest*, IV. i. 152.
[8] E.g., first-fruits, bedroom, to battle, jaunt, aspiration, intricate, gentlefolks, inaudible, knob, disagree, disastrous, to further, dwelling-house, mode, to moderate, instrument, stiffen, to stammer, an outbreak.
[9] E.g. 'daughter-beamed', *Love's Labour's Lost*, ii. 171.
[10] Such as the 'temple-haunting' martlet, *Macbeth*, I. vi. 4; or 'cloud-kissing' Ilion (*Lucrece*, 1370).

Let us now compare the state of the English language in periods before and since, and see what changes occur. Dictionaries of various dates afford us the surest information; but in order that they shall be comparable, we should choose, where possible, those not of an exhaustive and monumental sort, for they are apt to include too many versions of the same word (especially non-verbs) as used by different authors or in different dialects, and archaisms and obsolete words of earlier date. After Shakespeare's time, then, there is Dr Samuel Johnson's magnificent dictionary,[1] which we may take as representing the state of the language in, say, 1790; and Dr Charles Richardson's dictionary of 1844.[2] For the year 1900 we may take Collins' *Graphic English Dictionary*, of which I acquired my copy, new, in 1908. For the period before Shakespeare we have Mayhew and Skeat's dictionary of Middle English (A.D. 1150 to 1580),[3] which we may take to represent the language of, say, the year 1400. None of these dictionaries contains a material number of hyphenated expressions.[4]

Analysing the contents of each of these dictionaries we reach the following significant results:

Dictionary	Date Represented	Total Words	Percentage of Verbs	Nouns	Adjs.	Advbs.	Prons.	Preps.	Conjs.	Intjs.
Mayhew & Skeat (Middle English)	A.D. 1400	10,000	29	47	16	5·6	1	1	0	0
Schmidt (Shakespeare Lexicon)	1590	14,440	25·5	48	19	6·6	0	1	0	0
Samuel Johnson	1790	41,000	21	50	22	7	0	0	0	0
Chas. Richardson	1844	48,300	18	52	23·5	7	0	0	0	0
Collins' 'Graphic'	1900	63,000	14	54	25	7	0	0	0	0

In this table we have not gone back beyond Middle English, and have not included Anglo-Saxon (or Old English). The reason is that the dictionaries of Old English are in a great degree dictionaries of Old English poetry. In that period the language of poetry differed widely from the language of conversation – far more widely than at any time since. Indeed, except in that period and during some two centuries after the Conquest, and latterly in the 19th century, English poetry has been close to English prose and the language of every day. The history

---

[1] The edition of 1830, from the last folio edition corrected by the Doctor.
[2] Chas. Richardson, LL.D., *A New Dictionary of the English Language* (1844), 2 vols.
[3] Mayhew and Skeat, *A Concise Dictionary of Middle English* (1888).
[4] In Collins' dictionary a considerable number of hyphenated expressions are included as examples of the use of a word – e.g. 'hand-breadth' and 'hand-glass' under the entry 'Hand' – and they have been excluded in the above figures.

of the matter is much what it was in Greece, where poetry, as it begins with the epics of Homer at a similar stage of economic development, had something of a vocabulary of its own, shaped by tradition and remote from common speech. In Greece this consisted mainly of adjectives – 'rosy-fingered dawn, child-of-the-morning', 'cow-eyed' Hera, 'owl-eyed' Athena, 'white-elbowed' women, and other 'stock epithets' of great beauty. Aristotle says that it was the writers of drama who finally brought about the change, for 'they discarded all those words, differing from the language of everyday conversation, with which the early poets were wont to adorn their works'.[1] In England, by the time we reach the York Miracle Plays in about A.D. 1350, a date corresponding to that of the early Greek drama, the language of the verse has become wholly colloquial. The extent of this phenomenon in Old English verse was vastly greater than in early Greece. Its outstanding characteristic was its wealth of synonyms in the form of compound nouns (created in most cases by a combination of two nouns) and less frequently of compound adjectives. In a dictionary of Old English almost half the total of nouns are compound nouns, and almost as large a proportion of adjectives are compound adjectives, whether written with a hyphen or not. In Beowulf, for example, the sea is hron-rad (whale-road), holm-wylm (sea-surge), mere-straet (sea-path), and there are 14 other synonyms, and 35 synonyms for 'prince' and 'hero'. There are in Beowulf alone 20 compound nouns of which the first component is heaðo-(battle-). The following is a literal translation of a short passage[2] exemplifying well this characteristic:

> At whiles they vowed
> At the idol-fane buildings[3]
> Idol-honours,[4]
> And with words they prayed
> That to them the spirit-slayer[5]
> Might aid afford
> Against the nation-calamities.

It need hardly be said that the Anglo-Saxon did not speak this language. But if we are permitted to discard the compound nouns and adjectives from Clark-Hall's *Concise Anglo-Saxon Dictionary*[6] – and, of course, each component of a compound word is still counted as a separate word

[1] Ar. *Rhet.*, III, i. 9. See also ibid., III, ii. 5, and *Poetics*, IV. i. 4.
[2] Beowulf, 352 f.
[3] I.e. heathen temples.
[4] Sacrifices.
[5] The Devil.
[6] 2nd Edition, 1916.

– we get as near as may be to the true character of Old English, and the figures become comparable:

Dictionary	Date Represented	Total Words	Percentage Verbs	Nouns	Adjs.	Advbs.	Prons.	Preps.	Conjs.	Intjs.
Clark-Hall (Old English)	A.D. 1000	14,500	30	46	16	5·4	1	1	0	0
Mayhew & Skeat (Middle English)	1400	10,000[1]	29	47	16	5·6	1	1	0	0
Schmidt (Shakespeare Lexicon)	1590	14,440	25·5	48	19	6·6	0	1	0	0
Samuel Johnson	1790	41,000	21	50	22	7	0	0	0	0
Chas. Richardson	1844	48,300	18	52	23·5	7	0	0	0	0
Collins' 'Graphic'	1900	63,000	14	54	25	7	0	0	0	0

In the above table are to be seen on a large scale, in terms of the passage of time, phenomena which we clumsily described, in regard to Shakespeare's English, in terms of the relations between the 'heart' of his vocabulary and its 'extremities'. There are also to be seen in this table, in terms of the passage of time, phenomena which we described, in the previous chapter, in terms of the functional development between sentences of types 1, 2 and 3, and also between the minimum and the developed forms of each. This passage of a millennium in one small country has witnessed changes more wide-reaching than several millennia have produced in many other lands, for they span the ages from a primitive culture till today. The table discloses these changes with unmistakable clarity.

The first development we notice in the vocabulary is the increase in the total number of words. The reader will not require to be persuaded that as the material culture of a people develops and becomes more complex, and the size of the population and the extent of economic specialization grows, and as man's consciousness of the world around him and of himself increases, the vocabulary of the language must expand in a corresponding degree to record man's many and varied messages. Yet, curiously enough, this expansion does not readily lend itself to cogent proof or measurement. The vocabulary of a language is not altogether finite; but much that has been written on this subject is hasty and unconsidered. Max Müller gave currency to the statement, made 'on good authority by a country clergyman, that some of the

[1] The small number of words here is due to the exclusion of alternative forms. For example, the vocabulary of Stratmann's *Middle-English Dictionary* is substantially larger. This also has the result that the proportion of adjectives in Mayhew & Skeat is slightly smaller than in Clark-Hall's dictionary.

labourers in his parish had not 300 words in their vocabulary'.[1] Wood observed that 'the average man uses about 500 words'. At the other extreme, Sweet was impressed by the story that a missionary in Tierra del Fuego had compiled a dictionary containing 30,000 words of the language of the Yahgan, one of the most primitive peoples among the Food Gatherers. That story is equally remarkable, and the dictionary seems never to have appeared.[2] Smedberg, supported by others, came to the conclusion that the vocabulary of a Swedish peasant exceeded 26,000 words.[3] The vocabulary of modern English, whatever its limits, certainly far exceeds 100,000 words. It is impossible not to notice, on a general view of the dictionaries, that the vocabularies of languages grow with the advance of civilization, and difficult to doubt that in general the vocabularies of individuals expand with the growth of intelligence.

The vocabularies expand as a tree develops, by the annual deposit of new layers around the heart-wood. The relation that we saw in the vocabulary of Shakespeare, between the 'heart' and the 'extremities', remains much as it was: the change is made by the successive laying of new rings around the heart-wood. These rings are not of the same composition as the heart. They are the extremities, the Section C, of men's vocabularies – new words, being tried and not yet common, of which some are widely adopted and become familiar and of everyday use. The proportion of verbs in these outer layers rapidly diminishes. For example, in Mayhew and Skeat's Middle English dictionary there are about 10,000 words, of which 29% (2,900 words) are verbs and 71% (7,100 words) are non-verbs. In the Shakespeare Lexicon there are about 14,440 words, of which 25·5% (i.e. 3,684 words) are verbs and 10,756 non-verbs – that is to say, of the net increase of 4,440 words only 784 (18%) are verbs and 82% non-verbs. As between the dictionaries of 1844 and 1900 in the above table, out of the net increase of 14,700 words only 134 words (under 1%) are verbs and over 99% non-verbs. Consequently at each stage the proportion of verbs in the whole vocabulary diminishes.

But the other parts of speech do not increase in the outer layers in the same proportions. They increase much in the same way as in the

[1] Max Müller, vol. i, p. 308.
[2] See the remarks on this topic of Lucien Adam in his *Grammaire de la Langue Jágane* (1885), p. 1. Max Müller had the document in his possession in 1889, for he refers to it in a letter of the 12 May of that year (see *The Life and Letters of the Rt. Honble. Friedrich Max Müller*, (1902) vol. ii, p. 241) but I do not know what became of it.
[3] See some references in Jespersen's *Growth and Structure of the English Language*, 9th Edition (1946), pp. 200-1.

extremities (Section C) of Shakespeare's vocabulary. The nouns increase slowly, but the adjectives more quickly. Accordingly the latter gain ground upon the former. The ratio of adjectives to 100 nouns increases at each stage as follows: A.D. 1000, 35; A.D. 1400, 34; A.D. 1590, 40; A.D. 1790, 44; A.D. 1844, 45; A.D. 1900, 46. The development of the adverb is hidden by the decrease in the verbs which they define. The ratio of adverbs to 100 verbs is at each stage: A.D. 1000, 18; A.D. 1400, 19; A.D. 1590, 26; A.D. 1790, 33; A.D. 1844, 39; A.D.1900, 50.

One other matter of great importance should be noticed. Throughout human pre-history and human history, the pace of advance of civilization has quickened, and in this country we are familiar with the acceleration that has occurred since the commencement of the Industrial Revolution in 1750, and, in our own time, the increase in speed since 1914, and still more since 1939. The table above shows clearly the acceleration that has occurred over the last millennium. The percentage of verbs in the vocabulary of the English language falls per century during the period as follows: A.D. 1000 to 1400, ·25; A.D. 1400 to 1590, 1·1. A.D. 1590 to 1790, 2·25; A.D. 1790 to 1844, 5·1; A.D. 1844 to 1900, 7·8; The pace was slower before A.D. 1000. It has quickened much since 1900.

Before we leave this topic, there is one further experiment which can be essayed, and which will verify further the change that is in progress.

English is one of those languages which draws its vocabulary from two different sources. One part, the older part of the vocabulary, comes from the Gothonic (Germanic) sub-group of the Indo-European family, which includes Old English (Anglo-Saxon) and Old Norse. But for many centuries there has been an influx of Romance words (that is to say, words of Latin origin) coming either directly from the Latin or indirectly through the French. Commencing in the second half of the 12th century, when Middle English was formed, and at its height in the 13th and 14th centuries, and continuing in a lesser degree till the 19th century, there has been a great influx of words from the French. The entry of Latin words commenced in a small degree even before the Anglo-Saxons came to England.[1] During the Middle Ages, and especially through the Church, there was a continuous inflow of Latin words, but only on a large scale since the revival of learning in the 14th and 15th centuries. Accordingly the Gothonic vocabulary of English is older than the Romance, and, as we might expect, the proportion of verbs in the Gothonic is higher than in the Romance words.

[1] For example, the word 'wine', as distinct from the 'vine' that came from France.

I calculate that by A.D. 1900 the proportion of the Romance words in the English vocabulary had grown to 63% of the whole. The analysis of the two elements, as I take them from the same English dictionary of about 1900,[1] is as follows:

	Verbs	Nouns	Adjs.	Advbs.	Prons.	Preps.	Conjs.	Intjs.
Gothonic	20	51	20	9	0	0	0	0
Romance	9	56	28	6	0	0	0	0

This little test, then, produces the same results as before. Whereas the whole vocabulary contains the proportion of 14% of verbs, the Gothonic holds over twice as high a proportion as does the Romance. In the Romance the proportion of nouns has slightly increased from 51% to 56%; (i.e. 9·8%); the proportion of adjectives much more, namely from 20% to 28% (i.e. 40%); the ratio of adjectives to nouns from 39% to 50%; and the proportion of adverbs to verbs has increased even more, namely from 45% to 67%.

We have now examined the contents of several dictionaries in the course of the history of English, but only the vocabulary of one author. Let us compare it with that of other writers. Assuming that each speaks the language of his day – and in a measure all must do so to be understood – we must expect that there will be changes in accordance with the date of each author, the vocabulary of the later containing a smaller proportion of verbs, and more nouns and adjectives. But there are differences between authors beyond the differences of date – differences in the subject-matter of the work, differences between colloquial language and artificial or artistic styles, and differences between books written for adults and books written for children. Accordingly we should not expect to find that a comparison of the vocabularies of different authors would point to so clear a conclusion.

Let us, for example, compare with Shakespeare's vocabulary that of Milton's poetic works. I calculate the contents of Laura Lockwood's *Lexicon to the English Poetical Works of John Milton*, and compare them with Schmidt's *Shakespeare Lexicon*, as follows:

	Total Words	Verbs	Nouns	Adjs.	Advbs.	Prons.	Preps.	Conjs.	Intjs.
Shakespeare	14,440	25·5	48	19	6·6	·4	·5	·3	·3
Milton's Poetical Works	8,500	26·7	41	25	5·6	1	1	0	0

[1] Collins' *Graphic English Dictionary*. For the purpose of this comparison I have treated the few Romance words with Gothonic terminations (for example, the word 'denseness') as Romance. Mainly the development of each section of the vocabulary has been by its own methods (e.g. swiftness, rapidity).

Such a comparison tells us little. Milton's work is some 50 years later than Shakespeare's. A slight increase in the adjective was to be expected, but the size of the increase is due also to the fact that the language of drama is more colloquial and has fewer adjectives. The nouns, however, are fewer in Milton and the verbs more numerous, instead of the reverse. We now know the reason for this: in the Milton Lexicon, which only embraces his poetic works, the vocabulary is little more than half that of the Shakespeare Lexicon, and contains only part of Milton's vocabulary. Accordingly the chief omissions are of the less common words, the words on the outskirts of his vocabulary, especially the nouns (for his poetic writings are well furnished with adjectives); and the verbs loom somewhat larger by contrast. We gain nothing from this comparison except a confirmation, so far as it goes, of what we have already learned.

On the other hand, Edmund Spenser's vocabulary[1] contains the following proportions:

Total Words	Verbs	Nouns	Adjs.	Advbs.	Prons.	Preps.	Conjs.	Intjs.
8,500	29	44	19	6·7	0	0	0	0

Spenser wrote only a few years before Shakespeare (though partly in the language of a past day), and comparing his smaller vocabulary with that of Shakespeare we should probably expect to find what we find in these figures.

But Chaucer's vocabulary[2] produces the following proportions:

Total Words	Verbs	Nouns	Adjs.	Advbs.	Prons.	Preps.	Conjs.	Intjs.
8,000	25	52	16	6·7	0	0	0	0

This, for Chaucer's simpler age, is a somewhat large vocabulary, and it is that of a scholar as well as a poet. The difference is in the breadth of the author's knowledge and the variety of his wide province, and the proportion of nouns is for this reason very large and the proportion of verbs correspondingly small.

Let us now, from the published concordances of the vocabularies of the chief English poets of large output, calculate the proportions of the parts of speech and arrange them in groups in order of date:

Floruit	Author	Vocab.	Verbs	Nouns	Adjs.	Advbs.	Prons.	Preps.	Conjs.	Intjs.
1380	Chaucer	8,000	25	52	16	6·7	0	0	0	0
1575	Spenser	8,500	29	44	19	6·7	0	0	0	0
1590	Shakespeare	14,440	25·5	48	19	6·6	0	1	0	0
1650	Milton	8,500	26·7	41	25	5·6	1	1	0	0
	Average	9,860	26·5	46·2	19·7	6·4				

[1] A calculation of the contents of Osgood's Concordance.
[2] As shown in my calculation of the contents of Tatlock and Kennedy's Concordance.

Floruit	Author	Vocab.	Verbs	Nouns	Adjs.	Advbs.	Prons.	Preps.	Conjs.	Intjs.
1720	Pope[1]	6,000	28	44	22	5	1	1	0	0
1780	Burns[2]	9,250	24	45	25	4	1	1	0	0
1810	Keats[3]	9,500	24	41	27	6	0	0	0	0
1810	Shelley[4]	10,250	25	38	27	8	0	1	0	1
	Average	8,750	25·2	42	25·2	5·8				
1820	Wordsworth[5]	11,750	21·5	42	28·5	7	1	0	0	0
1850	Tennyson[6]	11,800	25	50	22	2	0	0	0	0
1850	Browning[7]	17,500	21	44	29	6	0	0	0	0
	Average	13,700	22·5	45·3	26·5	5				

These three groups may be described as consisting of four poets before the Industrial Revolution, four poets at its commencement, and three later poets. This table tells the same tale as before. First we notice, in spite of the size of Shakespeare's, a general increase in the vocabularies. Next we see some irregularity in the proportion of nouns in each vocabulary, and on the whole little change. This need not surprise us; and we saw, earlier in this chapter, only a slow increase over the centuries in their proportions. There is, as before, little change in the adverbs. But, as ever, there is a steady but quickening fall in the proportion of the verbs, and an even steadier and more rapid increase in the proportion of the adjectives, and in the combined proportions of nouns and adjectives (65·9, 67·2, 72·8). Above all we observed, as before, an increase in the tempo of change. The first group covers a period of 270 years, the second the next 160 years, and the third the next 40 years.

With each poet (though the figures are not exhibited) the proportion of verbs continues to be highest among the more commonly used words – that is to say, each verb is used, on the average, more frequently than each of the other words of the vocabulary. It is also impossible not to notice (though I have not exhibited figures) that as between one author and another there is far more difference in the

[1] Calculated from the contents of E. Abbott's *Concordance to the Works of Alexander Pope* (1875).
[2] Calculated from J. B. Reid's *Concordance to the Poems and Songs of Robert Burns* (1889).
[3] Calculated from Baldwin's *Concordance to the Poems of John Keats* (1917).
[4] Calculated from F. S. Ellis' *Lexical Concordance to the Poetical Works of P. B. Shelley* (1892).
[5] Calculated from Lane Cooper's *Concordance to the Poems of William Wordsworth* (1911).
[6] Calculated from A. E. Baker's *Concordance to the Poetical and Dramatic Works of Alfred Lord Tennyson* (1914).
[7] Calculated from L. N. Broughton and B. F. Stelter's *Concordance to the Poems of Robert Browning* (1924).

actual nouns, adjectives and adverbs that they use than in the verbs. The verbs are, to a larger extent, the common stock of the language. This will not surprise the reader; but the importance of this fact will be seen in a later chapter.[1]

These changes in proportions are not caused, or not solely caused, by increases in vocabulary. For example, in the second group of poets the vocabularies are in fact somewhat smaller than in the first. But we notice that the average proportion of verbs in our second group is 25·2%, whereas in Johnson's contemporary dictionary it was 21%; and the average vocabulary in that group is 8,750 words, whereas the vocabulary of Johnson's dictionary was 41,000. In our third group the average proportion of verbs is 22·5%, and in Richardson's contemporary dictionary 18%; and the average vocabulary of the group is 13,700 and of his dictionary 48,300. The explanation is that the configuration remains the same: no two men have the same vocabulary, but to an extent the verbs that each man uses are the common stock of the language – less so the nouns and adjectives. Even more is this true as between one *langue particulière* and another: as between one trade, profession or social class and another the verbs tend to be the common stock, while the particular vocabulary consists chiefly of the other parts of speech. This process of addition to the vocabulary of the language is merely an accentuation and exaggeration of the process by which language has always developed. In the most primitive communities, except as between the sexes and age-groups, interests were largely the same and there was little difference between the jejune vocabulary of one man and another. Throughout the ages the specialization and differentiation of occupations and interests and vocabularies has increased at an increasing speed, as the community grew in size and population and its total technology grew increasingly beyond the limits of one man's mind.

Let us take one example. Medicine is a subject of which I have no knowledge. I take by chance the issue of the *British Medical Journal* dated the 6th January 1951. Between pages 1 and 19 are six specialist articles commencing with that entitled 'Fractures of the Sphenoidal Sinus with Cerebrospinal Rhinorrhoea'; and on pages 19-20 are some Medical Memoranda. I collect from these pages all words whose meaning is unknown to me, or is known to me to be of purely medical use (excluding familiar parts of the body and other medical terms familiar

[1] Namely, that by and large the words of other parts of speech are derived from the verbs.

to a layman). I treat similarly the issue of the same journal for the 16th June 1951, pages 1343-1367. The following is the analysis of these words, differing little from article to article:

Date of Issue	Total No. of Words	Nouns	Verbs	Adjectives	Adverbs
6 Jan	192	56	2·5	40	1
16 June	180	53	2·5	44	1

This is an analysis not of the whole language of this occupational group, but of the words on the outskirts of its vocabulary. It represents a further step in the direction in which language is tending. The proportion of the verbs, which has been falling at an increasing pace since Anglo-Saxon times, and is now, in 1958, some 10% or less of the whole language, has here sustained a severe drop to 2·5%. The proportion of the nouns, which has grown so slowly till it reached 54% in the English of 1900, shows hardly any increase since then. But the adjective, which has grown so fast in recent ages, and had reached 25% in the English of 1900, has here topped 40%. The adverbs in this vocabulary are too few to show significant change. This is so extreme a case of a *langue particulière* that most of these words would not be found in an English dictionary. This thought reminds us of another aspect of this process of change. History starts with speech communities of only a few hundred souls.[1] The words we are now considering are hardly confined to the mighty English speech-community of some 250 millions: they are an international vocabulary.

We said earlier that among the differences between authors is the difference between books written for adults and books for children. We would expect, from what we have learned, that in the books written by or for children the vocabularies would be smaller, and the less common words of the language would be even less common in these vocabularies than in the books of adults, and accordingly the proportion of the verbs would be higher. This indeed we find, though I have not exhibited figures. The topic is, however, much larger than this: it extends to the whole story of the development of mind throughout the known human history, and will be looked at in that light in the following chapter.

[1] See the next chapter.

CHAPTER FOUR

The Vocabulary and the Parts of Speech in the different Languages

We have traced back changes in the proportions of the parts of speech throughout the history of the English language. Can we now do the same in regard to other tongues? Still more important, are there any means for pursuing this enquiry back towards the infancy of mankind, and does the same process continue? The history of English takes us back, in little over a millennium, from a modern civilization to a simple and backward culture. Can the enquiry be continued?

The only direct evidence available consists of the languages of primitive and civilized peoples around us and civilized peoples of the past. But we are enquiring into the languages of primitive peoples that no longer survive, back to the most primitive communities that we can imagine. We cannot use a chronological order of events, for we do not directly know anything of such languages, but at least we know something of the succession of the broad stages of material culture through which these peoples passed; and remembering that language is communally organic we may expect that changes in society may be related to changes in material culture, and changes in language to changes in society. Consequently if we place the primitive peoples known to us in their order of material progress, we may hope to reconstruct thereby the chronological pre-history of the past. The stages of material culture that we must choose must be fundamental changes, based on the degree of control of a society over its environment. Let us then arrange these past and present peoples in the order of these stages,[1] and examine the languages of some of the peoples of each stage. This is our only evidential means of pursuing into the past the examination that we have made into the developing English vocabulary.

Our first and most primitive stage, then, is that of the Food

[1] For further details of this classification, see the author's *Evolution of Law and Order* (1951).

Gatherers. They live mainly by taking their food where they find it – roots, honey, insects, game or fish. They have no permanent dwellings and live in holes, rock-shelters or caves, or protect themselves by windbreaks or rude shelters of branches or thatch. They are of the Old Stone Age: they have no spinning, pottery or metal, and only rudimentary weaving in the form of plaiting. The average size of the tribe is about 400 souls, and it commonly possesses a language of its own, distinct from all others and divided into some three or four dialects. Communications between tribes are few, but there are enough to create some resemblances between the tongues of a certain area, and the area tends to expand as the people advances. The tribe is commonly divided into a number of semi-nomadic local groups, each of about 20 persons and covering a delimited territory. It requires so much territory for its subsistence that the average density of population is about one person per 7 square miles. There is no social organization among the bulk of the peoples of this stage, neither clans nor totems, and no individuals exercise influence over a whole tribe. Many of these peoples have survived into modern times,[1] but most have left behind only a brief glossary collected by a traveller, and there is insufficient evidence to attempt an examination of the proportions of the parts of speech in a group of representative vocabularies.[2]

Next comes the First Agricultural Grade (A1), represented by peoples whose main subsistence is still by gathering and hunting their food, but who have achieved a rudimentary agriculture as a subordinate means of livelihood. They are of the Neolithic Age, and have added a primitive pottery and spinning to their plaiting or weaving. Some substantial houses are to be found among the most advanced of them, and there is a little exchange of a few natural products. The people now require less territory for their subsistence, and the density of population has grown to an average rate of about one person per two square miles. The local group is less nomadic, and has become the village, from which the half-settled community covers its territory. For the most part some social organization exists. Leaders have influence rather than authority. The average village contains about 300 persons and the average tribe about 1,500. There is also a parallel progress of peoples who have developed a hunting instead of a land-tilling culture (H2; the neolithic hunters of the past). In all these peoples there is a

[1] The best known are the Sakai and Semang of Malaya, Andaman Islanders, Bushmen, peoples of the South Chilean Archipelago, Shoshoneans and other peoples of California, Tasmanians and Australian Aborigines.
[2] See, however, *post*, p. 56-58.

slowly lessening isolation of mankind, and there are loose confederacies of considerable size. The languages of different tribes are now capable of classification, in some sense, into families of languages, in that there are sometimes resemblances of vocabulary, and sometimes grammatical resemblances. So, for example, among the more advanced of these peoples in North America, the Iroquois confederacy,[1] together with the Tuskarora and the Hurons, spoke languages of one Iroquoian family. The Siouan family of languages was spoken by peoples of the great plains, including the Dakota confederacy[2] as well as the Winnibago, Iowa, Mandan and Hidatsa. The Algonkian family of languages was spoken by many peoples of the Eastern forest regions, including such confederacies as the Abnaki, Delaware and Ojibway.[3]

Let us take as representative of the A1 and H2 peoples three languages[4] of which good, large vocabularies are available, being in two cases of comparatively early date before the influences of European civilization had progressed too far. One is the Blackfoot[5] (or Siksika) of the Northern Plains, roving Hunters with no permanent habitations, no pottery or canoes, and no agriculture save the sowing and gathering of a native tobacco. The language is one of the Blackfoot group of the Algonkian family of languages. Our second example is the Natick,[6] of Massachusetts, a people of the First Agricultural Grade, slightly more advanced than the Blackfoot. Their language is of the Central group of the Algonkian family. Our third example comes from a people still further to the south-east and still further advanced, the Choctaw,[7] of the Muskhogean family. This people has its home east of the Lower Mississippi, and it stands at the junction of the First and Second Agricultural Grades. The Choctaw dictionary contains a vocabulary of considerable size, but it has been swollen by the inclusion of many words betokening familiarity with the products of European civilization.[8]

[1] At its height in the 17th century, probably of a population of some 25,000.
[2] About 25,000.
[3] The latter about 30,000 in A.D. 1650.
[4] We have avoided the more polysynthetic of the North American languages, because of the greater difficulty of disentangling the word from the sentence.
[5] Uhlenbeck and Van Gulek, *A Blackfoot-English Vocabulary* (Amsterdam, 1934).
[6] J. H. Trumbull, *Natick Dictionary*, B.A.E., Bulletin 25 (1903). The author, a linguist, died in 1897.
[7] Cyrus Byington, *A Dictionary of the Choctaw Language*, B.A.E., Bulletin 46 (1911). Compiled mainly by Byington, a missionary, in the 50 years ending in 1868. In all these three languages the verbs for the most part perform the function of the adjective – e.g. it-is-green, he-is-lean, and so forth.
[8] E.g. words for book, paper, clerk, bookbinder, school, court, chapter, debtor, etc. The proportion of verbs has therefore fallen somewhat.

The Second Agricultural Grade (A2) is that of the peoples with whom agriculture (or, as it is better called, horticulture) has become the main means of subsistence. Nevertheless, they do not as yet possess herds or flocks. They, too, belong to the Neolithic Age of the past: they do not work in metals and they have not the plough. Their main implement in the gardens is still the digging-stick. Their wooden huts are substantial, and they have skill in wood-working, spinning and weaving, and some pottery. There is an increase of trade, which includes a not insignificant barter of small articles of handwork (such as baskets and bowls) as well as agricultural and natural products. There is a steady increase in the influence or authority of chiefs. In Melanesia there are still few chiefs; in Polynesia there is considerable increase in chiefly authority. Over the whole grade there is a chief or headman of the local group in half the communities, and a chief of the tribe in about a third of the tribes. There are still no tribunals and therefore still no law in the proper sense of the term, except a few criminal offences, such as incest and murder by magic, irregularly punished by the community. The increase in the extent of horticulture brings a rise in the density of population and the average rate is now between 5 and 10 persons per square mile.

The facts of language undergo corresponding changes. In America the situation is much as before. In backward Melanesia and New Guinea the number of languages spoken still challenges belief. A journey of 5 miles generally brings the travellers to a new dialect. A small tribe of 500 souls or an island of half that population commonly has its own language. And yet all the peoples of Melanesia, Micronesia, Polynesia and Indonesia speak languages grouped in one Malayo-Polynesian family, possessing, all in all, one general morphology and syntax. These islands and languages stretch from Formosa and Hawaii in the north to New Zealand in the south, and from Madagascar in the west to Easter Island in the east, a distance of 5,000 miles of sea from north to south, and 14,000 miles of sea from east to west, to be traversed by nothing but the frail barques of the islanders. In the midst of this vastness, the many scattered islands of the advanced peoples of Polynesia are occupied by tribes speaking tongues that are but dialects of one original language, growing ever wider apart. These facts speak eloquently of the increasing movement, change and adaptability of mankind, and they also suggest that while some tongues change more rapidly than others, the change grows faster as we mount the scale of civilization. For in the two centuries during which we have known anything of Polynesia, there is plainly evidence of changes in language. Yet the similarities between the tongues of the Polynesians are so close that, though communication has increased, the changes must have been little and slow in past ages.

We shall divide the Second Agricultural Grade, for greater clarity, into a more backward and more advanced stage, and into the former (Grade A2(1)) we shall put the Melanesians and their languages, and into the second (Grade A2(2)) the Polynesians. The Fijians form the boundary between the two. For additional clarity we take all our examples from these two groups of the great Malayo-Polynesian family of languages. As examples of the Melanesian group let us take the language of Bugotu[1] (Santa Isabel Island, in the Solomons), the language of Sa'a and Ulawa[2] (in the South-East Solomons), the language of the Duke of York Island[3] (in the New Britain group), and Mota[4] (Sugarloaf Island, in the Banks' Islands). The last-mentioned, originally the native tongue of some 800 persons, has become, through its use by the Melanesian Mission, a lingua franca known and used in widely distant islands. In our second stage of this grade we put the Fijian[5] (the most widely known of the Melanesian languages) and the languages of Tonga,[6] Samoa,[7] Hawaii[8] and the Maori.[9]

Hitherto we have spoken only of hunting and primitive agriculture, but a third way of life now appears, that of pastoralism, especially the tending of herds of large cattle. The institution of pastoralism is only a little later than primitive agriculture, and there have been a few pastoral peoples in the modern world, and no doubt many more in the past, of a somewhat lower grade of advance than that which we have now reached – for example, the Hottentots of South-West Africa, who till recently lived solely by a combination of pastoralism and hunting. But now we meet with peoples who subsist by pastoralism and agriculture as well as hunting, and they mark the beginning of our Third Agricultural Grade.

Forest – as, for example, in equatorial Africa at the present day –

[1] W. G. Ivens, *A Dictionary of the Language of Bugotu* (1940).
[2] W. G. Ivens, *A Dictionary of the Language of Sa'a (Mala) and Ulawa, South-East Solomon Islands* (1929).
[3] Brown and Danks, *A Dictionary of the Duke of York Language, New Britain Group* (Sydney, 1882), in MS.
[4] R. H. Codrington and Ven. J. Palmer, *A Dictionary of the Language of Mota* (1896).
[5] A. Capell, *A New Fijian Dictionary* (Sydney, 1941).
[6] *Dictionnaire Toga-Français*, par les Missionaires Maristes (Paris, 1890).
[7] L. Violette, *Dictionnaire Samoa-Français-Anglais et Français-Samoa-Anglais* (1879).
[8] L. Andrews, *A Dictionary of the Hawaiian Language* (1865).
[9] E. Tregear, *The Maori-Polynesian Comparative Dictionary* (1891).

prevents the growth of pasture and the rearing of herds. The pastoral peoples of the Neolithic Age had no means of cutting down the forest trees, and pastoralism could only exist in the semi-arid regions where rain-forest would not flourish. Yet pastoralism and some hunting can sustain a human population where agriculture is almost impossible through lack of rain, and where cattle and man can only live by moving from one shower to another; and it can flourish where these semi-arid regions are near to permanent rivers in temperate climates. In such favoured conditions the great civilizations had their birth. The chief areas of pastoralism (often combined with agriculture) were and are to be found at the junction between Asia and Africa, and the less favourable area of the steppes stretching between North-Eastern Europe and Western Asia. The increasing movement and adaptability of mankind are clearly reflected in the facts of language. Where Asia adjoins Africa the great Semitic-Hamitic group of languages had its birth, and while its speakers advanced to civilization these languages spread far and wide. In particular the Semitic family of tongues, originating in dialects of one proto-Semitic language, ousted 4,000 years ago the Sumerian of Southern Mesopotamia and covered Arabia, Babylonia, Assyria, Syria and Palestine, and has since spread far and wide in Africa, ousting the Hamitic from Egypt and many other countries. Another family of languages, the Bantu, originating perhaps in one language spoken in the region of the Great Lakes of East and Central Africa, has been carried south by such peoples and now covers the southern third of Africa. And somewhere in the steppes of Eastern Europe and Western Asia originated more than 5,000 years ago an Indo-European tongue which, while its dialects separated into distinct languages, was carried by such peoples to lands throughout the world, where later have flourished the civilizations of Greece, Rome, India, Britain, North America, Russia and many others; until now those who speak only one of these tongues, namely English, as their mother-tongue, total some 250 million persons.

We divide the peoples of this third Agricultural Grade (A3) into five stages according to their advance in material culture, which can be more nicely estimated by their progress in the development of law.

Our first stage (Grade A3(1)) is well represented by Nilotes and Bantu of North-East and East Africa, as they stood in the early years of the present century, and it was also the stage of the bulk of the peoples of Germany in the time of Julius Caesar and Tacitus. These populations are, on the whole, pastoral peoples with little subsidiary

PARTS OF SPEECH IN THE DIFFERENT LANGUAGES 45

agriculture. They have acquired the use and working of metal. Many of them form loose amorphous confederacies of between 50,000 and 600,000 souls. There are few real villages, and the population lives in well-separated homesteads. Religion shows a palpable advance. There is little progress towards central tribal authority, and only among a small minority of tribes is there a strong kingship.[1] The bride-price marriage is in full force everywhere. There are primitive tribunals dispensing justice, and by their rules of law we can define this stage with some precision as being that at which the sanction imposed by the courts for each of the four main civil injuries is the payment of a defined number of cattle. These civil injuries are homicide; wounding; adultery, rape and seduction; and unaggravated theft. Sanctuaries for homicides first appear. Legislation is as yet unknown.

As representative of this stage we take five languages from Nilotes and Bantu of North-East and East Africa – the Dinka[2] and Shilluk[3] at the junction of the White Nile and the Bahr-el-Ghazal, and the Lango[4] of Uganda (all three representing the Central Nilotic group of the Sudanic languages); and the Kikamba[5] and Kikuyu[6] (representing the Northern Bantu languages of this stage). The available vocabularies are mostly very small, and perhaps partly for this reason, and partly because of the difference in the methods of the writers of these dictionaries, the variations between the figures of individual languages are large; but the mean figures fall into their place in our table.

Our second stage in the third Agricultural Grade we call Grade A3(2), or that of the Early Codes. It is represented in Western Europe by the Germanic tribes when they first settled within the territory of the fallen empire of Rome – the Anglo-Saxons from A.D. 600 to 900. In Africa it is represented by the southern outposts of the Bantu world, as they stood at the beginning of the present century, including the Nguni peoples of South-East Africa. The strength of kingship has grown, and social classes multiply exceedingly. As these peoples are generally more settled in their territory, and their rulers are also administrators of the land by which all live, an incipient feudalism appears. The tribes began to group themselves into nations, which

---

[1] In Africa only among the Shilluk and (to a lesser degree) the Anuak; and among a minority of German tribes.
[2] J. C. Mitterrützner, *Die Dinka-Sprache in Central-Africa* (Brixen, 1866).
[3] Diedrich Westermann, *The Shilluk People* (1912).
[4] J. H. Driberg, *The Lango* (1923).
[5] *A Kikamba-English Dictionary*, compiled by the Language Committee of the Africa Inland Mission in Ukamba (Nairobi, C.M.S. Bookshop, 1939).
[6] L. J. and G. S. B. Beecher, *A Kikuyu-English Dictionary* (C.M.S., Fort Hall 1935).

slowly increase in size. The bride-price marriage is still at its height. The appeal of religion grows. Judged from the legal standpoint, this stage is that of the peoples among whom legislation – namely, the process of consciously changing the law – is first in evidence. The sanctions imposed by the Courts for each of the chief civil injuries (which remain the same as before) are still in most places the payment of a defined number of cattle, but a currency of some kind begins to take its place. There commences a great increase in the number of rules relating to theft.

As representative of the peoples of this stage, let us take the languages of three very different Bantu peoples. The most backward of these is the Zulu[1] of South-East Africa. Moving west and north we meet the Herero[2] of South-West Africa, and the Mayombe[3] near the west coast on the right bank of the Loango. The latter stand at the close of this stage, and the same point of development is represented in Europe by our dictionary of Old English.

Our next stage is that of the Central Codes, or Grade A3(3). It is the stage of the beginnings of civilization, In Western Europe our story continues in chronological order, and this stage is represented by the English from A.D. 900 to 1100. In Africa we move from the north-eastern and south-eastern outskirts of the Bantu world towards the centre and west of the continent, and this stage is exemplified in a very large number of Bantu peoples of Central Africa, and the bulk of the peoples of the Congo.[4] The ancient Hittite Empire[5] was of the same stage of advance.

The peoples are becoming more settled and their agriculture more intensive, and the density of population accordingly increases. The villages grow in size but are still very small. The average village is probably of about 20 households, but there are now a few growing towns. London in A.D. 1086 has a population of about 12,000. Towns mean markets, which now begin to be organized. The population of the English kingdom in A.D. 1086 is about 1,500,000, and many of these nations number over 100,000 subjects. The number and authority of local landowning nobles increases; the power of religion and the religious orders continues to grow. At the end of the period feudalism reaches its height. Legally this stage is defined as that in which the

---

[1] A. T. Bryant, *A Zulu-English Dictionary* (1905).
[2] H. Brincker, *Wörterbuch und Kurzgefasste Grammatik des Otji-Hérero* (Leipzig, 1886).
[3] Leo Bittremieux, *Mayombsch Idioticon* (Ghent, 1922).
[4] Most of these, however, have no cattle owing to the presence of tsetse fly or rain forest.   [5] Central and South-East Asia Minor, 14th century B.C.

sanction for homicide ceases to be pecuniary, and now begins to be criminal and commonly consists of the delivery up to the relatives of the slain man of a specified number of persons to take his place. We select, as languages representative of these peoples, the Sudanic language of the Azande[1] of Central Africa, and two Bantu languages of the same region, Buluba-Lulua[2] and Kongo.[3]

Our next stage – the last stage of the Third Agricultural Code – is that of the Late Codes, or A3(4). It gives birth to all the great civilizations and religious faiths of man. In England it is represented by the period from A.D. 1100 to 1300. It is the stage of advance of the bulk of the nations of West Africa, as they were at the beginning of the present century, and of most of the civilizations of the ancient world when first known to us – the Sumerians at the close of the 3rd millennium B.C., the Babylonians and Egyptians of 2000 B.C., the Assyrians of the Middle Period of 1400 B.C. On the edge of that world the Hebrews of the kingdoms of Israel and Judah were of the same age in 900-600 B.C., and such were the Athenians in the days of Draco (c. 620 B.C.) and the Romans at the time of the Twelve Tables.

The tempo of change continues to quicken, as it has from the beginning of our story. There is a great increase in the populations of these nations and empires. The English kingdom in A.D. 1300 numbers some 3,500,000 souls, and there are many nations of this and larger proportions. The density of population and the size of towns and villages advance. In most countries the average village holds about 300 persons. There is a great increase in industrial specialization and in the number and size of markets. Gilds of merchants and craftsmen are everywhere. From the middle of the period there is a market in land. The arts, especially of building, burst into maturity. The use of writing, hitherto confined to priests, is now the function of a separate order of scribes at the boundary of the ecclesiastical order, and schools for the laity appear. Feudalism is at its height but is beginning to wane. The bride-price marriage begins to fade, and the marriage-portion (a gift from the bride's father) grows important in its place. In legal terms the commencement of this age may be defined as the point at which the legal sanction for intentional homicide becomes capital. At the end of the grade all the four main wrongs of intentional homicide, wounding, adultery and theft have become criminal offences.

[1] C. R. Lagae, *La Langue des Azande* (Gand, 1921).
[2] M. M. Morrison, *Grammar and Dictionary of the Buluba-Lulua Language* (American Tract Society, New York, 1906).
[3] W. H. Bentley, *Dictionary and Grammar of the Kongo Language* (1887).

We may take as languages representative of the peoples of this economic stage that of the Baganda[1] of East Africa (belonging to the beginning of this stage), Hausa[2] (spoken to the north of Nigeria), Bini[3] (the language of the Edo people of Southern Nigeria) and Suahili[4] (of East Africa), a language somewhat difficult to place, for, originating as the language of Zanzibar, it has been spread by commerce far and wide as a lingua franca spoken among many less forward peoples. Last, but not least, we may take the Hebrew[5] of the Old Testament.

The ages following on that of the Late Codes may be briefly divided into two periods, the one leading up to the commencement of the Industrial Revolution (which we may call the Pre-Industrial Age) and that beyond, which was never reached by Greece or Rome, and which we may name the Industrial Age. The processes of change, which we have witnessed, continue at an increasing pace. The populations of cities increase to millions, and of States and Empires and speech-communities to hundreds of millions. The strength of central government grows ever greater, while in contrast the family weakens and the clan disappears. The specialization of occupations grows more and more intensive. Middle English may be taken to represent England about A.D. 1400. With Shakespearian English we may compare the Greek[6] and Latin[7] lexicons. Both are of a special character, for neither represents a language spoken at any one time. The Greek lexicon covers in some sort a period of nearly 2,500 years from Homer to the fall of Constantinople to the Turk. The Latin embraces an age of over 800 years from Ennius and Plautus to Fortunatus and Isidore. Hence the vocabularies are exceptionally large.

The whole table is then as follows:

[1] G. R. Blackledge, *Luganda-English and English-Luganda Vocabulary* (2nd ed., 1921).
[2] R. C. Abraham, *Dictionary of the Hausa Language* (1949).
[3] H. Melzian, *A Concise Dictionary of the Bini Language of S. Nigeria* (1937).
[4] L. Krapf, *A Dictionary of the Suahili Language* (1882).
[5] Brown, Driver and Briggs, *Hebrew and English Lexicon of the Old Testament* (1929).
[6] Liddell and Scott, *Greek-English Lexicon*. New ed. by Sir H. S. Jones (1940).
[7] Lewis and Short, *Latin Dictionary* (1907).

PARTS OF SPEECH IN THE DIFFERENT LANGUAGES

Language	Language Group	Area	No. of Words	Verbs	Nouns	Adjs.	Advbs.	Prons.	Preps.	Conjs.	Intjs.
\multicolumn{12}{l}{GRADE A1 AND BACKWARD HUNTERS}
Blackfoot (H2)	Algonkian (Blackfoot Group)	N. Amer. (N. Plains)	4,500	53	32	7	7	0	1	0	0
Natick (A1)	Algonkian (Central Group)	N. Amer. (Mass.)	3,000	48	34	8	9	0	1	0	0
Choctaw (A1-A2)	Muskhogean	N. Amer. (S.E.)	10,000	47	36	12	4	1	0	0	0
		Average:	5,800	49.3	34	9	6.7				
\multicolumn{12}{l}{GRADE A2(1)}
Bugotu	Malayo-Polynesian	Melanesia	2,750	53	33	6	4	2	1	0	1
Sa'a & Ulawa	,,	,,	7,750	52	34	4	5	4	1	0	0
Duke of York	,,	,,	3,900	41	37	14	4	2	2	0	1
Mota	,,	,,	5,750	40	44	11	3	1	0	0	1
		Average:	5,000	46.5	37	8.75	4				
\multicolumn{12}{l}{GRADE A2(2)}
Fiji	Malayo-Polynesian	Melanesia-Polynesia	4,500	39	35	20	2	3	1	1	0
Tonga	,,	Polynesia	7,800	48	26	19	3	1	1	1	1
Samoa	,,	,,	13,000	46	37	11	3	2	1	1	0
Hawaii	,,	,,	15,000	40	43	16	1	0	0	0	1
Maori	,,	,,	8,000	34	46	15	2	2	0	0	1
		Average:	9,700	41.4	37.4	16.2	2.2				

PARTS OF SPEECH IN THE DIFFERENT LANGUAGES

Language	Language Group	Area	No. of Words	Verbs	Nouns	Adjs.	Advbs.	Prons.	Preps.	Conjs.	Intjs.
			GRADE A3(1)								
Dinka	Sudanic (Nilotic)	N.E. Africa	2,500	44	36	12	3	2	1	0	0
Shilluk	,,	,,	2,500	44	47	4	3	1	0	0	0
Lango	,,	E. Africa	3,100	32	58	4	3	1	0	0	0
Kikuyu	Bantu	,,	6,500	42	53	3	1	1	0	0	0
Kamba	,,	,,	6,000	33	61	3	2	1	0	0	0
Average:				39			2·4				
			GRADE A3(2) – EARLY CODES								
Zulu	Bantu	S.E. Africa	12,500	45	49	2	2	1	0	0	1
Herero	,,	S.W. Africa	5,500	40	50	3	2	2	1	·5	·5
Mayombe	,,	W. Africa	8,750	40	53	4	1	0	1	0	1
Old English	Indo-Eur.	England	14,500	30	46	16	5	1	1	0	0
Average:			10,300	38·75			2·5				
			GRADE A3(3) – CENTRAL CODES								
Azande	Sudanic	Cent.-Africa	3,750	34	50	13	3	1	0	0	0
Buluba-Lulua	Bantu	,,	3,000	44	48	3	3	1	0	0	0
Kongo	,,	,,	10,750	36	54	4	2	2	0	1	1
Average:			5,800	38			2·7				

PARTS OF SPEECH IN THE DIFFERENT LANGUAGES

Language	Language Group	Area	No. of Words	Verbs	Nouns	Adjs.	Advbs.	Prons.	Preps.	Conjs.	Intjs.
\multicolumn{12}{l}{GRADE A3(4) – LATE CODES (=England 12th century)}
Ganda	Bantu	E. Africa	6,300	44	49	2	2	2	0	0	1
Hausa	Sudanic	W. Africa	17,500	29	60	5	5	1	0	0	0
Bini	"	S. Nigeria	3,000	33	57	6	3	1	0	0	0
Hebrew (O.T.)	Semitic	Palestine	6,000	29	57	9	2	1	1	0	1
Suahili	Bantu	E. Africa	13,500	31	60	5		·5	·5	·5	·5
		Average:	9,200	33·2			2·8				
Middle English	Indo-Eur.	ENGLAND A.D. 1400	10,000	29	47	16	5·6	1	1	0	0
		ENGLAND A.D. 1600–1700									
Shakespeare's English	"		14,440	25·5	48	19	6·6	0	1	0	0
Greek	"	Greece	101,250	30	36	29	4	0	0	0	0
Latin	"	Rome	42,500	18	45	25	10	0	0	0	0
		Average:	52,700	24·5			6·5				
English (Dr. Johnson's Dictionary)	Ind.-Eur.	ENGLAND A.D. 1790	41,000	21	50	22	7	0	0	0	0
English (Chas. Richardson's Dictionary)	"	ENGLAND A.D. 1844	48,300	18	52	23·5	7	0	0	0	0
English (Collins' Graphic)	"	ENGLAND A.D. 1900	63,000	14	54	25	7	0	0	0	0

Before examining these results we must notice some special difficulties that we meet with in comparing the vocabulary of one language with another, and especially the languages of different families of languages.

First, the ways in which man can express himself are legion. It is probable that in all languages may be found verbs, nouns, adjectives and adverbs, pronouns, a few conjunctions, and interjections; and in the bulk of languages, prepositions. But different languages and families of languages like or dislike a particular part of speech and tend to use another in its place. For example, even within the Indo-European family of languages, ancient Greek never took to the noun in the way that some others did. It persisted, for example, in using verbs and adjectives instead of abstract nouns, for example τὸ καλόν – 'the beautiful' (neut.) – for 'beauty'. Consequently the proportion of verbs and adjectives in Greek was at all stages higher than in English or even Latin. But this does not mean that the process of change in the history of ancient Greek was different from that in English. My calculation of the contents of Crusius' Lexicon for Homer,[1] and of the contents of Liddell and Scott's Lexicon of the Greek literature, produces the following comparison:

	Total Words	Percentage of Verbs	Nouns	Adjs.	Advbs.	Prons.	Preps.	Conjs.	Intjs.
Homer	6,750	41	27	23	8	1	0	1	0
Liddell and Scott	101,250	30	36	29	4	0	0	0	0

Accordingly, notwithstanding the difference between these figures and those of the English language, it is plain that, in Greek as in English, the proportion of verbs decreased and the proportions of nouns and adjectives increased.

The Indo-European languages do not stand alone in their early development of the adjective. It is at least as well developed in the Malayo-Polynesian group, and it is well developed even in Australia. But there are, on the other hand, languages, such as the Semitic and Bantu, that do not take to it. The verb and the noun still continue to serve the function of the adjective in most cases – for example, a verb will signify 'to be great', 'to be small', 'to be beautiful'. The Arab grammarians, indeed, did not recognize the adjective as a separate part of speech: to them there were only nouns, verbs and particles. In the Semitic and Bantu languages, the adverbs are even fewer, and almost

---

[1] G. C. Crusius, *Greek and English Lexicon for Homer*, trans. by H. Smith, revised by T. K. Arnold (New ed., London, 1876).

PARTS OF SPEECH IN THE DIFFERENT LANGUAGES 53

insignificant in number. For the most part, the verbs and nouns still perform the function of an adverb. For example, in Hebrew 'to rise up early' or 'to go quickly' is one verb; and 'he wept loudly' is bakah qol gadol ('he wept a great voice'). There is hardly a sufficient demand as yet to create the adverb as a separate part of speech. Consequently in the Bantu languages, for example, the proportion of verbs is high. Yet if we confine ourselves to one of these languages, and can follow its development, we observe the same changes in the proportions of the parts of speech that we saw in English.[1]

Secondly, there are some quite fortuitous and superficial differences between dictionaries of different languages. For example, if we imagine two languages alike in other respects, but in one the verb has developed by prefixing a particle, adverb or preposition, as in the English form *undo*, *outdo*, and in the other the verb has remained distinct and the adverb follows, as in the English form *break out*, *break in*, *break off*, *break up*, *break down*, then the dictionary of the former language will contain a somewhat larger proportion of verbs than the latter, because of the addition of those compound verbs. Again, in a Semitic language, the verb in one of its moods or forms has a causative sense, and this is so regular a feature of the conjugation of the verb that the dictionary will contain only one entry in respect of the verb. So in Hebrew, in the simple form of the verb, qaṭal = 'he killed'; and from it is formed hiqṭil = 'he caused to kill'; and the lexicon will contain only the simple form qaṭal. But in Bantu the verb may or may not have a causative form, and the form is not always of the same type. Consequently the lexicon contains a separate entry for each, and this tends to increase the proportion of the verbs in a Bantu as against a Semitic lexicon.

Accordingly any attempt to compare one family of languages with another must be rough and approximate in method and result. But when all has been said, these differences are but accidental. We have only to take the average of a sufficient number of languages, belonging to various families, and the accidentals will all disappear save one – the great irregularity in the development of the adjective. Some modern

[1] We can do this in regard to many languages of the simpler peoples, where we have dictionaries of different dates. For example, in regard to Maori, there is E. Tregear's Dictionary (1891), and H. W. Williams' Dictionary (1917), and I calculate the contents as follows (the figure in brackets represents Williams' Dictionary): Total words 8,000 (14,000), Percentage of Verbs 34 (31), Nouns 46 (50), Adjectives 15 (17). There are, in regard to Samoa, the dictionaries of Le P. Violette (1879) and Pratt (3rd and Revised Ed. 1893); and in regard to Fijian the dictionaries of Hazlewood (1850) and A. Capell (Sydney, 1941); and there are numerous other examples. If the later dictionary is smaller than the earlier, this must be allowed for.

grammarians would even abolish the use of the words 'adjective' and 'noun' in regard to the languages of the simpler peoples, and speak of 'dependent and independent nominals', or use similar terms. But if at each stage we add together the figures of nouns and adjectives, the regularity of development from stage to stage is complete.

The above table speaks eloquently for itself. It traces in other lands and peoples a story parallel and identical with that which we watched in England, and it traces the same process back, in economic stages and in time, to savage man at the close of the Palaeolithic Age. As the vocabulary increases the proportion of the verb diminishes as though by an iron decree, through peoples speaking a wide diversity of the families of languages, from a proportion, at the earliest point to which we can reach, of some 50% of the whole vocabulary, to a proportion in A.D. 1900 of some 14%, and in 1958 of probably 10% or less. The nouns increase first, and then the adjectives. The change in the adverbs is the most curious of all. We noticed in the language of Shakespeare that, as we moved from the heart of his vocabulary to the extremities, the proportion of adverbs at first diminished, and then at the outskirts increased again.[1] Here we see the same picture in terms of time. From the languages of North America to the remote tongues of Melanesia, and then from the Melanesian to the kindred Polynesian, the proportion of adverbs steadily drops. In the Sudanic and Bantu languages of the following stage it remains almost the same, and from that point it slowly mounts throughout our story. Among the most primitive peoples the adverbs are generally derived from the verbs. After the rise of the noun a number of nouns and noun-phrases increasingly perform the function of the adverb. But later, and very soon after the main rise in the adjective, adverbs (derived from adjectives) increase considerably in number[2]; so that whereas among the Polynesian languages there is only 1 adverb to 20 verbs, in Western Europe of A.D. 1900 the ratio has risen to a proportion of 1 adverb to 2 verbs.

In the North American, Melanesian and Polynesian languages the rise in the adjective is continuous, but in the Sudanic, Bantu and Semitic languages of the Third Agricultural Grade it is not easy to separate the adjective from the noun. If, however, we add together the adjectives and nouns – the dependent and independent nominals – the whole story is one:

---

[1] *Ante*, p. 27.
[2] In the various Indo-European languages the adverbs are formed from the adjectives in different ways, because this process is later than common Indo-European.

PARTS OF SPEECH IN THE DIFFERENT LANGUAGES

Grade	Verbs	Nouns and Adjectives	Adverbs
A1 and H2	49·3	43	6·7
A2(1)	46·5	45·75	4
A2(2)	41·4	53·6	2·2
A3(1)	39	56·2	2·4
A3(2)	38·75	55·75	2·5
A3(3)	38	57·3	2·7
A3(4)	33·2	62	2·8
England A.D. 1400	29	63	5·6
England A.D. 1600-1700	24·5	66·2	6·5
England A.D. 1790	21	72	7
England A.D. 1844	18	75·5	7
England A.D. 1900	14	79	7

Although, as we have said, there are few glossaries of the tongues of Food Gatherers large enough to enable us to arrive at precise figures of the parts of speech, it is reasonably plain from what we possess that the same process continues back among the peoples of that grade. The parts of speech are quite distinct, the verb dominates the whole, and there is little now but verbs and nouns. Professor L. F. Maingard, for instance, observes of the Khomani dialect of Bushman that 'although in Khomani there is no true line of demarcation between what we call "verbs" and "adverbs", although there are possibly no real "adjectives", although the so-called "adverb of time" can be analysed into a "noun", yet there are distinct "nouns" and "verbs" in the true sense of the word. It is not possible to discover a single instance of the two latter categories merging into one another.'[1] The position is much the same in Australia. The distinction between noun and verb in a sentence is everywhere clear.[2]

It is important to add to the bare bones of the above table a few illustrations of the spirit and essence of language among the most primitive peoples, where the proportion of the verb is at the height that has been mentioned. Various observers have remarked on the richness of the verb in these tongues.[3] Driberg points out that 'the verb is the most important part of speech in Lango not only for the functions natural to it but for the wealth of metaphor and colour which it imparts to the language'.[4] The Rev. Fr. L. M. Spagnolo observes that 'The verb plays the most important rôle over all the other parts of speech in Bari grammar, not only for its principal function of back-

---

[1] Prof. L. F. Maingard, *The Khomani Dialect of Bushman: Its Morphology and other Characteristics* (pp. 237-275 of J. D. R. Jones' and C. M. Doke's *Bushmen of the Southern Kalahari*, Johannesburg, 1937).
[2] See. for example, S. H. Ray's remarks on this topic in the Australian Encyclopaedia (title *Aboriginal Languages*).
[3] E.g. in regard to the Bushman languages, Dorothy Bleek.
[4] *The Lango*, p. 314.

bone of the sentence, but also because it is the richest in number of words, it gives origin to many other words (e.g. nouns, adjectives, adverbs, etc.) and it is apt, through a very complicated system of compositions, to supply the want of some adverbs or prepositions.'[1] Many authors have pointed out the power of the verb in the languages of North America; how it dominates the sentence[2]; its 'immense compositional power'[3]; how it welds together new combinations, and 'absorbs and incorporates all kinds of elements' within it.[4] An example of the like process can be taken from the language of a food-gathering people, the Aranda of Central Australia. Mr T. G. H. Strehlow, who has lived among this people and been familiar with its language since childhood, tells us how a native stalking a mountain kangaroo might say of it (using developments of the verb ilkuma, *to eat*) ilkutjakalaka (= it descended-eating), ilkulb-ilkutjakalanaka (= descended-slowly-eating-all-the-while) ilkuenalalbuka (= wandered-on-away-from-us-eating-on-its-way), ilkup-ilkuentjalbuka (= came-back-towards-us-eating-ravenously-the-whole-time) ilkup-ilkulanaka (= here-it-kept-on-browsing-and-browsing), ilkutjintjilka (= browsed-on-its-way-up) and so forth.

But these rich developments of the verb are explained by the mind and mental attitude of the native. He speaks of actions and movements, rather than of things or of qualities. Let us take, from one of the most primitive of the Food Gatherers, an instance of the speech of an Andamanese in a typical statement of action.[5] Let us first set out the text and a literal translation. We notice its crudity – its brief, colloquial, disjointed and imperfect sentences, its absence of conjunctions, and of the subordination of one sentence to another. But it has little or no meaning for us without its physical and affective context:

Ba kichika arla – l'-eate ngo on?   Wainga – len do on.
How many   day - - - past you come? Morning – in   I come.
Na   do reg dele. Kam wai   dol. Kam wai   do on.
Now I   pig hunt. Away indeed I.   Away indeed I   come (go).

[1] *Bari Grammar* (Verona, 1933), p. 98. The Bari are a Nilotic people of Grade A3(1).
[2] E.g. in regard to Tonkawa, H.A.I.L. Part 3, p. 106, by H. Hoijer; in regard to Takelma, H.A.I.L. Part 2, p. 63, by Edward Sapir; in regard to Suslawan, H.A.I.L. Part 2, pp. 459-60, by Leo J. Frachtenberg.
[3] C. C. Uhlenbeck *A Concise Blackfoot Grammar* (Amsterdam, 1938), p. 198; and see *The Lango*, loc. cit.
[4] Uhlenbeck, op. cit., p. 133.
[5] Abstracted from Portman, and cited in Sir R. C. Temple's *A Grammar of the Andamanese Language* (being Chap. IV of Part I of the *Census Report on the Andaman and Nicobar Islands*, 1902).

D' – arlog – len ka.   Wai do jala - - - - - ke. Reg – ba.   Kam
Me – behind – in there. Indeed I go-away – do. Pig – little. Away
wai   do ik   on.   Wai   ka   eda otjoi.   Do   lilti
indeed I   take come. Indeed there they roasted. I (in the) early-morning
doga - - - - lat. Reg doga. Do ela   l'igjit - - - - - ke.
big (pig) – for. Pig big.   I   pig-arrow sharpen - - - - do.
D' – okanumu - - - kan. Kaich d' - - - - arolo. Do - - - ng' - - - igdele.
I - - - - - go - - - - - - do.   Come me - - - after.   I - - - - you - - - hunt.
D' – okotelema ik   on.   Wai   d'a - - - be otjoi - - - - - ka
Me – before   take come. Indeed me - - - for cooking - - - were
bud-len. Tim roicha – beringa – ke. Ña   do
hut – in. Very ripe - - - good - - - do. Now I
ikpagi – ke. Ikre   ka.   Wai   eda ikkenawa.
several – do. Getting – were. Indeed they barked.

It is in fact an account of an imaginary pig-hunt, as told by an eremtaga (forest-man) of the Bea tribe for the amusement of his friends. 'The narrator sits on the ground, facing a half-circle of lounging Andamanese. After a short silence, he leans forward with his head bent down. Suddenly he sits erect with brightening eyes and speaks in a quick, excited way, acting as if carrying on a conversation with another person. 'After how many days will you return?' And then, answering as if for himself: 'I will come back tomorrow. I am off pig-hunting now.' A pause. 'I am going.' Very suddenly: 'You stay here.' Moving as if going away. 'I am going to another place.' Squeaking like a young pig, with pantomime of shooting it. 'It is only a little pig. I will take it to the hut.' Moving his shoulders as if carrying. 'They roasted it there.' Wave of the hands signifying that the pig was of no account. Pause. 'I started in the early morning after a big one – a big pig.' Motions of hands to show length and breadth of pig. To an imaginary friend: 'I will sharpen pig-arrows to take with me. Come after me and we will hunt together.' Imitation with the hands of a pig running, shooting arrows, slap on the left breast, squeals of several wounded pigs, and so on. A pause. 'You take them in front of me. Directions by pantomime to other persons as to the pigs. 'They were cooking them for me in the hut, cooking them well.' Brightens up and begins again. 'I will bring several more.' Pretends to listen. 'We have got them. The dogs are barking.' And so on for hours.

Here is another passage from Portman, less mimetic but just as simple and crude – Portman's version of the fire-legend in the Bea language.

Tôl – l'oko-tima – len Puluga mami – ka. Luratut – la
(Name of a place) – in God sleeping-was. (Name of a bird)
chapa tap – nga omo - re. Chapa - - - la Puluga – la
fire steal-ing bring-did. Fire God
pugat - - - ka. Puluga – la boi-ka. Puluga–la chapa
burning – was. God awake-was. God fire
eni - - - ka. A ik chapa – lit Luratut l'ot – puga – re.
seizing-was. He taking fire – by (the bird) burn - - - - - t.
Jek. Luratut eni – ka. A i-Tarcheker l'ot-pugari – re.
At-once (the bird) taking – was. He (a bird) burn - - - - - t.
Wota – Emi – baraij – len Chauga – tabanga oko – dal – re.
Wota – Emi – village – in The – ancestors made - - - - fires.
Tomolola.
Tomolola.

Portman's rendering is as follows. 'God was sleeping at Tôl-l'okotima. Laratut came, stealing fire. The fire burnt God. God woke up. God seized the fire. He took the fire and burnt Luratut with it. Then Luratut took (the fire). He burnt Tarcheker in Woti-Emi village, (where then) the Ancestors lit fires. (The Ancestors referred to were) the Tomolola.'

It is clearly borne in upon us that these differences in language do not represent mere stages of economic progress. They represent also stages of the intellectual development that goes with them. They can be closely paralleled in the language of our children.

CHAPTER FIVE

The Origin of the Nouns, Adjectives and Adverbs in English

It seems plain then, wherever we look, that from the time of savage man the advance in material culture has accompanied an increase in the vocabulary of language, a decrease in the proportion of verbs, and an increase first in the nouns, then in the adjectives, and then – mainly from the middle of the Pre-Industrial Age – in the adverbs. It is also clear, wherever we look, that although words may change or become obsolete and be succeeded by others, the process has been, in substance, an addition to the vocabulary of nouns, then of adjectives and adverbs – all, as it were, on the outskirts of language, for, on the whole, each verb continues to be used more frequently than each noun, adjective or adverb. Clearly the creation of the nouns did not take place at one time, nor the creation of the adjectives, nor of the adverbs. The process in all three cases has gone on throughout the period that we have watched; first the nouns; the adjectives later, and mainly from the period of the Late Codes and onwards, but at different dates among different families of languages, and in different oral or written 'literatures'; and the adverbs in part at a very early stage, and in part chiefly from the middle of the Pre-Industrial Age.

We have seen that even at the close of the Palaeolithic Age there was still as much of verbs as of all the other parts of speech added together, and assuming that the process of change continued the same throughout the age of savage man – and it is difficult to imagine any reason why it should not, or why this apparently eternal process should then cease – we should see, if we could look back to the beginnings of speech, vocabularies decreasing towards a vanishing point and consisting of a trivial number of words, each word being a verb and each word being also a sentence (for the complete communication is always a sentence and always contains a verb). Accordingly we should see both vocabulary and sentence diminishing to a nuclear verb.

We have also inferred that this unending process of change in the proportions of the functional parts of language is also the process of development of the intellect. The broad stages in that advance are, first in date, a consciousness of movements, second a consciousness of objects, and third a consciousness, or conception, of qualities. But we are not yet ready to consider this progress of mind: we must first examine, for a while, the forms of these parts of speech that we have been considering. It may serve to corroborate as well as to explain the conclusions at which we have so far arrived.

How is it, then, that there came into existence words of these new parts of speech, the nouns, adjectives and adverbs?

New words could originate in one of two ways. First, each could be a new word with the new meaning, whilst being different in form from any word already existing in the language. This, as a general phenomenon and process of development, is quite inconceivable. Even today, as a general system, it would be impossible. Even today, to be accepted by a community, a word must, as we said, be of an approved form, sounding well in the public ear; and its meaning must sit plainly upon it. It must sound as if it were born to have that meaning: it must mean what its sound seems to suggest. But in those ancient days of low and brutish intelligence, of few words and slow changes, how could a word get common acceptance with a particular meaning if there was nothing in its form to suggest its meaning? And if it was of a wholly new form, how could it be pronounced? Or, if it could be pronounced, why was it not already in use with its own meaning? The other way by which new words could appear is where old words come to be used with a new meaning, connected in some way with the old, or, if not the old words, at least words similar enough in form to the old words to suggest them and their meaning.

Of these two ways only the second is possible. As Bréal puts it: 'There could be no question (be it well understood) of creation *ex nihilo*: the application to new uses of matter transmitted by past ages, that is the form in which we see the building up of progress.'[1] Dwight Whitney says: 'Of the out and out invention of new words, language in the course of its recorded history . . . presents only rare cases.'[2] It is true that languages may contain a number of words unassociated in form or meaning with the rest, especially the names of imported goods or arts – as, for example, the word 'sack', which came from the ancient

[1] *Essai de Sémantique* (1897), chap. 7, p. 87.
[2] *Life and Growth of Language* (1896), p. 120.

civilization of the Near East and travelled everywhere with the thing it represented.[1] As a general method of development, in the languages we know of there is no evidence of any process but the second. There are so many words, in our own and other languages, that show an affinity of form and meaning with some earlier word, that if we cannot trace the origin of a particular word in some other word we rightly assume that there was such an origin, and say that its etymology is as yet unknown. When we hear that a particular word was formed, not from another word but by a conscious, independent act of voluntary creation, as the chemist van Helmont in the 17th century invented the word 'gas',[2] we treat it as an exceptional and remarkable thing. But the distinction between these two methods is not a distinction between the conscious creation of a new word and the insensible alteration of a word and its meaning. The second method, which we have mentioned, includes both the gradual insensible change of a word and the conscious creation of a word on the model of the form and meaning of other words. In both cases there must be an affinity of form and meaning with the old word, if the new word is to be understood and accepted, though we cannot assume any such conscious creation in the earliest days of language.

Let us then illustrate this process, by which words of new parts of speech are created, by taking a representative word of Modern English. Let us choose a word familiar to the Englishman of today – 'nationalization'. It is suitable for our purpose because it has travelled far, and bears on its shoes layer upon layer of the earths through which it has trudged. The present root or body of the word – 'na' – is the oldest part of it. It is verbal[3] in meaning, and signifies to give birth, to be born, to beget or be begotten. It has itself undergone more than one change. It came into English from the Latin, and in earlier Latin its form was 'gna' (as still in our English word 'co-gnate'[4]), Even the 'a' was not originally part of the root. Still earlier, in Common Indo-European, the root was 'gen', and it survives in innumerable words in English and the other Indo-European languages. Through the Germanic the

---

[1] But even imported words tend to become assimilated to the native, and to be understood through a real or fancied similarity to a native word. 'Ecrevisse' becomes 'crayfish', 'asparagus' becomes 'sparrow grass'.

[2] And yet (as Bréal suggested) with a vague recollection of the Low Country 'gest' (spirit).

[3] The word 'verbal' is used in this book, not as a synonym for 'oral', but as the adjective of the word 'verb'.

[4] The 'g' in 'gna' ceased to be pronounced as it has ceased in such English words as 'gnaw' since A.D. 1500.

word 'gen' came into English in the form 'Kin' and 'Kind'; and from the Latin, directly or through the French, such words as *genius*, *general* and *gender*. But in the word we are now considering only one letter, the 'n', survives in the root 'na'. By the addition of the common 'sc' it took the form of a present, frequentative or continuous tense, nascor (I am born), and there was a reduplicated form na-n-ci-sc-or, 'I get, obtain', just as in earlier English 'I get' may mean 'I beget' or 'I obtain'.

From this vague verbal root 'na' there came, through its participle 'natus', the noun 'na-tio' signifying 'a being-born, a birth, a breed, a people'. This noun is the verbal root with the addition of the suffix '-tio', one of the endings characteristic of Latin nouns of certain kinds (accusative 'nation-em'). To it was added the suffix '-alis' (accusative '-alem') a characteristic ending of Latin adjectives, forming the adjective 'national-em' ('of a nation') though this word is not to be found in a lexicon of the Roman republic or empire. From 'national-em' is then formed the verb 'national-ize' (sometimes spelt 'nationalise') by the addition of the suffix -ize, the Greek '-$ίζω$', an ending in use in that language for the purpose of turning, for example, an adjective into a verb. Lastly from this verb, by addition of the same Latin noun-suffix '-atio' (-ationem) is formed the noun 'nationalization'.

The history of this word, therefore, is that it was first verb, then noun, then adjective, then verb, then noun. We may expect to hear at any moment of 'nationalizational schemes' if the length of the word can be tolerated, and then the history will be verb, noun, adjective, verb, noun, adjective. Such a modern word as 'nationalistic' or 'naturalistic' has already turned the circle twice.[1] Words of the type of 'nationalization' are not uncommon in Modern English.[2]

This succession is highly significant. By means of these forms, each being characteristic of a part of speech, we are able to trace the history of the word, and to see, firstly, that it has within the last four thousand years or so passed through the whole history of language; and secondly that this history is forever repeating itself. The past history of language (assisted, for example, in the Indo-European languages by the existence of a certain succession of forms which it has left behind) has created in the mind a channel of association of thought and feeling through which thought and feeling may continue to pour, just as the waters

---

[1] na-(verb)-tion(noun)-al(adj.)-is(verb)-t(noun)-ic(adj.), the first three terms of the series being of Latin form, and the last three from the Greek through the French.

[2] E.g., nationalism (Greek '– $ισμός$'), sectionalism, secularization, generalization, pastoralism, conceptualism.

of a river will pour along a channel that its previous waters have cut.

We have heard, too, in recent years, of trades and trade unions being 'nationally' organized. In this word 'nationally' we see the history of progress from verb to noun, to adjective ('national'), and then to adverb by the addition of the suffix '-ly' by which in Modern English most adjectives are turned into adverbs. This little word shows by its form, like the geological strata in some little field, that it has passed through a history that is passed through everywhere. These words are very numerous in Modern English, but it is only in the languages of the modern age that we can see so clearly the whole process, for in the more primitive languages adjectives and adverbs are often very few. Moreover, in these Indo-European tongues, where a word commonly develops by affix, the history is especially plain to see.

There is another development in Modern English that we have not hitherto noted, and that is the advent of innumerable abstract nouns. Like the modern adverb, they follow behind the adjective, and their real increase is from the same date as the adverb – namely from the middle of the Pre-Industrial Age. Almost invariably, in English as elsewhere, they develop out of the adjective. The adjective expresses the speaker's and the hearer's consciousness of a quality: the abstract noun gives it an existence, a personality and a name. Like the adverb, the abstract noun is by no means unknown as early as Old English,[1] but there is a large increase of recent times.

Let us now take a more general glance at the various parts of speech in Modern English and see how the bulk are formed.

First, the nouns. Where we can trace their derivation, they are generally formed from the verbs. They are shaped in various ways – for example, by adding the suffix '-er' or other indications of the agent – from 'kill', 'killer'; from 'count', 'counter'; from 'pose', 'poser'; or by adding the suffix '-ing' to form a verbal noun – indeed the participle in '-ing' was originally a verbal noun. Then come all the nouns formed from Romance verbs (and sometimes Germanic verbs) by Romance suffixes. These words are the more modern, and accordingly a large proportion are abstract nouns – from the verb *judge, judgment; decide, decision; determine, determination; break, breakage*. Then there is a large number of words – mainly, but not all, Germanic in origin – which

---

[1] E.g. abstract nouns formed by an inflection of the vowel to 'e', often with a suffixed 'th' – so from *lang, leng* or *length*; from *brad, braed* (now *breadth*); from *strong, strength*; *wide, width; high, height*. Also the suffix *-ness* is used.

function both as verb and noun without change of form. When we can trace their origin, the word has usually been a verb – *to cut, a cut; to walk, a walk*. But there is also a large number of opposite instances, where a verb is formed from a very common and familiar noun – for example, the name of an animal (to dog, hound, wolf, fox, gull, pigeon) or the name of a part of the body or a garment (to finger, head, foot, toe, hand, arm, eye, elbow, button, coat, mantle). There are also a few other cases (for example, from the noun *battle, to battle*).[1] All told, these verbs which were originally nouns are only a small minority of the verbs. The change from noun to verb is against the general course of history and spirit of language; it is only possible because the noun, though younger than the verb, is still of great age, and, though the average verb is more commonly used than the average noun, these particular nouns are very common and familiar.

Then the adjectives. The vast majority of them are formed from the nouns in enormous numbers by the addition of Romance and sometimes Greek suffixes (*-ic, -an, -al, -ous, -ive* and others), and also Germanic (*-less; -lic*, now reduced to *-ly*, as in 'friendly', 'godly'; – *like* (O.E. ge-lic) as in 'godlike'; *-y*, as in 'juicy'; *-ful* as in 'blissful'). But in Modern English, with its analytical grammar, where the word usually shows its function by its position in the sentence and not by variation in form, there is a simpler method of turning a noun into an adjective, that is to say by putting it in the position occupied by the adjective in the sentence, namely immediately before the noun which it defines. So we get *flower* shop (not *floral* shop), *sea* (not *marine*) urchin, *boy* friend, and so forth. There is no limit to the extent of this process. So Darwin says in the *Origin of Species*, bk. 1, chap. 1: 'I have never met a pigeon or poultry or duck or rabbit fancier who was not fully convinced that each main breed was descended from a distinct species.' Among the nouns so used are the verbal nouns, for example, *driving power, killing bottle*. So that there is a variety of ways in Modern English of forming an adjective from a noun. We may say, for example, a cup *of gold*, a *golden* cup, or a *gold* cup – all have the same meaning. But in a minority of instances adjectives are also formed directly from the verb, especially in the form of the passive participle – *a deserted wife, a plucked hen*; and by analogy (as also in Latin)[2] a noun with the same suffix (*-ed*) may become an adjective – for example,

[1] I.e. from O.Fr. *bataille* comes O.Fr. *batailler* (M.E. *bataile* and *batailen*), But *bataille* itself comes from the low Latin verb *battere*.

[2] E.g. *rostratus* from *rostrum*, *scutatus* from *scutum*, *staminatus* from *stamen*. The same form is also used in Romance words in English, e.g. *roseate*.

a *two-handed sword* (though there is no verb 'to two-hand'), a *red-throated diver*, and so forth. And adjectives are very frequently formed from the verb by adding the Romance suffix *-able* or *-ible* ('readable', 'legible'). There are few, if any, reverse cases of concrete nouns being formed from adjectives,[1] but there is in comparatively modern times the process, to which we have referred, of the development of abstract nouns from the adjective, and finally, in modern times, a small minority of cases where the adjective itself becomes a starting-point for the development of a new verb.

On the recent development of the adverb in English we need not take up time. The few adverbs in Old English were usually, as in so many early languages, nouns (e.g. – *maelum*, 'by times'; so *styccemaelum*, 'piecemeal'; *daeges*, 'by day') or adjectives with the added suffix '-e' (for example, *heard*, meaning *hard*, adjective; *hearde*, adverb; *freondlic*, friendly, adjective; *freondlice*, adverb; *frecne*, daring, adjective or adverb). '*Lic*' was a noun signifying body, form (as in the modern *lych-gate*), and, as we have seen, its use as a suffix turned a noun into an adjective (freond, freondlic).[2] In Modern English both '*-lic*' and '*-lice*' have been reduced to '-ly', and the suffix mainly survives as a means of turning any adjective into an adverb. Further, with the general disappearance of the unstressed *-e* in the 15th century, some of the old adjectives and adverbs are now of the same form, as commonly in Modern German (so Eng. *hard, fast, sound*). An adverb does not become an adjective, or indeed change to any other part of speech: it is too recent a development. As we have seen, there are in Old English (as in languages of the most backward peoples) a few adverbs formed directly from the verb.

We may, then, sum up generally the vocabulary of Modern English by saying, with growing emphasis, that nouns are generally formed from verbs, adjectives are overwhelmingly formed from nouns, and adverbs in practically every case from adjectives, though earlier the few extant adverbs were formed from verbs and nouns.

[1] Except by omitting and implying the noun – e.g. *a Roman* (sc. *man*) from the adjective *Roman*.
[2] As in Greek, εἶδος, suffixed to a noun, formed adjectives ending in - ειδής and - ώδης.

CHAPTER SIX

The Origin of the Nouns, Adjectives and Adverbs in the Classical Languages

If we now turn to one of the older Indo-European languages and attempt to pursue these processes further into the past, we shall find them of the same character; but they can be measured with greater precision, for in Latin the words retain their function whatever their order in the sentence, and show it by their form. Let us, then, examine Lewis and Short's Latin Dictionary, and (accepting the authors' etymologies) count the words and their origins.

Of the verbs, approximately 60% are age-old verbs in which we can trace no substantial change of form or meaning, or are verbs derived from other verbs. The first-named class we shall call *radical verbs*, because they cannot be confidently derived from any other Latin word, and cannot be broken down into component parts. They include many of the commonest words in the language.[1] A further 26% of the verbs are derived from nouns.[2] These are far less commonly used. The remaining 14% are derived from adjectives.[3] They are also generally uncommon words.

Of the nouns, approximately 57% (the commonest of all) are derived from verbs,[4] 24% from other nouns,[5] and 20% from adjectives. The latter are almost all abstract nouns and late words.

Of the adjectives, 72% are derived from nouns[6] and 28% from verbs.[7]

[1] E.g. findo, seco, dūco, dīco, gero, pendo, sono, cădo, ruo, fĕro, păro, rapio, moneo, video, etc.
[2] E.g. auctorare, aucupare, depompare, comitiare, munerari, titulare, numerare.
[3] E.g. divinare, asperare, vacuare, continuare.
[4] In enormous numbers, ending chiefly in -*mentum* (e.g. argumentum from arguo), -*tor* or -*sor* (e.g. arator, assessor), -*tus* and -*sus* (e.g. exercitus, ascensus), -*lum* (vinculum, exemplum, templum), -*tum* or -*tium* (edictum, servitium).
[5] E.g. hospitium from hospes, aucupium from auceps; and the diminutives (e.g. rostellum, scurrula, scutella).
[6] In enormous numbers, ending, e.g., in -alis, -ilis, -eus, -aris, -ius, -anus, -icus, etc.
[7] E.g. in -*ax* (edax, audax), -*idus* (horridus, torridus, timidus, tumidus, frigidus), -*ilis* (agilis), -*bilis* (horribilis, flebilis), -*uus* (assiduus, arduus), -*ivus* (stativus).

ORIGIN OF NOUNS, ADJECTIVES AND ADVERBS

The adverbs are practically all derived from adjectives, but there is a handful of ancient adverbs derived from old, common verbs.[1]

We may sum up these changes in precisely the words in which we summed up the changes in English at the close of the previous chapter.

We can now attempt in two ways to gain a rough picture of the constitution of the vocabulary before these transferences of function had taken place. One is to substitute for each part of speech the parts of speech that preceded it. We calculated in an earlier chapter, that Lewis and Short's Latin Dictionary contained the parts of speech in the following percentages:

Verbs	Nouns	Adjs.	Advbs.	Prons.	Preps.	Conjs.	Intjs.
18	45	25	10	0	0	0	0

Let us now substitute for the figure of each part of speech the parts of speech from which it is derived. So, for the 18 verbs, we substitute 60% verbs (11), 26% nouns (5) and 14% adjectives (2); for the 45 nouns, 57% verbs (25), 24% nouns (11) and 20% adjectives (9); for the 25 adjectives, 72% nouns (18) and 28% verbs (7); and for the 10 adverbs, 9 adjectives and 1 verb.

The proportions of the parts of speech are then transformed to the following figures[2]:

Verbs	Nouns	Adjs. and Advbs.
44	34	21

These figures show a great increase in the proportion of the verbs. But the proportion is underestimated here, for many of the words in the dictionary have undergone more than one change of function. For example, a word like 'continuare' (to continue) comes from the adjective 'continuus', and this is where we have now left it. But 'continuus' itself comes from the verb 'contineo' (i.e. from the radical verb 'teneo'). If we continued this process of substitution, the proportion of verbs would be higher, the nouns and especially the adjectives and adverbs lower. But the above figures indicate sufficiently the character of the vast changes undergone by the Latin language, or the Indo-European dialect that preceded it, in the centuries or millennia before 200 B.C.

A second way of ascertaining the path taken by the language is simply to collect from the Dictionary all radical words of all parts of

[1] E.g. statim, cursim, ductim, passim (from stare, currere, ducere, pandere).
[2] Where a word is compounded of a preposition (or adverb) and another word (e.g. oppugnare or contineo), the preposition or adverb is disregarded. There are substantially no other compound words in Latin.

speech – that is to say all words that cannot be confidently derived from other Latin words, and cannot be broken down. There are approximately 775 of these. They are very short words, and are of the form CVCV, CCVV, CVV, CV, VCCV, CCV, VCV or V (where C signifies any consonant and V any vowel). But no less than 86% of these words are of one form, namely CVCV[1] – a fact to which we shall often have occasion to return – and even of the rest a further 8% are of the form VCV, suggesting that the initial consonant of the CVCV may have fallen out. The remaining 6 types constitute between them only 6% of the whole. The chief parts of speech are represented in the radical words in the following percentages:

Verbs	Nouns	Adjs. and Advbs.
46	37	14

These figures are not unlike those suggested by our first test, and they confirm the general picture indicated. They are very close to those contained in our tables on p. 49 as representing peoples of Grade A2(1). On many other grounds it is likely that the speakers of common Indo-European were no more advanced than this – that is to say, that they were primitive pastoralists or horticulturists. The most backward Indo-Europeans actually known to us are the Germans of Tacitus' time as described in his *Germania* and they were still only of Grade A3(1).

We need not examine similarly the course of history of the other Indo-European dialects. Long ago Panini and other grammarians of India, in their devoted studies of the Sanskrit of their sacred literature, recognized in its vocabulary a number of roots out of which that vocabulary seemed to have been compounded. The number of these roots, they thought, was 1706,[2] the overwhelming proportion bore the meaning of verbs, and they concluded that their language originated in verbs. Then from the time, at the close of the 18th century, when Sanskrit became widely known to the West, and brought with it the realization that Greek, Latin, Gothic, Slav, Celtic, Sanskrit and other languages were but dialects of an ancient tongue that had grown further and further apart, attempts were made by a succession of scholars to learn that language through the common elements to be found in its descendants. They used, therefore, the method employed by the biologist, who seeks to learn the characteristics of an extinct parent stock from the common features of its various descendants. In

---

[1] See, for example, p. 66 n. 1.
[2] Th. Benfey, *Kurze Grammatik*, § 151.

so doing these linguists arrived at two conclusions: the first, that in each language there are a number of 'roots' – that is to say, parts of existing words – each of which is to be found forming part of many other words in the same language; secondly, that the same roots are to be found performing the like functions, and with the like meanings, in other Indo-European tongues. They naturally concluded that these roots must also have been found in the parent language – that is to say, in the same Indo-European languages when they were closer together and were but dialects of one language. There was inevitably some variety in the results arrived at by different scholars, but they may be summed up by saying that the roots they found numbered several hundreds – something in the neighbourhood of 800 – and apart from an insignificant but compact number of roots with pronominal meanings (numbering little more than 1% of the whole), they all had the meaning of verbs, and none of nouns or adjectives. The forms of these roots were substantially the same as those of the radical words which we found in the Latin dictionary. One or two were of the form V (such as i = go). One or two were of the form CV (such as *da*, give – Latin *dā*, Greek *dō*). One or two were of the form CCV (such as *sta*, stand – Latin and Greek *sta*). But the vast bulk were of the form CVC – such as *gen* (or *gan*) to give birth, *ker* (or *kar*) to cut, *mer* (or *mar*) to break; divide; *per* or *par*, to pierce, separate.[1] They thought that all these roots were originally real and distinct words,[2] and dated from a stage in the growth of language in which that sharp distinction which we make between the different parts of speech had not yet been fixed,[3] and when the parts of the sentence had not been differentiated and grammar had not yet emerged.[4] They noted that these words always

[1] In the Latin dictionary we noticed that the radical words were mainly of the forms CVCV. But those were complete words, not mere roots, whereas *gen*, *ker*, *mer* and *per* are merely roots, and not necessarily complete words. In their simplest form as complete words in Indo-European they were perhaps usually, if not always, followed by a vowel. Throughout language there is a difficulty in deciding whether these original roots and radical words were of the form CVC or CVCV, but we shall see that, in all probability they were usually of the form CVCV. The difference is small. The final short vowel is easily lost, and is not sufficiently distinctive to be permanent; but in a large number of the world's languages, such as Italian and the Polynesian and Melanesian tongues, all words must end in a vowel. In these Indo-European roots it is important to notice that the vowel is usually short, and there is a certain prevalence of the vowel 'a' – a matter to which we shall often return.
[2] See e.g. Max Müller, *Lectures on the Science of Language* (1877), vol. ii, p. 92; G. Curtius, *Zur Chronologie der Indogerm. Sprachforschung* (Leipzig, 1873), p. 22; *Zur Kritik der neuesten Sprachforschung* (Leipzig, 1885), p. 132; W. Dwight Whitney, *Language and the Study of Language* (1868), p. 255; *Views of Language*, p. 338.
[3] Max Müller, ibid., p. 90; W. D. Whitney, *Life and Growth of Language* (1875), p. 200 (1896), pp. 201-3.
[4] See e.g. W. D. Whitney, loc. cit; Max Müller, ibid, p. 90.

contained a short vowel,[1] especially the vowel 'a'. Though, therefore, these roots – except for a handful of pronouns – plainly bore the meaning of verbs, probably few of these scholars thought of them as having originated as verbs. They considered them as complete words possessing verbal meanings, but as antedating the appearance of verbs, nouns or adjectives.

But round about the year 1880 a revolution occurred in linguistic thought, and we cannot leave this topic without mentioning it. Several discoveries were made in Germany and elsewhere on the Continent, emphasizing the truth that, irrespective of the meaning or function of words, sounds have a functional relation to one another and a history of their own. For example, when the speech organs are set to produce a particular speech-sound, that 'set' of the organs tends to have its effect in the production of the following or preceding sound, which is thereby changed. So, the sound *ka* may be relatively permanent, for the vowel *a* and the consonant *k* are both sounded towards the back of the throat. But if the vowel be *ĕ* or *i* (which are sounded in the front of the buccal cavity, just behind the teeth), the *k* tends also, for greater ease, to be pronounced in the same area, namely between the tongue and the hard palate, and consequently the set of the organs necessary to produce *e* or *i* tends to change the *k* to a *ch*. Similarly *ge* or *gi* will tend to become *je* or *ji*. This 'palatal law' helped to show that the vowel 'a', so common in Sanskrit writings, had earlier been in some cases 'e' (as it was in Greek). It was also learnt that stress or accent upon a sound, or the absence of it, affects the form of that sound and neighbouring sounds. In short there is such a thing as the 'blind' operation of phonetic laws, irrespective of the meaning or history of words. The result was a profound revulsion in certain quarters against the views of the pioneers. The school of the 'Junggrammatiker' claimed to explain all things by phonetic laws. It is astonishing now to see what influence they had in England, as elsewhere. For example, Sayce, Professor of Assyriology at Oxford and a learned linguist, in the preface to the second edition of his *Introduction to the Science of Language* (1883), announces the 'dethronement of Sanskrit',[2] joyfully echoes a phrase of Fick[3] about the 'empty clatter of roots and suffixes',

---

[1] G. Curtius, *Zur Chronologie*, etc., loc. cit.

[2] Why 'dethronement'? Sanskrit should never have been considered as more than one of the sister-languages, descended from dialects of Indo-European. Such was the view of Sir William Jones, expressed in his famous address of 1786.

[3] Fick was also the author of the 'discovery' that the strong aorist in Greek is a later development than the present tense. See *post*, p. 132.

ORIGIN OF NOUNS, ADJECTIVES AND ADVERBS 71

and claims that it must pass away with the influence of the Indian grammarians. 'In short,' says he, 'the Aryan verb was originally a noun, just as it still is in many languages of the world.'[1] It is true that when he says a 'noun' he means a verbal noun, that is to say the name of an action, not the name of an object; but the statement reads strangely in the light of the facts set out in the previous chapters of this book.

These roots, said Sayce, following his mentors on the Continent, can never have been words. Many of them, for example, require the addition of vowels to make them articulate.[2] Moreover, some of these roots are identical in form with other roots, but have different meanings – for example, there is an Indo-European root kar = cut, and kar = create, and this renders it still less likely that they were ever real words. Because they are but skeletons, the meanings of these roots are vague (to be born, go, stand, etc.) and it is impossible to suppose that language ever consisted of nothing more. It is true that they are substantially all verbal in meaning, but this is merely because verbs, too, are vague and general in meaning. Lastly, 'roots' need not be of any great age: a root can come into existence at any stage in the development of a language. As Bréal pointed out, if we consider the French words rouler, roulement, roulage, roulier, rouleau, roulette, roulis, we may fairly say that they contain the common root 'roule', which has a verbal meaning 'to roll'. But we know that rouler is derived from the Latin noun rotula (= a little wheel).

We need not pursue further the arguments of these two opposing views. It is submitted that there were errors on both sides. The pioneers were in error in some respects, but they had progressed along the right path, though not far enough. The more recent scholars made vast advances in other directions but lost sight of this path, and in consequence, since 1880, there has been little progress in the search for the origins of language. If, instead, we now look at the matter broadly and practically in the light of what we have learned of the history of language in the preceding chapters of this book, it is not difficult to appraise the true nature and importance of 'roots'.

As the peoples of the world progress towards civilization, their use and consciousness of their environment and of themselves becomes more intensive and detailed, and each speech-community becomes

[1] Apparently he had in mind particularly Egyptian and Polynesian, but he was in error.
[2] He referred especially to the Semitic roots, with their radical verbs of three consonants – so, for example, qtl is the common part of the radical which means 'kill', but cannot be pronounced without the addition of vowels. On the other hand, it would be better to say that the root (or stem) is qaṭala or qaṭal.

vastly larger, and in constitution more various, specialized and complex. Accordingly its communications increase in number and detail and its vocabulary expands. In the early days of language growth is infinitely slow: it increases ever in pace, and when the modern age is reached the speed becomes dizzy. But by what formal means can the number of words of a language be expanded in such a degree – from under 10,000 words in most peoples of Grade A2(1) to over 150,000 in Modern English?

First, there may be an increasing variation and differentiation of the vowels – in addition to, say, *bad*, we may have *bid*, *bed*, *bead*, *bud*. But that will not take us far. Vowels are comparatively few and unstable and their frontiers ill-marked. Indeed, such a variation and differentiation had already taken place to a large extent before the vocabulary reached the number of 10,000. Secondly, there may be an increasing variation and differentiation of consonants. That, too, had already taken place, and will not take us much further. Indeed, the number of different consonants in many languages of the simpler peoples is already very large and it does not increase in the languages we know of. On the contrary, it tends to diminish. Three further methods remain. One is, to increase the number of meanings of each word. This method has certainly been generally used, but it is not relevant to the present question, which is: How did vocabularies increase from under 10,000 to over 150,000 words? In a minority of languages an increase of vocabulary has been achieved by a variation of tones, so that in many Western Sudanic and Sino-Tibetan and Bushman languages, where the words are mainly monosyllables, each word obtains a different meaning according to the tone in which it is uttered – for example, it may be a high or low, a rising or a falling tone. As the language develops, the number of tones may increase, so that, for example, in Chinese, in the last 2,000 years, while the words are still monosyllables and are still to be numbered in mere hundreds, the number of tones has continually increased, till in modern Cantonese it has reached nine. In Ewe it has only increased to five. But the majority of languages – for example, the Indo-European, Semitic and Bantu – are not tone languages in this sense. One chief method remains: to increase the vocabulary of a language, the length of the words must be increased. Theoretically, by doubling the length of all the words of a language, the possible number is squared. English, whose history is so long in the time-scale of economic advance, affords us an unmistakable record of this process. Here, in any passage of

Modern English, is to be seen the old Germanic vocabulary of monosyllables and disyllables,[1] side by side with the later, Romance vocabulary of longer words; and the same process is to be seen at work in the vocabularies of the other Aryan tongues, ancient and modern, as their speakers advanced in civilization.[2]

But, as we have seen, these added, longer words contain only a very small and diminishing proportion of verbs. By and large, they are non-verbs added to a vocabulary of verbs. So we saw in the Latin lexicon – and we should see in any other Aryan language – that among the shortest words the proportion of verbs is highest. The form of these new and longer words is mainly derived from that of the verbs – the nouns mainly direct from the verbs; the adjectives mainly from verbs through nouns, but also directly from the verbs; and the adverbs at first from the verbs, then from nouns and latterly from adjectives. The reason why the form of the new and longer words is derived from the verbs is that, in order to be understood in their new meaning, they must be close enough in form to the old words to suggest the new meaning. They must therefore contain the whole of the old word, or a clearly identifiable part of it bearing the same meaning. It will be seen, on reflection, that more commonly they will contain the whole of the old word. For, firstly, any part of the old word – if it can be pronounced and is substantial enough to form a word – will commonly be already in existence as a separate word with a different meaning. Secondly, in all cases where the process of development is simply by the old word insensibly gaining a new meaning, the form will remain the same; and this is true of a large proportion of the cases. Indeed, it was probably true of all cases in the early days of language, when we cannot suppose that men, whose consciousness of their environment and of themselves was slight and vague, were capable of the conscious creation of words of new form with new meanings. Moreover, even in later days, wherever the process of development was by the combination of existing words, the new combination would commonly – at least until it became familiar enough to be understood in dovetailed or shortened form – contain the whole of each of the older words.[3] But

---

[1] As commonly occurs in language, there has also been some wastage and shortening of words by the lapse of time (for example, O.E. *hlaford* has become *lord*) and especially the disappearance of the final short 'e' in the 15th century, but these are relatively unimportant details of the general picture.

[2] This general tendency to increase the length of words is also part of the tendency to increase the length of the sentence – see *post*, p. 74.

[3] As, for example, in Ewe. In North America we see examples of both types of languages, chiefly the former.

where the new word contains only part and not the whole of the old word, as a rule it will contain the consonants rather than the vowels,[1] for vowels are unstable, and a word is not so easily recognized by its vowels as by its consonants. We recognize *bid* and *bade*, or *sing*, *sang*, *sung* and *song* as having a connexion with one another. Given their context in an English sentence we could complete without great difficulty the vowels in 'b-d' or 's-ng'. But no number of vowels alone will suggest the consonants of a word. If indeed – as we shall suggest – the vowels of the earliest words were substantially the same, there was then no possibility that a new word could retain any resemblance to the old except by retaining the old consonants – that is to say, by retaining the whole of the old word.

Hence the 'roots'. They are merely the results of the process of using old sounds for new purposes. By and large they are nothing more nor less than the old verbs (as in the Indo-European languages) or their consonants (as in the Semitic languages) which are found forming the whole or a part of each of a great number of nouns, adjectives and adverbs. At the same time the old verbs are often found surviving side by side with those words, unless the eternal process of the change, corruption, decay and loss of words hides the process from our eyes, or unless rarely (as in the Semitic radicals) the other eternal process of rule-forming or 'analogy' lengthens all words to one pattern or form.

But 'roots' will not be seen in all languages, but only in those in which the increase in vocabulary has been obtained on a large scale by the lengthening of words. The phenomenon of 'roots' is especially a phenomenon of the Indo-European languages. For, firstly, these languages have largely developed not merely by extension, but by the addition of suffixes, added for the purposes of grammar and for the extension of the vocabulary. This is one great process, and it is one with the development of the sentence by extension. Hence the 'roots' can be clearly seen, and as the endings of words tend to be less permanent in form than the beginnings, the 'roots' withstand corruption and decay the better. Moreover, the Indo-European languages, as we know them, and the material culture of the people speaking them, have developed faster and further than all others known to us, and in the result the vocabularies have expanded faster and further than in any other family of languages. The importance of this speed of development is that the eternal process of change, corruption, decay and loss of words has not had time to affect the growing vocabulary to the same

---

[1] E.g. in the Semitic languages.

ORIGIN OF NOUNS, ADJECTIVES AND ADVERBS

extent. We may also add that the mere existence of the same roots in so many words tends to resist the process of change and corruption and to perpetuate form and meaning.

If so, the pioneers were mistaken in thinking that the 'roots' date from 'a stage in the growth of language in which that sharp distinction which we make between the different parts of speech had not yet been fixed'. There is no evidence that such a stage ever existed. The roots are, by and large, verbs of earlier date. In the early days of language, from the verbs were derived the forms of the other parts of speech, and the same process, for the same reasons, has continued ever since. The verb, the action, is the productive, the fecund element of language and thought. On the other hand, the later scholars were in error in thinking that such 'roots' could never have been real words. Many of them survived with little change as separate and distinct words in the classical and even modern languages. They urged that it is only accidental that the analysis produces a verb: that what it produces is, naturally, something with a vague, general meaning, and verbs have a vague, general meaning. The only truth in this is that verbs have a general meaning, and it is partly for this reason that language originates with them. They pointed out that the same root is sometimes found with two different meanings – for example, there is kar, *to cut*, and kar, *to create*. That is so, for the good reason that *kar* was a word which originally meant 'to cut', and so (like the English 'cut') came also to mean 'to create by cutting' – as in England one *cuts* a caper or a garment. So too, for example, in Semitic: the verb *bara'* is used in the Hebrew Testament of God's creation of the world, but in some Semitic dialects it still means 'to create by cutting'. A hundred parallels could be cited from other languages.[1] Lastly, they urged that these roots need not be of any great age; and that roots can be created at any time. That, as we have seen, is very true. In Bréal's example the verb 'rouler' (to roll) was derived from the noun 'rotula' (a wheel). There are everywhere verbs formed from familiar nouns in everyday use. But the process of formation of verb from noun is the exception rather than the rule, and, in any case, when once the verb has been formed, it is the fecund element, ready to produce other parts of speech, as *rouler* produced *roulage, roulette, roulier. rouleau, roulis*. All this is no reason why we should confuse ancient with modern verbs. Roots common to Indo-European languages must be at least as old as Common Indo-European.

[1] And see *post*, p. 228.

Now, if we turn to the languages of the simpler peoples, we shall see these 'roots' as they had previously existed, namely, in the main, as verbs. But before we do so, let us look at one or two of the families of languages of the ancient civilization of the Near East. Though none of the peoples who spoke them were as backward in material culture as many of the Indo-Europeans, they will serve as an introduction to the languages of the simpler communities.

When we leave the Indo-European family of languages and turn to the miracle of the Semitic, how different is the picture we see! While most of the former, in the 3,000 years during which we have known them, have changed beyond recognition, so that apart from writing and a known history we should not have guessed that Modern French or even Modern English were two of these tongues, the Semitic languages during 4,000 years have remained substantially the same. The Assyrian of 2,000 B.C. is in some respects nearer to modern Ethiopian than either is to Arabic. In some respects the Hebrew of over 2,500 years ago has diverged further from the type than modern Arabic. Some modern dialects of Arabia are considered by many scholars more primitive and pure than any of the other tongues. While some Indo-European vocabularies have swollen to the gargantuan proportions of over 150,000 words, the Semitic remain small. The Hebrew Old Testament musters a total of only 6,000 different words. In the Semitic tongues we need not search for roots, for they are before our eyes. Practically every verb is a radical and practically every radical is a verb.

But all languages contain some archaic surviving features, and all languages are in some respects modernized and changed. The Semitic tongues, constant as they are in comparison with any other family of languages of which we know, are unique in the length of their radicals. They are generally (for example, in Arabic) of the form CVCVCV (as, *qaṭala* = he killed); or (for example, in Hebrew) of the form CVCVC (as, *qaṭal* = he killed). Almost all their verbs, that is to say, contain three consonants, separated by vowels, in place of the Indo-European two. But many scholars are agreed that in a common parent-language the Semitic verbs consisted of two consonants instead of three, and were therefore of the form CVC(V). There may also have been a few of the form VCV, though to the sensitive ear of the Semite a faint guttural consonant was audible at the commencement of the first vowel. The vowels of these ancient radicals, as well as of the present longer radicals, were, in their simplest forms, generally 'a'. Accordingly both the Semitic and the Indo-European tongues seem to lead us back towards a number of verbs almost unmixed with other parts of speech, almost all of the form CVCV, but a few of the form VCV, and the vowel 'a' curiously predominates.

The Hamitic languages show us a similar picture. In Egyptian the radical verb contained two, three or four consonants, but in the oldest known Egyptian the vast bulk of the radicals were of three consonants as in Semitic. It seems likely – and it is probably the opinion of most scholars – that Hamitic and Semitic have a common origin, but when they diverged the bulk of the radicals had already lengthened to the triconsonantal form.

CHAPTER SEVEN

The Origin of the Nouns, Adjectives and Adverbs in the Languages of the Simpler Communities—The Pronouns

In the last two chapters we gave reasons for thinking that, by and large, in English and the classical Semitic and Aryan languages the nouns, adjectives and adverbs originated in their form directly or indirectly from the verbs. Secondly we gave reason for supposing that verbs of earlier days survived as roots in the vocabularies of the classical languages, and we pointed out that those roots were overwhelmingly of one form, namely CVC(V), in which the vowels were short and the vowel A predominated. We were, therefore, considering two quite different aspects of the history of the form of words – the first, its functional history, and the second, its phonetic history. But it was important to consider both aspects together, for if the oldest words to which we can penetrate are, in the main, of one part of speech, namely verbs, and if they are also of one form, namely CVC(V), there is double reason for believing that the path we are treading is the broad path by which language developed, and that it leads back towards a common or like origin.

Let us now turn to the languages of the backward peoples around us, and consider them from the same two aspects.

First, then, as to the origin of the nouns, adjectives and adverbs. All over the world, in the languages of the simpler peoples, so far as we can test them, we find what we found in English and Latin, namely that the nouns are mainly derived from the verbs, the adjectives at first from the verbs direct and later from the nouns, and the adverbs at first from verbs, then from nouns and lastly from the adjectives; and the abstract nouns also mainly from the adjectives. It would be a tedious repetition to analyse the vocabularies of any great number of these languages and show these results. In some families of tongues, for example the Bantu and Semitic, some of these parts of speech are little developed, the adjective has not become differentiated on a large scale from the verb and the noun, and the adverbs are even fewer, and there is little more to be seen than the derivation, by and large, of the nouns from the verbs. But to the extent that adjectives, adverbs and abstract nouns are to be found, the general process is the same as that which we have mentioned. To obtain a better example of its working we should turn to one of the families of languages – for example the Melanesian and Polynesian – where the adjective is well developed. Let us take one example, the Fijian, at the junction of Grade A2(1) and A2(2), a Melanesian language nearer to the Polynesian than most. It is a useful and striking example, for in the Melanesian and Polynesian tongues, like Modern English in this respect and unlike Latin and Greek and Hebrew and the other inflecting languages, words are commonly to be found serving the purpose of different parts of speech without any change in their form. In his *New Fijian Grammar*[1] Mr C. M. Churchward expresses himself on this subject as follows:

'1. In Fijian, as in English, there are eight principal classes of words or parts of speech, differentiated according to their respective uses or functions. They fall naturally into four pairs: nouns and verbs (principal words), adjectives and adverbs (qualifying words), prepositions and conjunctions (connecting words), pronouns and interjections (substitutionary words)....

'2. It frequently happens, however, that one and the same word may serve, now in one capacity, now in another. This is quite common in English; it is still commoner in Fijian. Such interchange of functions occurs principally as follows.

'3. *First*, many words which are primarily nouns are used also as adjectives. Examples: kau (tree, wood) made of wood, wooden; vatu (stone, rock) made of stone; tagane (man) male; yalewa (woman) female. Thus na vale kau, the wooden house; na vale vatu, the stone house; na toa tagane, the male fowl (cock); na toa yalewa, the female fowl (hen).

'4. *Second*, most words which are primarily adjectives are used also as abstract nouns. E.g. savasavā (clean) cleanness, cleanliness; dina (true) truth; balavu (long) length; titobu (deep) depth. Thus na kena titobu, its depth; na savasavā, cleanliness; na dina, truth.

'5. *Third*, most, perhaps all, words which are primarily verbs are

[1] (1941), p. 16.

used also as nouns. E.g. vosa (to speak) speech, word, statement or language; qito (to play) game; bula (to live) life; maté (to die) death etc.

'6. *Fourth*, verbs, either alone or preceded by the adverb dau (habitually) are sometimes used as adjectives. Na waqa vuka, the airship or aeroplane (lit. the flying boat). Na taurata dauteitei, the planter (lit. the habitually-planting man).

'7. Some verbs are even usable as adverbs. E.g. yaco, to arrive, as in vunau yaco ("to preach arriving") = to be a fully accredited preacher; cakacaka yaco = to work efficiently; and lako, to go, as in vunau lako (to preach as one goes along) etc.'

Any Melanesian language will clearly show the like process at work, and so, too, will any Polynesian tongue. So, for example, G. Pratt in his *Grammar and Dictionary of Samoan*[1] points out that verbs are mainly primitive words, that is to say words that cannot be traced as deriving from other parts of speech.[2] Many nouns are also primitive, but others are derived from verbs by addition of ga, saga, taga, maga, or 'aga,[3] and the simple form of the verb is sometimes used as a noun.[4] Of the adjectives, some are primitive, some formed from nouns by addition of an 'a' (like the 'y' in English) or by doubling the noun or prefixing fa'a to it. As the English '-ly' and '-like', the fa'a often expresses similitude.[5] But verbs are also used as adjectives without change.[6] Adjectives are made into abstract nouns by adding an article or pronoun, as lelei, good, ó le lelei (goodness – cf. the Greek τὸ καλόν). The Papuan languages of New Guinea show the same process at work. For example, in Motu (a language spoken in and around Port Moresby) we are told by Lawes[7] that some nouns are primitive (as au, a tree; nadi, a stone), or they are derivative, being derived from a verb. Verbs become nouns by prefixing i or he to the verbal root, and in certain cases adding also the suffix -na and the word tauna or gauna. But in many cases the verb is used also as a noun without alteration of form. Abstract nouns are formed generally by adding 'na' to the adjective. The adjective is known by its position in the sentence. Commonly it is a noun or a verb, showing by its position behind a noun

[1] 3rd Ed., 1891.
[2] Ibid., p. 14. These we have called radical words.
[3] Ibid., p. 3.
[4] p. 4.
[5] p. 7.
[6] p. 8.
[7] Rev. W. G. Lawes, *Grammar and Vocabulary of Language spoken by Motu Tribes (New Guinea)* (3rd Ed., Sydney, 1896).

that it is used in this instance as an adjective. Almost any adjective can also be used as an adverb.[1]

Here then, in these languages which we have chosen as instances, we see at work a process by which, in the long lapse of time, the words (with or without change of form – and, if there is a change of form, usually by lengthening of form) will become less and less of verbs and more and more of the other parts of speech, in the order which has been described.

Now let us turn to the other matter which we considered in the last two chapters, namely 'roots' and their form.

When we looked at the Indo-European and Semitic languages, we spoke of 'roots' because, though we surmised that they had previously existed as separate and distinct words, they were chiefly to be found as a part of a longer word, and they were the part that constituted its origin. When we turn to peoples more and more simple and backward, we find that the vocabularies are still very small and the words of the other parts of speech – that is to say, words which have been derived from verbs – are far fewer, and hence what we have called 'roots' are seen more and more as distinct and independent verbs. They are also to be seen as parts of other words (mainly non-verbs) but far less so than before: they are more and more to be seen as verbs which cannot be derived from other words. Accordingly it becomes less appropriate to call them 'roots', and more fitting to call them 'radical (or primitive) words'. The primitive words are not by any means all verbs, but the proportion of verbs among them is far greater than in the derived, non-radical words of the vocabulary. The number of primitive words, that is to say words whose derivation cannot be traced, is often large. We have already noticed the reasons: among the simpler peoples the extension of the vocabulary, including the formation of non-verbs from verbs, is slow, and meanwhile the normal wearing and decay of words proceeds apace.

Let us begin with the Sumerian language, the language of the Late Code civilization of South Mesopotamia, that was superseded by

[1] Op. cit., pp. 3-7. The same process can also be seen in the languages of North America, though it has not proceeded so far. For example, M. J. Andrade observes of Quileute (the language of Hunters of the N.W. coast of the State of Washington) that 'the words which we should classify as adjectives in Indo-European languages are identical in their morphology and syntax with the Quileute verbs, and this applies even to the numerals'. He also notes that 'it is more common to form nouns with elements whose meanings we should regard as primarily verbal, than to form verbs by the reverse process', H.A.I.L., part 3, p. 179. Leo J. Frachtenberg says the same of Suslawan, remarking that 'all stems expressing our adjectival ideas are in reality intransitive verbs' (H.A.I.L., part 2, pp. 459-60). See also *ante*, p. 50 (n.)2.

F

Semitic in that area in the second millennium B.C. Here we can appropriately speak either of 'roots' or 'stems'. The majority of the roots are of the form CVC, but there is also a large minority of the form CV. It was a pronounced characteristic of Sumerian, as it is of modern French and many other languages, that final consonants disappeared except where the following word began with a vowel. So common, indeed, was it, that in many cases (as in modern alphabetic writing) it was customary to write in the consonant by a separate phonetic symbol, although it was not pronounced, so as to make clear the meaning of the word. It seems likely that it is this process of the dropping of final consonants, continued over a long period, that has changed many roots of the form CVC to CV. An analysis of the roots supports this view. As the CVC forms are earlier than the CV, the proportion of verbs among the former is greater than among the latter. I estimate from glossaries that the proportion of verbs in roots of the form CVC is a little over 50%, and in roots of the form CV approximately 40%. The proportion of verbs in the non-radical words is very small in comparison.

Most of the peoples of the Third Agricultural Grade surviving in the modern world are to be found in the continent of Africa. All the native peoples of that continent are of this grade, excepting, on the one hand, the modern peoples of Egypt and the Mediterranean littoral, and, on the other hand, the few surviving Bushmen and Hottentots of South Africa and Pygmies of Central Africa. We can find, therefore, a succession of African peoples of this grade, more and more primitive than the advanced communities which we considered in the previous two chapters. But Africa is more important to us than that. The bulk of Africa is part of one great cultural field which includes the areas of the Semitic, Sumerian and Aryan-speaking peoples. We shall notice again, in regard to language, great general resemblances with the Semitic and Aryan fields, save in so far as the backwardness of Africa in the progress towards civilization produces its own differences.

Looking at native Africa generally, we see that the radical words in the great bulk of languages are overwhelmingly of the type CVC(V).[1] There are also a few peoples in whose languages the radicals are generally of the form CV, and a few among whom they are of both forms.[2] There are reasons for thinking that in Africa the CV radicals, where

---

[1] See Homburger, *Negro-African Languages*, p. 78.
[2] Op. cit., p. 79. And see Appendix B in *A Study of the Ewe Language*, by D. Westermann (trans. by A. L. Bickford-Smith, 1930).

ORIGIN OF NOUNS, ADJECTIVES AND ADVERBS 83

they occur, are later than the rest. The peoples among whom they occur are situated furthest from the Indo-European and Semitic worlds. Their languages are a few of the West Sudanic group of languages in West Africa, and of the Bushman languages of South and South-West Africa. They are tone languages, in which the variation of tones has taken the place of the final C(V) and made it possible to make shift with a smaller vocabulary. In most of these languages the radicals are of both types, CV and CVC(V). The languages in which the radicals are uniformly of type CV are confined to the cradle of the Negro race, in the lands bordering on the north coast of the Gulf of Guinea. Here the number of tones is increasing to meet the need of the vocabulary to expand. For example, in Ewe, which has five tones, 'almost every combination of a consonant with a vowel appears with a high and low tone, each of which has a different meaning'.[1] But even in some of the West Sudanic tongues (for example, those of Senegal) the radicals are normally of the type CVC(V), and over the whole of Africa, excluding West Africa and the Bushman languages, the radicals are uniformly of this type.

For example, moving by degrees backwards from the Semitic world, we turn first to the Bantu-speaking peoples, who cover the whole of the southern third of Africa. They represent stages varying between that of the Akikuyu and Akamba of East Africa (Grade A3(1)), the Zulu and other Nguni peoples of South Africa (Grade A3(2)) and the peoples of Central and West Central Africa (mainly Grade A3(3), or the Central Codes). We may take the Zulu as representing the simpler of these peoples and one of the least changed of the Bantu dialects. Throughout the Bantu languages the radicals are of the form CVC(V)[2] The terminal vowel is uniformly 'A'. As in Indo-European, the first vowel of the radical does not generally change in the different parts of the verb and noun,[3] but there is evidence that at an earlier date the vowel changed in the grammar of the verb, much as it does in Semitic.[4] In the view of the present writer there is abundant evidence that originally the first vowel was a short 'a'. Even in the present state of the language it is still generally a short vowel. As examples of the radical in Bantu may be taken such Zulu words as *caba*, to chop, break, cut; *ceka*, cut; *capa*, soften the skin by rubbing; sometimes however with a nasal vowel, as *canda*, chop, split; *centa*, scrape, and so forth.

[1] Westermann, p. 26. E.g. ka, to scatter, ká, to touch; ke, root, ké, to drop down.
[2] Generally CVCV except where the final vowel has been dropped in the North-West Bantu or Semi-Bantu (Johnston, vol. ii, pp. 495, 512).
[3] Johnston, vol. ii, p. 495.   [4] Homburger, p. 81.

To find the more primitive peoples, we must move to North-East Africa at the borderland of the Negro, Bantu, Hamitic and Semitic fields. Here we find the naked Nilotic peoples of the Sudan and the Lango of Uganda. They are of Grade A3(1), pastoral peoples with little subsidiary agriculture – Shilluk, Anuak, Nuer, Dinka and others, speaking a sub-group of 'Sudanic' languages. In all these tongues the radicals are overwhelmingly of the form CVC,[1] and the vowel is short. Let us look for a moment at Driberg's glossary and grammar of Lango,[2] in order to appreciate how uniform and unmistakable are the phenomena which we are considering. In Lango the vast majority of the radicals are of the form CVC, the vowel being short, and practically every verb is of that form. Out of 930 verbs in the glossary only 16 begin with a vowel, although nearly half the words in the vocabulary begin with a vowel. Of the words beginning with a vowel only 1·5% are verbs. Of words beginning with a consonant 52% are verbs. In Lango, then, the verbs are mainly radicals, and the radicals mainly verbs. The position is the same in Dinka, where the bulk of the radicals are of the form CVC, and practically all of them are verbs. 'Nearly all Dinka words are primitive roots, which are not infrequently – without great alteration of quantity, etc. – also used as nouns, adjectives or prepositions.'[3] The Dinka are the most primitive of the Nilotes.

Let us move still further backwards in our economic grading. The peoples of the Second Agricultural Grade are chiefly to be found in Oceania. Here again the radicals are overwhelmingly of the form CVCV, both in the Polynesian (Grade A2(2)) and Melanesian (A2(1)) languages and the vowel A predominates. We have seen that the proportion of verbs grows greater here, and even more than in Africa it is appropriate to speak of radicals rather than roots, for they chiefly exist as separate words though they are also found, as in Indo-European, forming part of other words.[4] In the whole of this area, however, there is a notable indistinctness of speech sounds,[5] and in the result the form of the words shows a rapid decay and change, and in particular a growing weakness and progressive disappearance of consonants. Consequently in many cases an old radical or root, found, for example, in Indonesian in the form CVCV, becomes in Melanesian or Polynesian CV.[6] As Ray remarks, the extreme degradation of the root in some Melanesian languages renders its identification uncertain.[7] The

---

[1] Adding frequently a semi-vowel, as in Lango bwong, gwen, tyen, lyech.
[2] In Driberg, *The Lango.*
[3] J. C. Mitterrützner (1866), *Die Dinka-Sprache in Central-Africa,* p. 29.
[4] Ray, p. 39.   [5] See e.g. Ray, p. 40.   [6] Ray, p. 53.   [7] Ray, p. 54.

same phenomenon is to be witnessed in Polynesian. For example, the Maori tō ('to drag') and ke ('different') appear in cognate Polynesian dialects as toso and kese, the s having fallen away in Maori. In some of these languages, indeed, the consonants have become very few.

Let us now move backwards in the economic scale of progress to the Hunters and peoples of the First Agricultural Grade, the majority of whom are to be found in America. Again we observe the same phenomena. In most languages the most common form of the 'roots', 'stems' or 'elements' is the form CVC (the vowel being generally short), though there is a substantial minority of languages in which they are most commonly of the form CVCV, and a substantial minority in which the most common form is CV. There is no space here to give examples.

Lastly, we may take as examples of the most backward of the Food Gatherers the Bushman languages of South Africa and the languages of the Andamanese. In Bushman the most common type of verbal stem is the type CV, but there is also a substantial number of the type CVCV. In the languages of the Andaman Islands the radicals are mainly of the type CVCV.

Now let us pause and consider, what is the significance of the facts, set out in this and the preceding chapter, in regard to roots and radical words. What is the significance of the persistence of the same general forms – namely the type CVC(V) (the vowel being predominantly short and predominantly A) and to a lesser extent the type CV?

If words were biological entities, we should infer that these types, being found far and wide at all stages of evolution, represented characters of a common parent stock. By analogy we might infer that words originated in these forms, and accordingly that the explanation of their existence was historical. If then it were urged in answer to this hypothesis (as Sayce urged in regard to Semitic roots) that these types are to be found not for historical reasons but because they are merely the type-skeleton of the commonest words – that the majority of words and syllables begin with a consonant, and therefore roots begin with a consonant; and as they are arrived at by analysis and abstraction, they are brief and contain a short vowel, which is but the common factor of all vowels – if this were argued, we might heartily agree with it, but go on to say that the explanation might still be historical also. Nothing is more likely than that the commonest, most general features of language are its original features. Indeed, over short periods it can be seen everywhere very plainly that the origin is historical. If a number of words possess a common root, that is to say a common syllable or pair of syllables with one and the same meaning wherever it appears, the root must be older than all these words, or at least older than all but one of them. We might add that Sayce's explanation utterly fails to fit radical words as distinct from roots.

But we shall better understand the significance of these phenomena if we remember that language is not merely, in a sense, a biological unit – the sounds made by living creatures – but also the product of function. Let us return to our metaphor of the heartwood of language. We noticed in the vocabulary of individuals (for example, Shakespeare) a heartwood of the most common words, in which the proportion of verbs was larger than in the rest of the vocabulary. Then we looked at the course of development of English and other languages over the centuries and over the grades of advance, and noticed that the relation between earlier and later language was similar to that between the heartwood and the extremities, namely that the history of language was the deposit round the heartwood of outer rings in which the proportion of verbs grew less and less. The heartwood in later language tended to retain the characteristics of the earlier language, for example, the higher proportion of verbs. It is the same with form. These radical words whose forms we have examined are overwhelmingly verbal. In all the languages mentioned in this chapter, covering all grades of advance up to that of the Late Codes, so far as I can measure them the proportion of verbs in the radical words of types CVC(V) and CV remains constant at the enormous figure of about 50%, be it more or less. Moreover, these radical words are generally the commonest words in each language: they are the centre of the heartwood, and they tend to retain the same type of form throughout history, even while they tend to retain the same functions, namely the same proportions of the parts of speech. In short, as we have found again and again, and shall find in later chapters, the commonest in language is generally the oldest, and the characteristics of the commonest, in function (that is, meaning) and form, are generally the characteristics of the oldest.[1] Conversely, the oldest in language is generally the commonest, because it is generally the most familiar. Moreover, we can easily see that if the

---

[1] G. Stern, in *Meaning and Change of Meaning*, suggests as a conservative factor in the preservation of meaning 'the frequency of words in a specific meaning; in other words the strength of the linguistic tradition. It is well known that the most common words of a language retain most tenaciously old and otherwise discarded forms and inflections. It is reasonable to assume that a strong tradition has similar effects on meanings', p. 185. See also ibid., p. 193. This is the same point.

heartwood has originally consisted of verbs, and tends to continue to consist of verbs, and if the radicals or rootwords tend to survive with unaltered function, they will also tend to survive with unaltered form – otherwise what becomes of the old forms? Either they must disappear leaving a lacuna, or they must tend to keep the old meanings. These are the tendencies of language in the course of its history.

But, it might be said, this is not enough to account for what has occurred. Assuming, for the moment, that these root-types are the types of the earliest words of language, how is it that, while language is forever changing, this relation should continue during countless generations between the radicals and the rest of language – that the former should remain of these brief types, while other words expand to greater and greater length. The answer is chiefly to be found in a fundamental characteristic of language that has not yet been noticed in this book, namely the principle of the conservation of human energy. Man – and especially primitive man – does not say more than is necessary to enable him to be understood. The rest – if there is anything else in the language – is left unsaid, or slurred, or shortened. These radical words, as we have said, are generally the most familiar words in the language. Accordingly the conservation of energy finds here its chief field – the words are limited to the minimum necessary to make the speaker understood. We shall later see much more of the working of this process.

Before we finally leave the topic of roots, let us return to a matter that we mentioned in the previous chapter but did not pursue. It was said that the great bulk of the Indo-European roots were verbal but that there was a small, compact number of roots with the meanings of pronouns. Personal pronouns have their main function in connection with verbs, and it is therefore not to be wondered at that among a vast number of verbal roots a small group of pronominal roots should appear. Moreover, it has been noticed by many linguists, and may almost be termed a commonplace, that of all the parts of speech the personal pronouns are the least liable to change their form. These two considerations materially reinforce our conclusions that, firstly, the verbal roots were originally true verbs, and, secondly, that these roots are generally of considerable age. *Noscitur a sociis* – a word, like a man, is known by the company it keeps. The extent to which the forms of the personal pronouns resist change is truly remarkable. Not the pronouns of the third person: indeed many of the world's languages have no pronouns of the third person, though they may have various classes of demonstratives. But all languages have pronouns of the first and second person. And there is truly only one person of the first person singular – one speaker of each sentence. I do not recollect any language which finds it necessary to mark him out even by the distinguishing signs of gender, Even the second person is not so distinct; there may be more than one hearer, and there are a few languages that (like the Semitic) make distinctions of gender in the pronouns of the second person.

It is chiefly the pronoun of the first person singular that resists change in the world's languages. Vast, for example, as are the changes undergone by the Indo-European languages during the last four millennia, the pronoun of the first person[1] moves within a very small compass – me, ma, mam, mi, mu, etc. – the consonant merely moving from m to n, and the vowel showing a somewhat wider range.[2]

The Sumerian pronoun of over four millennia ago is substantially the same. The forms of the independent pronoun of the first person singular are, as subject or object of the verb, ma, ma-e and mē, and as indirect object ma-a; as suffixed possessive pronoun (Eng. my) subject or object -mu, and as indirect object -ma.

In the Semitic pronoun the consonant is n. The pronoun of the first person singular in Arabic and most other Semitic dialects is 'ana, but in Hebrew and some modern dialects of Arabic it has become 'ani.[3]

---

[1] I omit in the following examples the pronoun of the nominative singular (Greek and Latin ego, Skt. aham, Goth. ik, Mod. English I). This is a different Indo-European word.

[2] *Sing*: *Accus*.: Skt. and Zend mam and mā; Gk. mě ěmě; Lat. mē; Old Slavic mě; Lithuanian mane; Old High German mihi (Low, mik); Hittite amm, mu.
    Genitive: Skt. mama; Zend mana; Gk. emeîo, moû, emoû; Lat. mei; O. Sl. mene; Lith. mané.
    Dative: Skt. máhy-am, me; Zend me; Gk. moi, ěmoi; Ombr. and Old Latin mehe; Lat. mihi; O. Sl. mi; Mod. German mich; Hittite -mu.
  Plural: *Nom*.: Greek hē-meis; Gk. Lesb. am-mes; Armenian mekh; O. Sl. my; Lith. mes; Lat. nos.
    Accus.: Skt. nah; Zend no; Gk. he-mas; Lat. nos; O. Sl. ny; Goth. uns.
    Gen.: O. Sl. nasu. *Dat*.: O. Sl. namu.
  Dual: Skt. nau; O. Sl. na; Gk. (accus.) nō.
  Suffixed to verb as subject-pronoun – M weakening to N.
    Present tense: -M, e.g. verbs ending in -mi (Skt. as-mi; Gk. ei-mi for es-mi; O. Sl. yes-mi; Lat. sum for es-mi; Mod. Eng. am). Also such forms as Gk. luoimi; Lat. regam, amem; Hittite -mi.
    Secondary or past tenses: *Sing*.: Gk. -n (e.g. ebalon, estēn, eiēn); Lat. -m (e.g. amabam, amaverim, etc.).
      Plural: Gk. -mes, -mos, -men; Lat. -mus; O. Sl. -mu; O. H.G. -mes.
      Middle and Pass.: Gk. -mai, -metha, -mēn; Indo-Iran. madhai; Skt. -mahe; Lat. -mur.
  In Abyssinia, 'ana in Ge'ez, 'anē in Tigriña, and 'ennih or 'eñe in Amharic.

The objective pronoun suffixed to the verb is generally -ni throughout the Semitic languages.[1] These and similar forms for the pronoun 'I' are widespread in Northern and Eastern Africa. For example, among East African languages, sometimes called Hamitic and sometimes Sub-Semitic, it is ane (Bishari) ani (Galla; accusative ana), anu (Saho), an (Bilin and Dambasa), ana, ani and an in Somali. Still more remarkable is the persistence of these forms among some of the most backward peoples of Africa. Among the naked Nilotes and so-called Half-Hamites of North-East Africa, we find, for example, in Nandi ane, in Suk ani, in Nuer 'an, and in Lango an.

The rest of the Sudanic tongues – a varied group stretching from East Africa to the Atlantic – present the same general picture as the Indo-European, Sumerian and Semitic tongues. It would be wearisome to multiply instances.[2]

The Bantu languages corroborate these views and widen the vast landscape. Different as they are, in their present form, from the languages that have been mentioned, there is a substantial identity between their personal pronouns of the first person singular and those of the Hamitic, Semitic, Sudanic and Indo-European languages. Far as they have spread from their original home in the area of the Great Lakes, they have changed little in this respect. Sir Harry Johnston[3] considered that the original forms of these pronouns in the Bantu mother-speech were probably: for the subject pronoun, mi, n, ne, ni; for the object pronoun, -mi, -n-, -ni-, -ñgi- ; for the possessive pronoun, -ñgu, -ñge, -m, -mi, -ni, -ne. These are common in the modern forms, which also include such forms as nene, nanu, -a-nge, -a-ne, a-ni, -a-nye.

In the far South and South-west of Africa, the same words are found in the languages of the Bushmen, Food Gatherers who were widespread about the continent during many millennia. Here are the pronouns of the first person singular in three northern Bushman and six southern Bushman languages, whose vocabularies have been collated by Miss D. F. Bleek.[4] Northern: (1) m, mihi, mi; (2) ng, na,

[1] Arabic, Hebrew, Ge'ez, Aramaic, Assyrian (the latter -ni or -ani, -anni, -inni).
[2] E.g. in Hausa (with its Hamitic affinities) ni, nai, plural mu; but generally in West Sudanic tongues the consonant is m – Basa: me, mi, em; Nupe: mi; Yoruba: emi, mo, ng, mi; Ewe: nye, me, m, ng, ye; Pul: min, mi, -am; Wolof: man, ma.
[3] Johnston, vol. 1, p. 32.
[4] D. F. Bleek, *Comparative Vocabularies of Bushmen Languages* (1929), p. 49. The tribes are as follows (I omit clicks):—Northern: (1) K'au en, (2) Kung, (3) O Kung. Southern: (1) Kam-ka ke, (2) Ng-ke, (3) Batwa, (4) Auni, (5) Masarwa, (6) Nu en. She also records two central tribes, Masarwa (Tati) and Naron, in which the words are of different form. Cf. also *The Naron* (by the same author), 1928, p. 61, in which she gives the Auen pronouns as mihi, mi.

m, mi; (3) mi, mihi, ma. Southern: (1) ng, n, ng-ng (emphatic), m (before labials), and occasionally ka; (2) ng, n, ni, ma, a; (3) ng, ang, am; (4) ng, ng-ng; (5) ng, na; (6) ng, ng-ng (emphatic), m, na. Professor L. F. Maingard gives the pronoun of the Khomani dialect as (subject) n, ng, nga, na, and (object) ng; (emphatic) ng-ng.

From Central Europe across present-day Asia, the same phenomenon is seen everywhere. In the Finno-Ugrian family of languages, scattered between Lapland and Finland, Hungary and hither Siberia, we find again the pronoun of the first person, in its varied uses, represented by m weakening to n. For example, in Hungarian könyv = a book, könyvem, my book; ház, a house, házam, my house; var, he sows, varam (definite form of imperfect) I sowed; én is the personal pronoun of the first person singular, and mi the plural. In Finnish minä is the singular of the first person pronoun, and me, the plural; the singular possessive (Eng. *my*) is -ni, and the plural (Eng. *our*) is -mme. The negative personal pronoun (= not I) is en, and the plural (= not we) emme. The first person singular of the verb is -n, e.g. tu-on (originally tu-om), I bring, to-in (originally to-im), I brought. Similarly in the kindred Samoyed languages, the main predicate-affix everywhere is -m, and the possessives are usually variations of m[1]: Lûca, Russian; Lûcam, I am Russian; paránām, I burn. The singular pronoun is usually 'man'. Tavgui, kula-ma, my raven; matuyua-ma, I have cut. But in some of these languages, in some parts of the verb and noun, the final -m has plainly become corrupted to a labial vowel or consonant – e.g. Yurak, lamba-u, my ski; madâ-u, I cut. In Yenissei-Samoyed l'ibe-bo = my eagle; mota-bo, I cut.

The phenomenon is the same in the Turkish-Mongolian-Tungusian family of languages, which stretches from Europe to furthest Asia. Generally the pronoun of the first person singular is represented by m. In the various Turkish languages scattered between Europe and North-East Siberia the various uses of the pronoun or pronominal adjective are all expressed by suffixes which are compounds of m or n, for example Turkish achar-im, I open; ach-di-m, I opened; qiz-im, my daughter; bâbâ-m, my father. In the Mongolian languages the pronoun in its various uses is compounded of m and n (min = I; man = we); and the possessive adjective is formed of the genitive of the pronoun, menu = my, manu = our, shortened in speech to various compounds of m. In the Tungusian group the position is much the same, but in

[1] See table of pronouns in M. A. Castrén, *Grammatik der Samojedischen Sprachen*, ed. Schiefner (St Petersburg, 1854), pp. 210-13.

the Tungusian language (as we saw it in Samoyed) the m sometimes changes to b: pronoun bi, (Turkish ben, acc. béni) possessive suffix -f, -u; while Manchu still has mini (my), mani (our), being genitives of the pronoun. In the language of the Ghiliak (Hunters of North Sakhalin) the pronoun is again ni (I) – ni vind, I go.

In the Dravidian languages of Southern India and Ceylon, the different uses of this pronoun are generally represented by variations of the letter n: Tamil, nan (=I), nam (=we), en (=my); e.g. sey-d-en, I have done; en kaigal, my hands; nam seydem or seydom, we have done, valu-nam, we live. In Old Tamil yan signified I, en (disjunctive) me; kon-en, I am King (lit. King – I). In Canara the singular of the pronoun is nanu, ná, plural návu (we), accusative namma (us).

In the Sino-Tibetan-Burmese languages, according to Karlgren, in Ancient Chinese the nominative and genitive of this pronoun was nguo, accusative nga (Burman nga-ga̭, accusative nga̭-go. In the Lo-Lo group, in Miri ngā was the subject pronoun (accusative ngom); in Dafla ngâ, (I) ngam (me). In Tibetan nga is the pronoun of the first person, and the genitive (nge) is the possessive pronoun.

In the Mon-Khmer group, the pronouns of the first person singular are añ and khñŏm.

Throughout the tribes of Australia, from coast to coast, it appears that the pronoun of the first person singular is represented by nga or some compound thereof – e.g. ngai, ngaia, ngato, ngatoa, ngaiya, yinga, ngi, ngaiyu. The position is much the same among at least many tribes of Papua.

It is only in South-East Asia and Oceania, and to a smaller extent in America, that many exceptions are to be found. In Malaya and Indonesia generally this pronoun is represented by *aku* (reminiscent of the Indo-European *ego*), and it is also found in some parts of Melanesia with the usual weakening of the consonant. Yet in some Melanesian groups, at least, the nasal consonant is again much in evidence.[1]

In North and South America the nasal n[2] (or sometimes m) signifies this pronoun in perhaps the majority of the vast number of native languages.

What, then, can be the explanation of these remarkable phenomena?

[1] For example, in New Hebrides (Tasiko: nu, ne; Aulua: anu (ne); Paama: mau (na); Ambrim: ni, etc.). See Ray, *A Comparative Study of the Melanesian Island Languages* (1926).
[2] Eg. Chinook, Maidu, Blackfoot, Fox, Mexican, Suslawan, Coos (Kusan).

Nothing, it is suggested, but the postulate that some such word or words represented the pronoun of the first person singular when language first evolved it, and that they have remained the same, with slight variation, ever since. But it may be said: Is it not possible that the nasal consonants possess some fundamental physical or psychological association with the reference to the speaker's self? It may well be so; but this only reinforces the view just stated. Or it may be suggested as the true explanation that the nasal plosives n and m are among the slowest to change of all speech-sounds, and especially at the commencement of a word. This is wholly true; but it only reinforces the same view, for it affords a reason why, if the word for I and Me in the early days of language was ma or mama, na or nana, or some such form,[1] that form should, with variations of the vowel, be retained.

The pronoun of the second person singular is far less constant, though some forms, especially ta and ka, with variations of the vowel, are significantly widespread about the world. But we must not pursue the matter further. We began this digression in merely seeking to say that, if the roots of Indo-European consisted of a few pronominal roots as well as ancient verbs, this, in view of the vast age of some of the pronouns, is not in the least to be wondered at. The pronoun which we have been considering, as well as others, would of course appear in a list of roots and radicals in all the widespread languages referred to in this chapter.

[1] As the instances show, the number of variations is limited. I believe, for example, that no form 'ama' is anywhere to be found.

CHAPTER EIGHT

Grammar

Language, in its every facet, embodies or reflects fundamental traits of the human mind and so makes them manifest. For example, the mind does not (at least at first) have real or full knowledge of any object in nature, but only of some character or aspect of it, which first impresses the mind; and accordingly language expresses a character or aspect and not the object. What applies to objects in nature applies equally to actions, except the simplest of them. So the word for 'sheep' in Attic prose – πρόβατον (próbătŏn) – signified originally 'that which walks forward (or, in front)'; the English 'breakers' of the sea bear their character plainly upon them; the Greek κρίνειν (krīnein), *to judge*, meant originally to *separate* and *sort out*; and the English 'cuckoo' and 'curlew' are the calls of two birds. And provided that the allusion is understood by the hearer, either from the context (that is to say, the function for which the word is used) if the usage be new, or from previous usage if it be old, the purpose of language is served. As soon, however, as the reference or allusion is familiar, the word ceases to signify the character or aspect, and symbolizes one of a class of objects (for example, a sheep), or of actions (for example, judging) possessing that character or aspect. Till then the usage might well be described as a 'figure of speech', except that this term suggests some abnormal process, some elaborate artifice, and in fact this is the usual and natural process. For language and mind are primarily concerned, not with articles or animals, but with characters or aspects, and hence not with individual articles or animals but with classes possessing those characters. It may be useful to a shepherd to be able to refer to one particular sheep as 'Gertie'; it is much more useful to mankind to have a word signifying any member of the class 'sheep'. And whether it is more useful or not, there are (for the reason mentioned) few words in language that do not symbolize a class.

When the mind is simple, whether in early man or modern child, the total of these 'figures' or references is small, and they increase slowly. But there is also a retarding, controlling and organizing factor in the growth of language: a new 'figure of speech' must, as we said, meet with the approval and acceptance of a community before it can become a permanent part of the language as the symbol of a class of things or actions. Otherwise it remains a figure of speech.

We have instanced three kinds of 'figures of speech'. In one (as in κρίνειν, *to sort out, to judge*) a new class of action may be named by the name of an old, more familiar class of action, so that a verb changes or extends its meaning. In the second a class of objects is referred to by its movement (like *probaton, and breaker*) so that the verb becomes a noun when the figure of speech becomes a symbol. The third is the uncommon case where a creature is referred to by mimicry of its call, so that an animal cry becomes a noun. Looking at language generally, it is easy to recognize that the most widespread 'figure of speech' is that arising from the apparent *resemblances* between movements or things. *Differences* are of infinite number, and the usual relation of two movements or things is to be different from one another. Resemblances are of the utmost importance to man in his behaviour and his language. In his behaviour he recognizes the resemblances without effort: and as language refers to the aspects of things, two things having a common apparent character may acquire the same name (or a name that is partly the same) and it may thus be understood in both contexts. Hence language obtains a wide field of reference and is able to symbolize a wide area of nature. And as language refers primarily to an apparent character, and it is apparent to opinion, feeling, emotion and memory, the limits of the class of objects referred to as possessing the same character will tend to be vague and indeterminate.

We can more easily perceive this vagueness of outline in the early language of children or in foreign tongues than in our own. For example, Dr C. W. Valentine's boy B, at the age of 1 year 2 months, having often seen pictures of dogs and barked at them, now barked at pictures other than those of dogs. At the age of 1 year 6 months – which is the approximate mental age at which language originates – having learnt to call birds ku-kuk, he called a pinafore with birds depicted upon it ku-kuk, and later called a pinafore without birds ku-kuk. The same child at 1 year 5 months, having already begun to call Dada at the sight of his father, pointed to a print of a clean-shaven man and said Dada. At 1 year 6 months he called pictures of women as well as men Dada, and even pictures of statuary; and at 1 year 7 months pictures of bearded men, and one of a woman in evening dress.

The same child, at the same age, having learnt to call his grandfather Ga-ga (grandpa) called his grandfather's photograph Ga-ga, and later his father's photograph, and pictures of men generally.[1] There are innumerable examples of similar observations in the literature relating to the language of children.[2] We might be prone to say that the child was mistaken in calling the pinafore ku-kuk, or the photograph of a woman Dada, but that is not the truth of the matter. The truth is that the same apparent character that impressed the mind and elicited a certain speech-sound on a previous occasion elicited the same sound on the later occasion. We can now see that the term 'figure of speech' that we used in regard to $πρόβατον$ and 'breakers' was inapt. When a man calls a sheep $πρόβατον$, 'that which walks forward', or a child calls the photograph of a woman 'Dada', the process is the same. Any difference in the process is a mere matter of degree. Sheep are seen as having the same character as other things that walk forward, or, in other words, are classed with them and elicit the same name; the photograph of a woman is seen as having a common character with pictures of men, and is classed with them and called by the same name, Dada. The same is true of the successive steps in the widening and changing of the use of Ku-kuk. So, if we were to enter in a lexicon the child B's word ku-kuk, we might write:

Ku-kuk. Origin probably Cuckoo, the call of the bird Cuculus Canorus, Linn. Hence
1. By extension, Any bird.
2. Trop. Any representation of a bird, and particularly any pinafore containing a representation of a bird.
3. By extension, Any pinafore.

This is typical of an entry in any lexicon of a word in any language. In the light of a common apparent character two classes of objects are classed together, and the meaning of the name of one of them is extended to the other and becomes a symbol for the enlarged class, and can thence be extended to other objects classed with the latter. Similarly if we consulted Liddell and Scott's Greek Lexicon in regard to the word $πρόβατον$ we should find the following entry (in brief):

Originally of small cattle, sheep and goats which, in primitive mixed herds 'walk in front' of the larger animals. Among the Ionians

[1] C. W. Valentine, *The Psychology of Early Childhood* (3rd Ed. 1946), pp. 393-4.
[2] See a collection of references and a discussion thereon in M. M. Lewis, *Infant Speech*, 1936, chap. XI.

and Dorians all four-footed cattle. In Homer generally, cattle,[1] flocks and herds. But in Attic prose and comedy (though never in tragedy) almost invariably of sheep. Generally, slaughtered animals, whether for sacrifice or food. Proverbially, of stupid, lazy people. Also name of a sea-fish.

As language develops there will be many of such references, and the boundaries of the class which they embrace are extended here and there into strange places. For example in Malay there are many classes characterized by special names, of which the following are examples:

oran ('person') is the name of a class including human beings and angels.
ikor ('tail') is used for animals, including some which have no tails like frogs and flies.
buah ('fruit') for fruits, houses, towns, ships, islands, lakes.
bidzi ('grain') for grains and little objects more or less round.
batan ('stem' or 'trunk') for long objects.

These names are used as determinatives together with the person or object referred to. So buda' dua oran means *infants two, persons*; kuda tiga ikor means *horses three, tails*; and rumah dua buah means *houses two, fruits*.

In some languages these names of classes become mere prefixes to the noun. For example, an Andamanese language, according to Portman,[2] referred to different classes of things, each named by a distinctive prefix:

ot-, signified round things (e.g. cushions and sponges).
ôto-, long thin pointed or wooden things.
aka-, ôko-, hard things.
ar-, upright things.
ig-, weapons, utensils, things manufactured.
ad-, speech (noises) of animals; and so forth.

So in Haida, nouns are classified into long, slender, round, flat, angular, thread-like, animate and other classes.[3]

---

[1] The learned authors are experiencing a difficulty in defining πρόβατα (which means bovines and sheep, but mainly sheep) in terms of the English word 'cattle' (which means bovines and sheep, but mainly bovines).
[2] Cited by Sir R. C. Temple in *A Grammar of the Andamanese Language* (being chap. IV of part I of the *Census Report on the Andaman and Nicobar Islands* (1902), pp. 16-17.
[3] J. R. Swanton, *Haida*, H.A.I.L., part I, p. 216.

These tables have a special interest. In the Sumerian cuneiform tablets certain picture-signs, each with a general significance, preceded characters which stood for the names of objects of certain classes. For example, dingir (a star) before another word signified that the latter was the name of a god. There were a number of other class-signs, for example

itu preceded names of months.
na   „   names of stones.
duk   „   earthen vessels.
giš   „   wooden objects.
tug   „   cloths.
sal   „   females.
id   „   rivers; and so forth.

It has long been suspected that these class-signs were not merely a device of writing but represented prefixes actually pronounced, and such a language as the Andamanese is itself enough to turn the suspicion into belief.

It will readily be noticed in regard to these characters, and the classes displaying them, that they do not by any means pretend to cover all the world's phenomena. No philosopher has succeeded in classifying the universe into a small, complete set of categories. These classes are partial and imperfect, and the boundaries between them are not fixed by logic, but, if they are fixed at all, are fixed by mind – emotion, interest, shape, memory, opinion and so forth – and also to some extent by convention. The child that calls by the name of Ga-ga not only grandfather but also pictures of men, and calls by the name of Dada not only father but pictures of men and women, can only fix the boundary by a decision if it is to be fixed at all. The boy B, having learned to say ba (baa-lamb) at the sight of a sheep, at 1 year 5 months said ba to cows. Yet he would readily change ba to moo when told.

It is obvious that, in the life of primitive man, many of such class-references will be formed, and the boundaries fixed, by function, that is to say by usage determined by local economic needs and circumstances. For language may be defined as an instrument for coping with our environment, or, more accurately, for getting our fellows to help us to do so. It is also obvious that such class-references may differ as the poles between two peoples of the same degree of advance. We have left far behind us the phenomena which are uniform between peoples of the same grade of material culture.

For example, the Aranda, Food Gatherers of Central Australia, have names for the following classes:

garra – all animals that walk on land and can be eaten.
deba – all birds that fly in the air.
deba-deba – all flying insects, also all minute, living creatures.
pinara pinara – all beetles.
apina – all snakes.
irbanga – all fishes.
manna – all edible plants and fruits, grass seeds, and vegetable foods generally.
inna – all trees, bushes and shrubs.

Garra does not include lizards which cannot be eaten, though it does include all edible lizards and goannas large and small. Ants are neither beetles nor flying insects. Berry bushes are neither grass nor shrubs; and they are classed as manna only if their berries are edible. Emu and turkey are not birds but garra, for they spend most of their time walking around on solid earth, and are hunted with spears and boomerangs for their flesh. There is no word for lizard, but there are 9 words for individual members of the lizard family exclusive of goannas.[1]

Similarly in a Melanesian language there will commonly be, say, 9 names for coconuts in different stages of growth, and no name for the coconut.[2] In the Trobriand, according to Malinowski, there will be names for the trees or objects of importance to the native, and other trees will be just background, 'just bush'. An insect or bird which plays no part in the tradition or the larder would be dismissed as 'mauna wala' – 'merely a flying animal'.[3] In Khomani Bushman there is no word for *animal*, but a rich and impressive catalogue of the numerous and different species of antelopes that the native shoots.[4] In a Semitic language there may be many names for lions of different sexes and ages, but no word for 'lion'. In Nandi (Grade A3(1) – mainly pastoral) there are 35 words for oxen of different kinds, ages, markings, colours, offspring, history, etc. Even in English, though there are words for bull, cow, bullock, steer, heifer, calf and so on, it is doubtful if there is a word for the group. 'Cattle' often includes other species.

In all languages there are various classifications of actions as well as

[1] Strehlow, p. 65.
[2] See e.g. A. M. Hocart, *The Psychological Interpretation of Language*, B.J.P., V, 1912.
[3] B. Malinowski in *The Meaning of Meaning*, 6th Ed., p. 331.
[4] Maingard, p. 259.

objects. Properly speaking, any name of an action – move, break, make, strike – is the name of a class of actions. In addition, in Maidu,[1] for example, there are prefixes to verbs referring to the parts of the body with which they are associated, so that the prefix ha(n) signifies actions performed with the shoulder or back; hi-, actions performed with the nose or snout; in-, actions performed by sitting on; is-, actions performed with the foot; and ka-, with the flat hand. In Kwakiutl is a series of suffixes denoting the instrument with which an action is performed – for example, with a sharp object. In the language of the South Andaman Island there is a sevenfold classification, expressed by prefixes, as to the parts of the body referred to, and this extends to nouns, verbs and adjectives.[2]

Different language-communities see different resemblances between persons and objects in nature. A minority of languages (for example, the Indo-European and Semitic, but not the Sumerian or the bulk of the languages of Africa) contain a classification according to sex, but the classification is just as partial and imperfect, and the boundaries are equally vague and have often been extended beyond merely logical limits. In some languages this classification extends to all nouns, in many (such as Chinook[3] and Bushman[4]) only to a few. In several of the world's languages the masculine includes large and strong animals and things, and the feminine weak and small animals and things, so that in both the last-mentioned languages the right hand is masculine and the left hand feminine. In Hebrew, on the other hand, for some mysterious reason we find the reverse. In the majority of languages where there is sex-gender (including the Germanic), the sun is feminine and the moon masculine: in Latin and Greek we find the reverse. The unreason of the genders in Indo-European languages is familiar to all. In the older of these languages the classification was threefold, into masculine, feminine and inanimate, and extended to all nouns, pronouns and adjectives, but not actions. In most North American languages and many others (such as Hittite and Andamanese) there is a twofold classification of animate and inanimate. In Blackfoot, for example, the classification runs throughout the grammar and includes the verbs. Here some parts of the body are animate and some inanimate; some trees animate and some inanimate. Earth, sun, moon and stars are animate, being invested with a sufficient personality.[5]

---

[1] Hunters, N. E. California, see R. B. Dixon, in H.A.I.L., part I, p. 694.
[2] Ellis, pp. 53-4.   [3] Boas, *Chinook*, p. 597 f.
[4] Maingard, p. 239; but see Bleek, *Naron*, p. 53.   [5] Uhlenbeck, pp. 18-19.

Again many languages have a classification into singular and plural, and many not. In some languages it extends to all objects and persons, pronouns and adjectives, and all actions; in some languages not. In many languages the classification is into singular, dual (especially referring to various parts of the body) and plural. The Yahgan (perhaps the most primitive of all peoples) have a classification into singular, dual, trial and plural.[1] In Chinook there is a fivefold classification into masculine, feminine, neuter, dual and plural.[2]

In some languages, on the other hand – sometimes because the original ratio of the classification has been lost – there are classifications merely according to the form of the words: and here we reach pure grammar. Language has become an institution and lives its own life. Man is no longer classifying in language the things of nature, but is classifying in language the things of language. So in Latin one of the chief classifications of the noun is according to the form of the word-endings – nouns ending in the singular (nominative) with -a and in the plural with -ae; nouns ending in the singular with "ŭs" and the plural with "ūs", and so forth. In the Bantu languages, on the other hand, the classification is according to the form of the prefixes. So in Buluba-Lulua there are eight classes of the nouns, in the first of which the singular begins with mu- and the plural with ba- (e.g. mu-ntu, a person; ba-ntu, persons); in the second the singular begins with mu- and the plural with mi-; in the third the singular and plural both begin with n-; and so forth. Classifications of verbs according to form are also frequent, for example in Latin. In most of such languages (for example in Tsimshian) there are classes according to form as well as classes according to function.

We who are familiar with two or three Indo-European grammar-books, are conscious of the different character and treatment of nouns and verbs – and certainly languages do not confuse these two main parts of speech. But in nature there is no necessary separation between the two: if George strikes, there is one picture to be seen, namely a man moving in a certain way. It is not surprising therefore that, in the respects which we have noted, nouns and verbs are often placed in the same contrasted classes – in the singular or plural, animate or inanimate. And having observed that, on the whole, nouns originated as verbs, we feel even less surprise at seeing them still grouped together in the same classes. Still more clearly, an adjective and its noun form

---

[1] Adam, p. 29.
[2] Boas, *Chinook*, p. 597.

one fact in nature – a fat man is one object – and we are not surprised that almost everywhere nouns and their adjectives find themselves in the same classes, especially when we remember how recently the adjectives have emerged from the nouns.

But verbs also perform some very different functions from the nouns, and have their own distinct classifications. Verbs – that is to say, actions – are classed according to the person acting, or according to the tense of the action, the mood or voice, and even according to whether the action be positive or negative, and affirmative or interrogative. In these respects again one group of languages differs from another as far as the poles. In many or most languages 'tense', in the sense of 'time', is irretrievably bound up with other aspects of the action. For example, if one says in English 'I was eating my dinner when he came in', the difference between the two verbs is not one of time. Both are past; the difference is that 'was eating' is an incomplete, and 'came' a complete action. In so far as tense means time, many languages (such as the Semitic and Sumerian) have strictly no tenses at all, and classify actions according as they are complete or incomplete. At the other extreme, in a few languages (such as Hupa) both verbs and nouns have their tenses, and there may be a past or future house or wife as well as a past or future action indicated by the suffix -nun applied to noun or verb[1]; and such a language as Buluba-Lulua has all the Modern English panoply of auxiliary verbs and even more, and achieves even more varieties and niceties of tense and aspect – I am biting (present actual), I am biting (present progressive), I am now biting, I have bitten, I bite, I bit, I had bitten, I was biting, I had been biting, I keep biting and biting, I kept biting and biting, I shall bite, I am about to bite, I am just about to bite, (if) I bite, I would have bitten, that I may bite, why don't I bite? (two forms); and, in most of these cases, corresponding negative conjugations.[2] In most languages it is impossible to express many of these distinctions, and they must be inferred as well as may be from the context. In Hebrew it is sometimes mere guesswork whether present, past or future is intended.

But probably all languages classify actions according as they are by the speaker (first person), by the person addressed (second person) or by some other person or thing (third person); and again according as the person is singular or plural. No other parts of speech are so classified, except the pronouns which name the class of person. But a great

[1] Goddard, p. 105.
[2] Morrison, pp. 79-91.

number of languages (chiefly those of America, South-East Asia,[1] Australia and Oceania[2]) cannot tolerate the ambiguity which the Indo-European, Semitic, Sumerian and most African languages suffer, between the first person plural (we) that includes the person addressed (=I and you), and the first personal plural that excludes that person (=I and he, she or they). The former is in part a first, and in part a second, person. So, for example, the former is expressed in Blackfoot, by a pronoun resembling in form both the first and second person singular:

nistóa, I.
ksistóa, you.
ostói, he, she or it.

nistúnàn, we (exclusive).
ksistúnùn, we (inclusive).
ksistóau, you (plural).
ostóauai, they.[3]

Blackfoot[4] and Andamanese distinguish between a third and fourth person (the latter being a person subordinate to the main third person of the sentence). So in Blackfoot 'That man said to his wife' would be rendered

ánistsiu   omá   ninau otoxkéman
Said (3rd pers.) that (3rd pers.) man (to) his-wife.

But to render 'That man was told by his wife' we should say 'His wife said (4th person) to that man (3rd person)' and the sentence would run:

otánik   omá   ninau otoxkéman
Said (4th pers.) (to) that (3rd pers.) man his-wife (i.e. 4th person).

Blackfoot even knows a fifth person.[5]

But in the complete communication – the sentence – there are both actions and persons (or things), both verbs and nouns, combining together. The picture of George struck by John and staggering under the blow is quite different from the picture of John in the act of striking. Many languages contrast the two classes of nouns that are the subject of action and nouns that are the object of action. In the earlier Indo-European languages and some of the modern, the classification is

[1] E.g. Eastern Dravidian languages (Telugu, Tamil, Kui and Kurukh; but not Canara, Gondi and Brahui); Munda languages, Annamite and Mon-Khmer group.
[2] The Malayo-Polynesian family (Indonesian, Melanesian and Polynesian).
[3] Uhlenbeck, p. 70.
[4] At least in the singular of most inanimate nouns (Uhlenbeck, p. 24).
[5] Ibid.

marked by the use of two contrasted noun-endings (the forms of the pair varying according to the form of the noun-stem). In Modern English and French and innumerable other languages the distinction is marked by the relative position of the words in the sentence. In most of these languages the noun when subject of the verb precedes it and the object follows the verb. In some languages (such as Maori, Fijian and Hebrew) the subject usually follows the verb. So that in some languages the contrast of subject and object is marked by accidence; in some by syntax.

But as soon as the sentence has been sufficiently developed, that is to say lengthened and made more precise, the different parts of it become more or less specialized in their functions, and from the verbs issue nouns, then adjectives and adverbs. In some languages, as we have seen, words are classified according to form into different parts of speech, one of a number of affixes or variations of vowel designating a particular part of speech. In some languages, such as Modern English, Polynesian or Melanesian, the same speech-sound may function as one of several different parts of speech and the order in the sentence (syntax) will chiefly indicate it – for example a word which is normally a noun becomes an adjective when it precedes (or follows) another noun.

The sentence, among all the peoples of whom we know, is now a complex organism, and in order to make its meaning intelligible and to copy it, some means is requisite for showing the relations between its component parts. Every method referred to earlier in this chapter is called in for this purpose. If we take the following simple pair of Modern English sentences – 'Go! And let no crusted Tory ever darken these innocent doors again' – we see that the first sentence, 'Go!' is a request for action containing but one term. No means is necessary – neither accidence (i.e. variation in form of words) nor syntax (i.e. variation in word-order) to show the relations between its terms. But in the second sentence it is plain to see that the place of every word is fixed and unchangeable (with the possible exception of the adverb 'again'). By this means the relation of each word to every other is defined – 'no' and 'crusted' are shown to be adjectives describing the noun 'Tory' which they precede; and 'these' and 'innocent' to be adjectives describing the noun 'doors', which is also the object of the verb 'darken' which precedes it. In the earlier Indo-European languages these relations are shown mainly by formal congruence of word-endings. By their means not only is it shown that one noun is the subject and the other the object of the predicate, and not only must the subject and predicate agree in their endings as respects gender and number (and, if the subject is a pronoun, as regards person), but an adjective must be shown to belong to the same class as its noun in respect of gender, number and case. In Bantu the classes are different, and the formal badges of congruence are prefixes. To take two striking examples, if one wished to say in Kongo 'These are the great white stones which we saw yesterday', it would run:

O	matadi	mama	mampembe	mampwena
The	stones	these	white	great
i	mau	mama	twamwene	ezono.
(it) is	they	which	we – saw	yesterday.

Matadi (stones) is a noun of class 8, forming its plural by the prefix ma-; and this reappears as prefix to all the adjectives and pronouns qualifying, representing or referring to it in this sentence. Indeed, the pronouns are to a large extent composed of the prefix. Similarly in the same language, if we wished to say: 'The coat you lost yesterday has turned up.' 'Where is it?' 'This is it. I saw it in the house' – the passage would run:

E	kinkutu	kiaku	kiavididi	ezono	kisolokele
The coat		you	lost	yesterday	it-has-turned-up.
Akiegi?	I kiau kiki.		O mo nzo		mbwene kia.
Where-is-it?	Is this it.		In the house		I-saw it.

Kinkutu, as is shown by the prefix ki, is a singular noun of class 5, hence these repetitions of the prefix.[1]

We have set out above a few of the fundamental and familiar classifications to be found in language. There remain a great many minor and more occasional and more subtle groupings by means of which some of the finer and more delicate distinctions are marked, but there is no space for them here. We have collected in this chapter a number of classifications of diverse nature, which are commonly treated as distinct topics, and we have done so because, looking at language generally, it would be artificial to make separations between them. For example, the classification of natural objects into cattle, trees, shrubs and the like cannot be distinguished from that into male and female creatures, or animate and inanimate. The classification of natural

[1] Bentley, p. 526.

objects into male and female or animate and inanimate cannot be distinguished from the purely grammatical classification into masculine and feminine, or animate and inanimate. The same applies to the classification into singular, dual and plural, or into first, second, third and fourth persons. Accidence is not wholly to be distinguished from syntax, in as much as the functions performed by accidence in one language are performed by syntax in another, and often the same function is performed partly by accidence and partly by syntax in the same language.

Are there, then, any general truths which can be stated of these various phenomena?

One of the fundamental characters of man's way of life consists of what we may call 'rules of conduct'. They mirror fundamental characters of his mind. Whether infant or adult, primitive or modern, he must continue in the ways he knows. Some of them are or become instinctive or at least mechanical. Moreover, it is easier to do what he has done before than to strike a new path. Still more, he is for ever obtaining confidence for himself in the uncharted seas of life by creating for himself paths of movement and rules of conduct where there was uncertainty before. If he is called upon to do something of public import that he has not done before, he is happier when he finds someone who assures him that there is only one proper and recognized way of doing it, and tells him what it is. Thereby he substitutes certainty for uncertainty and confidence for anxiety – confidence that he is in a fair way to gain public approval or at least escape public contempt. At its least important, we recognize this process in the formation of rules of etiquette, or general social behaviour: at its most important, in matters fundamental to a society's existence and welfare, we recognize the same process in the creation of compulsory rules of law. In language, rules of conduct are almost as crucial as in law. Public approval and disapproval in the matter of language are of the highest consequence to a man, and he must conform to the language of the community to be understood. The more precise are the rules of speech in a community, the more certainly will he be understood if he observes them, and the more expressive are the shades of varying meaning that can be imported by a recognized deviation from the norm.

As between the rules of law and rules of mere etiquette we observe without difficulty that the former are more firmly based on the needs of the society; they are its framework and structure. To a large extent they are common to peoples of the same stage of material advance –

especially such crucial laws as those of homicide. The rules of etiquette and other rules of social conduct exist because man must make rules of behaviour; but they differ as the poles from one people to another, and they change with ease. In language there is the same relation between on the one hand, such fundamental facts as the proportions of the parts of speech, and, on the other hand, rules of grammar or even style. The former are in general common to peoples of the same stage of advance in civilization; the latter are rules of convenience and convention, less firmly based on economic necessity, readily changing, and varying to an unlimited extent from people to people. That is why grammar is so important to the linguist. He endeavours to trace the kinship of two particular tongues: if he finds similarities in the rules of grammar, then because such rules are to a large extent arbitrary and fortuitous, as well as difficult for foreigners to learn, he regards the resemblances as evidence of a common origin. The fundamental matters marking similarity in the stage of economic and mental progress would be useless to him for the purpose.

The grammar of a language – its accidence (or morphology) and its syntax – are among the most difficult of all things in language for a stranger to acquire. Yet they are learned by every native child, learning the whole mind, as it were, of the language, and beginning in the middle of his second year with no previous knowledge of speech. He builds up his grammar with the rest of the language, but after he has built up the beginnings of his vocabulary. He starts, as we have seen, with classifications of objects in nature – Dada, kukuk, bow-wow, and the rest – and when he begins to put sentences together he needs all the assistance of the rules of grammar; and finally, after the classifications of things in nature, come the more technical classifications of things in language, as language becomes to some extent (like law) a separate, self-sufficient institution.

The first general characteristic of grammar is its uniformity. The regularity of its forms merely reflects the fact that they represent rules of conduct. This regularity and uniformity runs throughout language. We have seen a striking instance of it in the Semitic verb-stems, which, having once in time long past been generally of the form CVC(V), have not been content (like ancient Egyptian) to extend themselves here and there to form biconsonantal, triconsonantal and quadriconsonantal forms, but have all, or almost all, expanded by enlarging the same pattern to CVCVC(V). This uniformity is a thing to which all language tends in greater or less degree. We say 'I see, I saw', but the child or the unlettered adult may say, on the common model, 'I see, I seed', and there is a tendency, for simplicity, gradually to rid the language of all exceptions and irregularities.

The Aranda, in the centre of the 'museum continent' of Australia, afford a good instance of this, In their language, as we are told by T. G. H. Strehlow, in a striking passage, the inflexion of the verb, noun and adjective is entirely regular. There are only three patterns of the verb, and they are almost identical; and every verb in the language, according to its stem, follows one of these three patterns. There are no exceptional forms or exceptions to rules. 'Whatever irregularities there may have been in the Aranda conjugations originally have all long since been smoothed out by the principle of analogy. In other continents the principle of analogy, though continually at its work of simplification, has been countered partly by education, partly by the disturbing influence of borrowing from foreign tongues. But in Australia, where no invaders disturbed the ancient peace of the continent, where no conquests superimposed the language of one tribe violently upon another (at least not within historical times) where no written records put a brake upon the human love of yielding to analogy,[1] the process of simplification went on unchecked from the very beginning, and in the Aranda language, at least, we see the final stage of a long process of linguistic evolution: we come here upon a speech where the inflexion of the verb, like that of the noun and the adjective, is absolutely regular. Beside the conjugation of the Aranda verb even the simplest European inflexional system of verbs is hopelessly archaic and irrational. Aranda in this regard is far more modern than English or any other Indo-European language. On the other hand the Aranda verb revels in a bewildering wealth of inflexional terminations and reduplicated forms, by means of which every shade of meaning that the native wishes to express in his own natural environment can be communicated to his listener with the utmost precision imaginable.'[2]

The second general characteristic of grammar (strange though the statement may appear to a schoolboy) is that it exists to render speech easier. The uniformity, to which we have referred, enables words to be used in contexts in which they may not often or ever have been used, and yet to be fully understood. So a verb may be used in a certain context – or, as we say, a particular 'part of the verb' may be arrived at – in accordance with the rules of grammar, and be easily understood,

---

[1] And, we may add, where no economic advance brought its changes.
[2] Strehlow, p. 105.

though the verb, or that part of the verb, is not in common use. Accordingly the full force of grammar is shown in the least common words. The commonest words, as we have seen, are the verbs, and it has often been remarked that irregularities are found specially among the commonest verbs. We have been painfully familiar from childhood with the following monstrosity of French grammar:

Aller = to go.

Present Indicative	Imperfect	Future
Je vais	J'allais	J'irai
tu vas	tu allais	tu iras
il va(t)	il allait	il ira(t)
nous allons	nous allions	nous irons
vous allez	vous alliez	vous irez
ils vont	ils allaient	ils iront

This is not by any means unique. For example we find in Masai[1]:

A-lo = to go.

Present	Past	Imperative
A-lo = I go (am going, or shall go)	A-shōm-o = I went	Ma-shōm-o = let me go
I-lo = thou goest	etc.	Shōm- or I-nno } = go
E-lo = he(or she) goes		
Ki-pwo = we go	Ki-shōm-ó = we went	Maa-pe = let us go
I-pwo-pwo = you go	etc.	E-njom = go ye
E-pwo = they go		

A-lōtu = to come.

Present	Past	Imperative
A-lōt-u = I come (am coming, or shall come)	A-ē-uo = I came	Wō-u = come!
I-lōt-u = thou comest	etc.	
E-lōt-u = he (or she) comes		
Ki-pwōn-ú = we come	Ki-ē-tuó = we came	
I-pwōn-u-nu = you come	etc.	Wō-tu = come ye!
E-pwōn-u = they come		

But we need hardly go further than the English 'I go, I went' – or the English verb 'to be': 'I am, thou art, he is, we are', etc.; 'I was, we were'; 'I have been'. The only regularity in all the above verbs is in

[1] Hollis, *Masai*, p. 91 (E. Africa, A3(1)).

the personal pronouns and the pronominal endings of the verbs – a thing which will not surprise us, remembering what we noticed of the history of these pronouns in the previous chapter. These verbs, 'to go' and 'to be', are among the commonest verbs of these languages; but if we sought the imperfect or the future of a little-used verb, we should need the regular forms of grammar – or, as they are often called, analogy – to reach them. For example, though Aranda has this 'bewildering wealth of inflexional terminations and reduplicated forms by which every shade of meaning that the native wishes to express . . . can be communicated', 'Aranda . . . limits itself normally to the use of the indicative moods of the two most common tenses – present and past.' Accordingly it is only by the aid of the regular variations of form provided by grammar that the less familiar uses of the verb could be expressed and understood.

To a lesser degree we can see the same phenomenon in the case of some of the commonest nouns. For example, we notice in English no resemblance between the names of male and female of the domestic animals and birds – horse and mare, cock and hen, dog and bitch, cow and bull, boar and sow, ram and ewe, tiercel and falcon, stag and hind, buck and doe. In other species the name of the female must generally be formed by rule from that of the male – lion and lioness, male rat and female rat.

The third characteristic, that follows from the previous two, is that a language is not wont to adopt rules of grammar from a foreign source. That could only lead to more, not fewer, exceptions and irregularities. Grammar exists to aid and not to hamper or perplex. Foreign rules of grammar are outside the meaningful generalizations evolved by the native speech. For example, in Somali the definite article, when applied to a masculine noun, is represented by the suffix -ki. That part of Africa has in recent centuries been much exposed to Arab influence, and has imported from the Arab goods and notions and their names. The Arabic for 'the door' is al bab (masc.) and now the Somali is albabki[1]: the Arabic definite article 'al' has no meaning to the Somali. But we need not look outside England for the same phenomenon, for we speak of 'an alkali' (though in childhood we were familiar with a 'lemon kali'). In various parts of the world the English definite article is similarly adopted by the native with its noun in ignorance of its meaning.[2]

[1] J. W. C. Kirk, *A Grammar of the Somali Language*, 1905, p. 14.
[2] As is the French definite article with French words in the Chinook jargon.

A fourth characteristic is that grammar becomes increasingly necessary as language develops. As the vocabulary expands, so that each word, on the average, becomes less and less used, rules are necessary for declining the noun, forming the feminines and plurals and conjugating the verb. Above all, the precision and complication of the growing sentence rely more and more on the aid of accidence and syntax.

A fifth characteristic arises from the differing functions of the parts of speech. The verb is the heart of the sentence, and being more general in character than, for example, the noun, is capable of application in a wider variety of circumstances – a variety of times, manner and aspect. As there is greater variety in the functions, there is greater variety in the forms of the verb. Though in many languages there is little or no inflexion of the noun, adjective and adverb, there is almost everywhere considerable inflexion of the verb. In Aranda (which has, for example, no gender of the noun) there are 1,200 different possible forms of each verb.

In all this building-up of accidence and syntax, this conflict and variation from one language to another, is there anything to be found which is common and universal in language? There is nothing.

But there is, indeed, one use of language, one function-form, in which there is a common and universal *absence* of grammar. The second person singular of the imperative, namely the request for action, is the simple form of the verb — without affix and without rules of syntax. This is the third fundamental fact that we have found in language – the first, the fact that every complete communication includes a verb, and the second, the universal decrease in the proportion of the verb. This third fact is so important to our study that we must investigate it, and the reasons for it, in some detail.

CHAPTER NINE

The Request for Action

Throughout the world and throughout its known history the shortest and simplest form of the verb is the request for action, the second person singular of the imperative. In the few languages where (as in Semitic and Hamitic) there is a separate form for the masculine and feminine according to the person addressed, it is the masculine.

We may take the Latin as an example. Here the verbs are of four forms — the first (as illustrated by the infinitive) is of the form *amā-re*, the second of the form *monē-re*, the third *regĕ-re*, and the fourth *audī-re*. All the various tenses and aspects, moods, voices, persons and numbers of *amāre* (*amat, amabit, amavit, amandum* and so forth) are expressed by amā and a suffix[1]; the parts of monēre, by monē- and a suffix; of regĕ-rĕ, regĕ- and a suffix; and of audīre, audī- and a suffix. And the part that is constant — the root, or what the Latin grammarian calls the 'stem' — amā, monē, regĕ and audī- is the second person singular of the imperative.

It is true of all the Indo-European tongues that the simplest form of the verb is also the request for action. For example, in classical Greek the stem + ε is the imperative, e.g. băle, luĕ.[2] Modern English is a very different case, for it has lost practically the whole of the grammatical apparatus of the Indo-European verb, but the same remains true. For example the English for festinare is 'to hurry'; for festino, 'I hurry'; for festinat, 'he (she, or it) hurries'; for festinavi, 'I hurried'; for festinans, 'hurrying'. Accordingly the constant in each of these uses of this verb is 'hurry'. In English the variation of form is in some cases by the addition of a pronoun, and in some cases by a suffix,

---

[1] In the first person singular of the present, amō is an abbreviation of ama-o (as the Greek τιμῶ for τιμάω); and, exceptionally, the subjunctive amem is a variation of amam.
[2] Probably the presence of the final ε is explained by the fact that the oldest verb-stems were in the form CVC (like βαλ-) and not CV (like λυ-), and as Greek (like Modern Italian) tended to avoid ending a word in a consonant, the imperative was βαλ-ε, and the later forms CV took the same final ε.

whereas in Latin it is always by a suffix; but in all parts of the English verb 'hurry' is the constant element or stem, just as is festina, and if I say to a person 'Hurry', it can mean, and will be understood to mean, only one thing, namely the second person singular of the imperative. 'Hurry', indeed, is also a noun, but if I say 'Hurry', and nothing more, it can only mean the request for action. There are few languages of this type in the Indo-European family, but many outside.

It is true also of the Semitic languages that the shortest and simplest form of the verb represents the second person singular (masculine) of the imperative. These languages represent a different type of inflexion from that of the classical Indo-European. In almost all cases the constant part of the verb consists of three consonants – for example qṭl, kill; lmd, learn. But consonants cannot exist without vowels, and the different functions of the verb are expressed by variations of the vowel and also by added consonants prefixed, infixed or suffixed. The second person singular of the imperative has never an added consonant, and typically consists, in the simple conjugation, of the verb-root with the stress-accent at the end,[1] qṭal. But the stress has an effect on the vowel: it must be strengthened to hold the stress. The nearest form to qṭal is the Hebrew, which avoids beginning the word with two successive consonants (an innovation which the conservative Semitic tongues resist) by inserting a half-vowel between the first two: – qeṭal, lemad. But, as in other instances in the history of language, the stress upon the final 'a' causes a progression of the vowel to O [ɔ] and then U, or (less commonly) through e to i. Accordingly, while in Hebrew the form is generally lemád or lemód, in most Semitic languages (e.g. Arabic and Assyrian) there is a further change to U, and in some of these languages to e and i.[2]

This process of change from a to O and U is countered where the last consonant is a guttural.[3] More interesting, there is also in the imperative, throughout the Semitic languages, an omission of the first consonant in a large number of cases.[4]

In Sumerian the root of the verb is one of the methods of expressing the second person singular of the imperative – for example, zu, know! There are also, in this as in many other languages, other ways of expressing it, but we are at present not concerned with them.

[1] As in the Greek λαβέ.
[2] E.g. Abyssinian qeṭel. Cf. Hebrew galéh (redeem), gǎš or gēš (approach), tēn (give).
[3] So in Hebrew meṣá' (find!), šemá' (hear!). Also the imperfective (formed from the imperative) yilemód or yilemád (he will learn), yimeṣá' (he will find).
[4] E.g. Hebrew from yšb, šēb; from ngš, gǎš or gēš; from lqk, qak.

The same is true of ancient Egyptian and the rest of the Hamitic family, for example Hausa, kāmā, seize! and Somali, sheg, tell! It is also true of the whole Bantu family,[1] for example in Zulu, geza, wash! bona, see! tanda, love! It is true also of the great and varied group of Sudanic languages, for example, Lango[2] and Acholi,[2] Dinka[3] and Nandi[4] in East Africa, and Ewe[5] and Nupe[6] in West Africa. In short, throughout Africa the second person singular of the imperative is generally the verb-stem alone.[7]

In the families of languages stretching from Eastern Europe to further Asia it is the same. For example, it is so in the Finno-Ugrian group: in Finnish the second person singular of the imperative is the stem, and indeed the stem in a closed or abbreviated form (stem otta, imperative ota; stem anta, imperative anna; stem teke, imperative tee). In the kindred Samoyed languages, too, the second person singular of the imperative is the stem (e.g. mada, cut!). It is so in the Turkish-Mongolian-Tungusan family – for example, in Turkish the stem is the second person singular of the imperative, e.g. yaz, write! sev, love! ghel, come! The same applies in the Sino-Tibetan-Burman languages; for example, in colloquial Tibetan the imperative is the stem of the verb. So, too, in the Dravidian languages of Southern India and Ceylon – for example in Tamil, Canarese and Telugu, the second person singular of the imperative is the stem. In Japanese it is the shortest and simplest form of the verb – for example, oku is the stem of the verb 'put', and oke is the imperative, put! It is the simple stem in Ainu, e.g. kik, strike!

In the Malayo-Polynesian languages the position is generally the same. For example, in Indonesian the root signifies the imperative. In Maori the simple form of the verb is the second person singular of the strong imperative (the mandatory or precatory) – karanga, call! haere, go! mahi, work! In Samoan the plain root of the verb has the same significance (e.g. ta, cut!) as it has also in Tongan (fai, do!). In Mota, Lifu, Roviana and Iai (Melanesian languages) the simple form

---

[1] Johnston, vol. 1, p. 20; vol. 2, pp. 496, 513.
[2] The 2nd pers. sing. of the imperative is the root of the verb, and the only form that drops the final -o where it occurs.
[3] If the verb root ends in a vowel, the root is also the 2nd pers. sing. of the imperative. If it ends in a consonant, add a short 'e' at the end, but in roots ending in m, b or n it is never pronounced, and some persons do not pronounce the e, or hardly pronounce it, in any circumstances, see Mitterützner, p. 29 f.
[4] The 2nd pers. sing. imperative is the simple verbal root.
[5] E.g. yi, go!
[6] The verb in its simplest form.
[7] Homburger, pp. 138-9, and p. 79.

of the verb is the imperative; and the imperative can be expressed by root alone in Fijian also. In the Andaman Islands it is the same, and it appears to be the same throughout the Australian continent. In South America it appears to be the same; for example among the Yahgan the plain verbal stem signifies the second person singular of the imperative. In North America the same appears to be true. For example in the Algonkian languages the second person singular of the imperative is the simplest form of the verb – so in Blackfoot, nitáipi = I enter; pit, enter! In Zuni the stem of the verb indicates the imperative; and so, too, in Takelma – nà, do! or say!

What is the reason and origin of this remarkable phenomenon? For every fact in language there is always more than one reason. The main reason for the fact which we are now considering is to be found in the central purpose and function of language. Language, as we have seen, is the means whereby man in society influences his environment: it is the means whereby he enlists the efforts of his fellows for his benefit. Language is a bodily activity, and at the same time a means of extension of man's bodily activity. It is a tool by which he achieves his ends, but in this case, instead of using his own limbs, he is by language enabled to use the limbs of his fellows. In primitive language, before mind and language have advanced to lay stress on other activities, and the uses of language have widened and deepened, this situation is all the more manifest; but it is there to be seen throughout. Accordingly, as language is *prima facie* used for this purpose, so it is also *prima facie* taken by the hearer to be intended for this purpose and to bear this meaning. And as this is the central purpose of language, we may take it that the verb, in the history of language, has been employed as a request for action more often than for any other purpose (a fact that to the modern reader of books would seem incredible). Now we noticed earlier in regard to the verb that each verb was more commonly used than each word of the other parts of speech, and this had the result that, by and large, the verbs were the briefest of words. Man has no language to say more than is necessary to say, and indeed he abbreviates the words he uses to the minimum necessary to express his meaning. Accordingly, as we saw, the familiar verbs, and particularly the radicals, remain the briefest words of the language. Similarly the use as a request for action has been the commonest and most familiar use of the verb, and accordingly the briefest form of the verb is the form of the request for action. Accordingly it is true to say that when a Roman said 'festinat' instead of 'festina', the purpose of the added 't' was to indicate that he did not intend a request for action. Similarly if I say 'I go', the function of the addition 'I' is, in truth, to indicate that I do not intend a request for action but a statement in the first person, for if I had intended a request for action I need merely have said 'go'. For the same reasons the imperative is in some languages (e.g. Finnish) not the stem but an abbreviated version of the stem.

We can illustrate this view and corroborate this explanation by a connected phenomenon. The simplest form of the verb is understood to mean a request for (or suggestion of) action. But the same is not true in the corresponding negative. 'Go' is a request for action; 'go not' is not a request for action. Accordingly though there are many languages in which the sense of 'go not' is given by a negative together with the imperative of the verb; and though there are many verbs which have themselves a negative meaning, such as 'desist', 'cease' or 'abstain'; and though there are many languages (for example the Bantu) which are rich in negative moods or conjugations of the verb; nevertheless, in a large number, and perhaps the majority of languages, the negative of the request for action is never (as in Semitic) or rarely (as in Indo-European) expressed by the imperative, but rather in some other way, usually by the subjunctive and a negative,[1] or sometimes by the imperfective[2] and a negative, or sometimes by a periphrasis.[3] Similarly the first or third person of the so-called imperative is not an imperative at all, because it is not a request to the hearer for action, and is commonly expressed by the subjunctive or future – for example, dicant, qu'ils disent (let them say!).

We can better illustrate and reinforce this view by an analogous phenomenon. The noun in many (perhaps a third) of the languages of the world is found in varying form according to its function in the sentence. In the Indo-European languages these different 'cases' are expressed by varying word-endings. Now in most of these languages (as in the bulk of the world's languages where such variation of form occurs) the same form serves both for nominative (referring to the subject of the sentence) and vocative (referring to the person addressed). But where there are separate forms for nominative and vocative, the shortest and simplest form of the noun is the vocative singular, which consists of the mere stem or little more. So in Latin the vocative is the stem: dominĕ, master! (the ĕ so that the word should

---

[1] As, for example, in Latin and Kongo.
[2] E.g. Semitic; so Hebrew O.T., translated 'Thou shalt not ...'
[3] E.g. Latin 'noli' ..., or English 'do not ...'; or Mota, where the verb 'pea' (= *to be not*, or *to be nothing*) is added.

end in a vowel) and in the corresponding Greek there is the nominative ἄνθρωπος (anthrōpos), and the vocative ἄνθρωπε (anthrōpĕ). In the most conservative of the Indo-European languages, namely classical Greek and modern Lithuanian, examples of this phenomenon are many.[1] In English the case-endings have practically disappeared, but the position remains the same. I may speak of *the friend, a friend, this friend, that friend,* but if I say to a man: *Friend, chief, prince, stranger,* the word is intended and understood to be the vocative.[2] Case is not sufficiently developed in Semitic to show a differentiation between nominative and vocative (and indeed there are substantially no case-forms except in Arabic and Assyrian), and there seems to be no difference between nominative and vocative in Sumerian, but in the kindred field of Africa we see the same phenomenon as in Indo-European. Wherever in Africa there are case-forms and there is a difference between nominative and vocative, the vocative is generally the simplest form of the noun.[3] For example, in Bantu, prefixes mark the differentiation, and in Zulu *inKosi* signifies a Chief; *'nKosi* is the vocative, Chief! In Herero *ohongaẓe* is *paternal aunt*; *'hongaze* is the vocative. In the rest of the world the position is the same: where case-variation is found, nominative and vocative have usually the same form. If there is a difference, generally the vocative is the shortest, simplest form of the noun. Accordingly this phenomenon is not frequent, but it is met with here and there, for example in North America. In Chinook, where as a rule the noun contains a pronominal element, this is missing in the vocative of some nouns, these last consisting chiefly (as might be supposed) of terms of relationship – āo, younger brother; āq, son; āc, daughter; māma, father,[4] etc.

Functionally this is to be explained in the same way as the form of the request for action. The vocative of the noun is part of a request for action. It is the functional complement of the verb. *George, help! George, hurry!* If I hear my name called I turn automatically – to see what is wanted of me. My reactions to language are conditioned by my life in the society to which I belong, and I know – almost instinctively – that my name is intended for me, and for me to take some action.

[1] E.g. Greek ναύτης (nautēs), vocative ναῦτα (nauta); πρέσβυς (presbūs), vocative πρέσβυ (presbu); πατήρ (patēr), vocative πάτερ (patĕr). Lithuanian wejas (wind), vocative wéje; zodis (word), vocative zodi; gaidys (hen), vocative gaidi. Hittite, too, has a vocative of proper names, consisting of the mere stem.
[2] This phenomenon does not apply in the plural – *friends*, or *amici*, can be nominative or vocative. But then language is usually addressed to one person, not more.
[3] See e.g. Homburger, p. 55.
[4] Boas, *Chinook*, p. 612.

Accordingly, if instead of saying 'Balbě' I say 'Balbus', it is simply to indicate that I am not making a request – for which Balbě would suffice – but a statement.

But the hearer is equally a person for whom the function of language is to increase his sphere of activity and attain the assistance of his fellows. Accordingly, though he understands *hurry! go!* as a request for action, there are circumstances in which he is liable to resent it. Man, living as he does in society, must respect the interests and viewpoints of others if he is to gain their assistance. Accordingly there is also a wide use of other forms than the 'imperative' to indicate a request for (or suggestion of) action, and gain the speaker's ends. If the Englishman had no writing and no grammars, and an anthropologist or linguist from elsewhere were to visit and study this backward island, what would he record as the form of the verb used by the native to express a request for action? Probably four forms. The first, which he might describe as the commonest, would be the stem or shortest form of the verb – *Go! Hurry!* A second, which he might describe as also common, would be the use of the subjunctive – 'You might clean the kitchen today.' 'You might bring me the file.' A third, which he might describe as 'quite often used', would be a periphrasis of some kind – 'It would be nice if you would do the kitchen today.' 'Would you mind handing me the file?' 'Please bring me the file.' Lastly he might mention as being rare, except in the negative, and limited to certain types of relations, the use of the future: 'You will proceed with your Company to point A. . . .' 'You will do nothing of the sort.'

This is precisely what we find in a general view of the world's languages. In one language one of these means of expression is in more general use, in another language another; and looking at the world's languages as a whole, this is probably the order of frequency. But observers often give us only the commonest form. We began this chapter by saying that 'throughout the world and throughout its history the shortest and simplest form of the verb is the request for action'. This is only true subject to qualifications. In a considerable number of languages the subjunctive is found as a separate form of the verb, and we read in many of the grammars of these languages – perhaps one-twentieth of the world's languages – that the imperative of the verb is the same as the subjunctive. We must view this statement against the background mentioned above. In these languages, for reasons which have been mentioned, the subjunctive is used as the recognized form of the request for action, and the observer who compiled the grammar mentions no other form as used for the purpose. But this does not mean that the simple stem of the verb would not also be understood to bear this meaning; and sometimes this is plain from what the grammarian says or does not say.[1]

The less common method of expression recorded by the visiting anthropologist in England was, we said, the periphrasis 'It would be nice if you would', etc. As in English, this is less common in the other languages of the world, but it is frequent in, for example, North America. So in Tsimshian the most frequent method of expressing the imperative is by ām [= (it would be) good (if)] and the subjunctive; or by the subjunctive alone.[2]

Last was mentioned the use of the future tense as the request for action. This is found here and there about the world, as, for example, in Motu.[3]

There are, however, two more forms to be noticed, both in English and elsewhere. In English an exclamation is often used together with the verb-stem to express the imperative – Oh! get on! Oh! hurry up! This usage is also found in some other languages, chiefly in Polynesian, where the exclamation is E, an exclamation in wide use in those languages especially in verse.[4] For example, in Maori one of the forms of the imperative is the plain verb-stem, but another, in active forms, is the verb stem preceded by e – for example, E noho, stay! sit! In some other languages the exclamation follows the verb, but this must not blind us to the fact that the simple verb-stem is also the imperative. We see the same phenomenon with the vocative of the noun. An English grammar may tell us that the vocative of the English word 'friend' is 'O friend!' This, of course, is not so; 'Friend!' serves the purpose just as well. The exclamation serves to call attention to what follows, as well as to give the speaker time to choose his brief word. Similarly in Latin or French if we call *puer!* or *garçon!* it means *boy! slave!* or *waiter!* with or without the prefix O.

There is one other usage to be noticed. We have mentioned one means of avoiding the resistance of the hearer and securing his help by

---

[1] Conversely the verb stem (as we are told) is occasionally used as the subjunctive, e.g. Shilluk and Nandi (Nilotic), Serer and Dyola (South of the Senegal).
[2] H.A.I.L., part I, p. 407.
[3] New Guinea. We are told that the form used for the imperative is the same as for the future.
[4] In many Polynesian languages the same exclamation, used before or after the noun, signifies the vocative (e.g. Maori, Hawaian, Tahitian, Mangarevan; and also Fijian). In several of these languages it is used to mark the end of a line of verse, and in Malagasy to mark the end of a sentence.

THE REQUEST FOR ACTION

expressing the request for action in the indirect and gentler form of the subjunctive. But, as we well know, the same result may be achieved in many cases in English and other languages by a forceful and commanding tone and volume calculated to overbear his resistance, or to produce action on his part before he has time to resent. In some languages this result is achieved by a special tone or accent; and just as, in English, a military command is usually accented on the last syllable (as 'attentión' or merely 'shun'), we see the same accent in the imperative of a large number of other languages (such as Semitic) where the imperative is a dissyllable.[1] In a small number of languages this effect is achieved or heightened by an added particle of emphasis. For example, although in the Finno-Ugrian family of languages the root of the verb is generally also the second person singular of the imperative, in Mordvin the imperative is the stem with the affix k – so, *era* (stem of the verb 'to live') imperative *erak*, live! *vano* (to see); *vanok*, see! This element k has a wide use as a particle of emphasis or reinforcement in that family of languages.[2] In Hungarian the particle is -j.[3]

These various exceptional cases are sufficient to explain why only some 85% of the grammars of languages indicate that the verb-stem, or the shortest and simplest form of the verb, expresses the request for action. I believe that substantially in all languages the shortest form of the verb is understood to mean the request for action.

This is therefore one of the most striking of all the phenomena of language. Earlier in this chapter we gave a reason for it, namely that the request for action is the fundamental and characteristic function of language, and is, as such, at the same time the most frequent and familiar use of the verb; and that, as man says no more than is necessary to be understood, when the verb is used in its characteristic and most familiar form it is at its shortest and simplest. But there are other important reasons.

We have now returned to the point where we began this book. Let us look round and remind ourselves of the journey that we have taken. We started by pointing out that there were three types of sentence in language – the request for (or suggestion of) action, the statement and the description-statement: as examples (1) Look!

---

[1] In Hebrew the first consonant is omitted in the imperative of some verbs.
[2] In Ostyak it is ke – for example, manlem, I go; manlem-ke, Yes, I go. Ollem, I am, ollem-ke, Yes I am. In Hungarian this, the full form, is abbreviated: varom, I sow (it); varok (for varomke), I sow.
[3] Varj, sow! irj, write!

(2) George runs. (3) George is fast. The request for action consisted at its simplest of one term, a verb; the statement consisted of two terms, a subject-noun and a verb; and the description-statement of three terms, a subject-noun, a verb and an adjective, We examined from various aspects these three types of sentence, and noticed in every instance that the second was more advanced than the first, and the third than the second. The first performs the basic function of all language, namely, that by it man in society, through the person addressed, wields and gains control over his environment. In the statement, and still more in the description-statement, the exercise of this function is indirect. Again, the request for action represents the simplest form of mental process, the nearest thing in language to the interjection or call produced by an animal. The third type, 'George is fast', is a thought in the mind of the speaker, involving analysis and synthesis. The second type, 'George runs', is hardly a thought; a mere mental reflection of the perceived physical event of George running. But Type 1, 'Look!' is not a thought at all, but expresses a desire. Again, in the third type there is a subject, and a predicate that states something of him, and the subject is the heart of the sentence. In the second type we may regard the sentence in the same way, or say, from the opposite point of view, that there is a verb extended and made more precise by the addition of a subject. In the first type there is verb alone and no subject. Again, the first type is characteristic of language in that it is intimately and directly related to the physical environment: the second type may or may not be so; and the description-statement is not simply related to the environment. It always involves some analysis and some synthesis with other persons, objects or events. Again, the first type is at its most common outside literature; the second is common in and out of literature; while the third is the language of literature and especially advanced literature. Again, the first type expresses all the generality of the verb of which it consists: it expresses a mere class of action; in the second it is lengthened and becomes more precise by the addition of a noun; in the third it is further lengthened and made more precise by the addition of an adjective. Accordingly the proportion of verb in the parts of speech of the sentence decreases from Type 1 to Type 2, from Type 2 to Type 3; and in the minimum request for action we see the sentence at its simplest and shortest, while the description-statement is the most complex and varied. Lastly, the verb itself weakens in force from Type 1 through Type 2 to Type 3. In the first it performs the whole function of language, it is a tool bringing about the action of

others; in the second it is a mere event; in the third the verb is reduced to the mere copula 'to be', and almost all meaning of action is gone.

We then investigated the changes in the development of language, from peoples who were the most backward in terms of civilization (that is to say, in their control over their environment) to those most advanced, and saw many or most of the changes between Type 1 and Type 2, and Type 2 and Type 3, progressively appearing. In this line of advance we saw a machine-like fall in the proportion of verbs in the language, and a steady increase, first in the proportion of nouns and then in the proportion of adjectives. We saw this process of change not merely between earlier and later language, but between fundamental and less fundamental language – for in the same language, at the same point of time, the most common words contained the largest proportion of verbs, and in the less common words there was an increase in the proportion of nouns and in the least common words in the proportion of adjectives. We saw the development of language as the addition of annual rings to the heartwood, the heartwood remaining largely of the same composition. Accordingly, the verb was not merely the earliest but functionally the central or basic part of the language. We then saw the same progressive changes in the history of the form of words, the verb, by and large, being extended to form a noun, and the noun being extended to form an adjective. Finally we saw that the roots or primitive words of the language – that is to say, the parts of words, or whole words, whose derivation could not further be traced – consisted in the main of verbs, that is to say, the shortest and simplest form of old, common verbs. We then considered accidence and syntax, and noticed that they became necessary and developed as the sentence grew longer and more and more complex and precise, for they indicated the relations between the different terms of which the sentence consists.

And now we see that the verb-roots signify requests for action, and are the heartwood of the verb, the shortest and simplest form of the verb, the commonest and functionally basic part of the verb, the earliest and most primitive form of the verb, without accidence or syntax. They are also the shortest and simplest form of the sentence, and the earliest and most primitive and functionally basic form of the sentence – and therefore of language, for every complete communication is a sentence and the sentences make up the language. We now see why the imperative retains the same form in modern language: it is merely another instance of the heartwood of the language retaining the same general nature while additions grow up around it. In short we see the imperative of the verb, the request for action, as the beginning of the verb and of the sentence and of language – language originating as a word which is also a sentence.

The suggestion that the imperative of the verb is the oldest part of language has been made by more than one writer. For example, Michel Bréal expressed such a view in his Essai de Sémantique (1897), suggesting that the imperative is the oldest part of the conjugation, and that where there is identity between indicative and imperative (contrary to what we are taught) it is the indicative which is the borrower.[1] He ends his chapter upon the subjective element by saying: 'We begin to see from what point of view man ordered his language. Speech was not made for the purposes of description, of narrative, of disinterested considerations. To express a desire, to intimate and order, to denote a taking possession of persons or of things – these were the first uses of language. For many men they are still practically the only ones.'[2] Elliott Smith also suggested that language originated in the imperative of the verb. In a well-phrased passage in his *Evolution of Man* he writes: 'Primitive speech, apart from mere emotional cries such as animals endowed with a true sense of hearing emit, no doubt began with imperative verbs, differing only in their variety and fuller meaning from instinctive cries. But when names were invented, at first by the definition of a visual experience for which a verbal symbol was devised, it became possible for men to communicate the one with the other in sentences of two words after the manner of Alfred Jingle in Pickwick Papers.'[3]

In other words, our sentence of Type 2, the statement, emerged from Type 1. Let us consider how this can have come about.

[1] Michel Bréal, *Semantics*, trans. by Mrs H. Cust (1900), pp. 235-6.
[2] Ibid., p. 283. The passage is somewhat marred by the inclusion of the words 'to denote a taking possession of persons or of things'. What property was there for early Food Gatherers to take possession of? Certainly not land, and practically no goods. And no persons except an eloping bride. For no man is the only use of language 'to denote a taking possession'.
[3] G. Elliott Smith, *The Evolution of Man*, 2nd Ed., 1927, p. 173.

CHAPTER TEN

The Infinitive

In order to see by what steps the request for action may have become the statement, and the imperative verb produced the noun and the indicative verb, let us proceed by the same method as we used in the previous chapter. Let us look generally at the languages of the world and see whether there are any further uses of the verb which are expressed by the verb-stem alone in a large bulk of languages. Examining the evidence to this end, we see two further uses of the verb-stem, and only two[1]: one is the infinitive; the other is the third person singular of the aorist indicative (and, in the rare cases where there is a separate form for the masculine and feminine,[2] the masculine). These two uses of the verb-stem are not so frequent as its use as an imperative: the use as infinitive is found in, perhaps, nearly a half of the world's languages, and the second use in, perhaps, a little more than half of the world's languages. In short, these uses are very frequent, and so frequent as to call for explanation. It is not rare that the three uses are found in the same language, where confusion can be avoided by some means, for example by variation of vowel or tone. But sometimes the verb-root is used as infinitive or third person singular of the aorist in a language where it is not used as imperative. The reason is usually that the imperative customarily includes a particle of emphasis, and the typical case is represented by the Finno-Ugrian family of languages. For example in Hungarian *var* is the stem of the verb meaning 'sow'; *var* also means 'he sows' (indefinite form); and varj, 'sow!' In a large number of languages we find two of these three uses present. But since the uses as infinitive and third person singular of the aorist are slightly removed from the central function of language, it is not enough merely to notice the proportion of cases in which the simple stem or root of the verb expresses one of these two functions; in order properly to assess the evidence, it is equally important to notice the number of

---

[1] We have noticed above, p. 118, the rare use of the verb-root as subjunctive – possibly confined to a few Sudanic tongues. It may originally be the infinitive, for it is especially characteristic of the Sudanic languages that the verb-root is used as the infinitive.

[2] In Semitic, and some languages of Hamitic affiliation, for example Hausə.

languages in which the infinitive or third singular aorist, though not expressed by the mere stem, is represented by the shortest and simplest form of the verb next to that of the imperative; and if there is an addition to the stem, it is important to see, if possible, what is its meaning. This is particularly important in regard to the infinitive, for the infinitive marks the frontier between verb and noun, and in languages in which nouns have characteristic forms distinct from those of verbs, the infinitive may be given a form (for example, a case-ending) characteristic of a noun, so as to indicate that the root is here used as being also a noun. For the same reason, in a larger number of languages, in which nouns have no distinctive forms, there is commonly used with the infinitive a separate word, so as to indicate the noun – often, for example, a word corresponding to the English 'to' or (as in Maori, Greek or German) a demonstrative or definite article.

We need not go further than Modern English to find an example of a common kind. Here, for example, the verb-stem 'break' signifies the imperative and also the infinitive (e.g. I will break it); though as infinitive, being noun as well as verb, it is frequently preceded by the preposition 'to', and the expression 'to break' can be described, in terms taken from Latin Grammar, as a noun in the dative case (to break = for breaking, for fracture). But, it may be said, in earlier English the infinitive was quite distinct in form from the imperative, and in O.E. ended in -an, so that 'to break' was in O.E. *brecan*. That is true, but even so the ending -an in O.E. was simply a case-ending, indicating that the stem was to be understood here as a noun, and Modern English, where the case-endings have almost all disappeared, is the more typical of language generally. Indeed, it is generally agreed that in the Indo-European languages the suffixes of the infinitives are merely case-endings, originating from the use of the word as a noun, and later permanently incorporated as the meaning of the suffix was forgotten.[1] It is easy to see how this arose. If a verb can be used as a noun, it can be used as subject or object of a sentence, but more commonly it will be used as an indirect object. For example, 'he desired to run' means 'he wished for running'. In the course of time a particular preposition or a particular case-ending is so commonly used with the stem in this sense that its origin is overlooked, and it is re-

---

[1] A conclusion first reached by Bopp in *Conjugationssystem der Sanskritsprache* (1816), and followed by later scholars. See references in Callaway, *The Infinitive in Anglo-Saxon* (1913), p. 1. In the same way, in the Romance languages, as the meanings of the Latin case-endings, in the nouns generally, became forgotten, one case-ending (in commonest use) became encrusted with the noun as part of it (e.g. the accusative singular).

garded as a mark of the infinitive. For example, in the phrase 'he desired to run' the word 'to' has its proper sense; but the phrase 'to run' also somewhat resembles a direct object (he desired to run = he desired a running). And in the sentence 'To err is human' the word 'to' has completely lost its meaning, and indicates merely that 'to err' is an infinitive or verbal noun. Similarly in the German *Das Wandern ist des Müllers Lust*, the case ending -n in *wandern* has entirely lost its significance and indicates merely the infinitive. So in the Indo-European languages generally the infinitive-endings are merely case-endings which have become permanently incorporated. Some may be neuter accusatives or nominatives, but the great majority (as we might expect) seem to be datives or locatives.[1] And as each dative-ending or dative-preposition becomes encrusted with the stem, and its original meaning is forgotten, new indicia are added; and so in English.[2]

Another typical case is the Sumerian, where the verbal root signifies the infinitive (as well as the imperative) – so, du = to build – though more commonly it is followed by one of a number of suffixes. In Semitic the infinitive is the shortest form of the verb, and equally so with the imperative, and generally hardly differs from it. So in Hebrew, generally, lemód, teach! infinitive lámod, to teach; construct lemód (the difference being a mere matter of accent). Where the second vowel of the root in Hebrew is a or o, it is o in the infinitive. In most Semitic languages, however, where the a has given place to u in the imperative, the a is retained in the infinitive.[3] And just as, in the Semitic languages, the first of the three consonants of the root is dropped in certain cases in the imperative, so it is also dropped in the infinitive. But the infinitive is a noun as well as a verb, and in these cases it is commonly lengthened to three consonants by the addition of a suffix characteristic of a feminine abstract noun; and commonly, the preposition 'to' is prefixed. In the Hamitic languages, too, the infinitive is generally the verbal root, or the shortest and simplest form of the verb next to the imperative. So it is the root in Ancient Egyptian; and in Somali it is the root with the suffix -i, as sheg, tell! shegi, to tell; Galla, root + u, kemu,

---

[1] E.g. in Greek such dative forms as ἰστάναι, λῦσαι, λύεσθαι; and such a Latin form as rĕgi (= to be ruled, i.e. for ruling; cf. rĕgi = for a ruler) and similar Sanskrit forms. Also the Latin form -ĕre (from -esei) and Lithuanian -ti. Cf. also the Latin oratio obliqua, as in Max Müller's example, *miror te nihil ad me scribĕre* = I marvel at you for writing nothing to me.

[2] So, starting with *beran* (= to bear), there is the added dative-ending (*beranne* or *berenne*), and in addition the prefix 'to' (*to beranne* or *to berenne*) and finally an added 'for' (*for to beranne*).

[3] As, Assyrian, imper, *purus*, infin. *parās*. The commonest Arabic form is qaṭl.

to give; in Hausa the verbal noun is the root, kāmạ, seizing; harbā, shooting, though in certain connexions the suffix -a or -wa is added.

In Africa we see much the same situation throughout the continent. With few exceptions, throughout the Bantu languages, as in Modern English, the infinitive is the root, preceded by some variation of the word ku, which corresponds to the English 'to' – so *ku bona*, to see; *ku tema*, to cut; *ku tanda*, to love, in many Bantu languages.

The Sudanic languages afford a very clear example, for in most of these languages the infinitive is the simple root. In the Nilotic groups of these languages this is the case; for example in Lango (ol = to be tired), and Acholi (stem alone in verbs of neuter form), Dinka,[1] Bari and Nandi; also in Azande; and in West Africa it is common, for example in Ewe (simple root, e.g. yi = to go), Nupe (where the infinitive is usually the root preceded by the preposition nyi = to), and Bambara (Mande). In the Bushman languages the simple form of the verb (that is to say, the root) is the infinitive (e.g. mu = to see).

In the Malayo-Polynesian family of languages the infinitive is generally merely the verb-stem treated as a noun, e.g. Fijian (lako, to go), Samoan (ta = cut! or to cut). In Maori the infinitive is the verb-stem, but is always attended by an article or demonstrative.

The position is much the same in Asia, and America, but perhaps we have given sufficient examples.

What then is the explanation of all this?

We suggested, in the previous chapter, a number of explanations of the general use of the verb-root as an imperative, but they do not seem applicable to the similar phenomenon in regard to the infinitive. One explanation that we gave was that the typical and fundamental use of language is to influence the actions of others for our benefit. We said that words are therefore *prima facie* used and understood in this sense, and accordingly it is not necessary to add any qualification to a verb to give it the meaning of a request for action. Such an explanation will not serve us in regard to the infinitive. We also gave the kindred reason that, in the history of language, the use of the verb as a request for action has been its commonest and most familiar use, and accordingly the imperative is the shortest and simplest form of the verb. This reason will not serve us here. We gave further the explanation that the request for action is the shortest and most primitive form of the sentence – Type 1, as we called it. This reason, too, will not serve us here. The infinitive can never serve as a sentence. What then is the

[1] But often in Dinka the root is preceded by ba, be, bûg, etc. (as English 'to').

explanation, or rather what are the explanations? for there are always several reasons for every fact in language.

The first step towards answering this question is to notice the close relation between the imperative and the infinitive. In the modern Indo-European languages everyone is familiar with the use of the infinitive as a request for action in public notices and elsewhere; and there is a wider use in the negative in Italian (non credere, do not believe). We are also familiar with the use in classical Greek in statutes and public notices, and such poetical uses as, for example, in the epitaph on the men who died at Thermopylae.

This use of the infinitive is not confined to the Indo-European languages. For example, it is found in Old Egyptian; and in Swahili (Bantu), when the verb-root has only one consonant, the request for action is commonly lengthened out to the usual two syllables by using the infinitive (kula, eat![1] kufa, die!) But looking generally at these Indo-European usages we notice that these imperatives, expressed by the infinitive, are weak imperatives, or are addressed not to one person but to the world at large. The boundary between a general request for action and the infinitive is vague. In such English proverbial sayings as 'Love me, love my dog', 'Waste not, want not', it is difficult to see whether the verb is infinitive or imperative. We might equally have said 'To love me is to love my dog', or 'To waste not is to want not', but that would take too long.

We have noticed a number of instances where the infinitive is used as an imperative, but no cases where the imperative is used as an infinitive. The reason is probably that the infinitive has usually a specialized form; but whenever the verb-stem is used as an infinitive, it is probably the old imperative. The use of the imperative as infinitive is the history of language. The main reason for the use of the verb-root as an infinitive is that the infinitive is merely an imperative which has lost some of its force, and, as we shall see, it is the fate of all language to lose its force. It has still part of the function of an imperative: for example, like an imperative it can have an object but no subject; but it has lost a vital part of its force – it cannot function as a sentence. Accordingly, the main reason for this widespread phenomenon of the verb-stem functioning as infinitive is that in the earliest days of

[1] Ku la = to eat. The inclusion of the word ku in the request for action is also common in some Bantu languages of the Congo. So in Buluba-Lulua, where the imperative is the verb-stem, and ku is *prefixed* to the verb stem to form the infinitive, it is often *suffixed* to the verb-stem to form an emphatic imperative in the 2nd person singular – so ambaku (speak!), yaku (go!) – see Morrison, p. 64.

language the imperative verb took its first step of expansion by becoming also an infinitive, and for this reason the verb (since become a verb-root) still functions widely in the world as an infinitive, though less widely than it functions as imperative.

But, it may be said, is it not simpler and more probable to assume that the infinitive preceded the imperative? If the main use of language is to influence the action of others, and if words are *prima facie* understood in this sense, it is obviously only necessary to use an infinitive – for example a word meaning 'moving' or 'taking' – and the person addressed will take it as a suggestion to him to move or take. Certainly this is the foundation of the use of the infinitive in the Indo-European languages – it is used to convey tentative suggestions of action.

But to make such an assumption in regard to the beginnings of language is to substitute theory for history. Words take their meaning from their use: they do not take their use from their meaning.[1] If language began with an infinitive which later became an imperative, then, before the existence of the sentence of Type 1 (the request for action), language consisted of something which was not a complete communication – for the infinitive is not a sentence – and relied on some other kind of words, not yet in existence, to form a sentence, a communication. How then could the infinitive or language have existed? No, the infinitive is merely the imperative, retaining the meaning of the verb, but having lost the imperative function through being used in a different context. No longer was the verb being used to perform directly the function of language – to enlist the assistance of fellow-men.

A second reason for the phenomenon, and the second reason for saying that it is of great antiquity, is that the infinitive represents the first step taken by the verb – namely the imperative – towards becoming a noun, and the first step, therefore, taken by sentences of Type 1 towards becoming Type 2. The infinitive marks the boundary between verb and noun: it is both verb and noun: it is the name of an action. In those languages where there is no formal apparatus distinguishing verb from noun this is not so plainly apparent: the same stem may be used for either purpose, as in the Malayo-Polynesian languages. But even there we noticed that, for example, in Maori the infinitive, though it is the verb-stem, is always attended by an article or demonstrative. In other groups of languages we noticed that the infinitive is usually attended by a word meaning 'to', and in Semitic we

---

[1] Except, of course, that the speaker in his choice of words with which to express his meaning, is always confined by the necessity to make himself understood.

observed that in some verbs there are two forms of the infinitive, one verbal and the other possessing a termination characteristic of the feminine abstract noun; and the prefixing of a preposition meaning *to* is widespread in both cases. In Indo-European languages we noticed that the infinitive has commonly either a noun case-ending or the preposition 'to', and often the definite article. And we must remember that the imperative, in its progress towards creating nouns, is not content to become an infinitive. Modern English is full of examples to the contrary. There is not only the imperative 'break!' and the infinitive 'to break', there is something else which is almost the same thing – namely, the noun 'a break'. This too is a process of high antiquity. In classical Greek, for example, where nouns must have their characteristic terminations, there is not merely the ancient βαλέ (bălĕ), throw! and formed from it, the ancient infinitive βαλεῖν (baleîn) for βαλέ-εν (bălĕ-ĕn). There is also the feminine noun βολή (bolē'), a throw; and the masculine noun βόλος (bŏlŏs), a throw, a missile; and the neuter noun βέλος (bĕlŏs), a missile. The process by which the imperative, in the expansion of language, gave rise to the nouns was by the intermediacy of the infinitive, and the first nouns were verbal nouns.[1]

But, it may be said, is there not another explanation of the wide use of the verb-stem as infinitive, the explanation that has been offered earlier for other phenomena in language? The infinitive is the verb at its vaguest, without time, without quality, person or number, tense or mood; and similarly the verb-stem is in form what the infinitive is in meaning, the mere notion of verb without prefix, infix, suffix or other variation particularizing the action? Why need so fantastic an antiquity be claimed for what is illustrated in English and other modern tongues? Have not these relations of meaning and form between imperative, infinitive and noun been shaped and built up and retained by usage?

All these observations are wholly true, and the answer is the same as we have given in earlier chapters. These relations remain because language remains the same, merely gathering new forms and usages around its extremities. But these relations originated for the same reason, for language originated as what has since become a heartwood. Whatever vagueness there is in the heart of language is the vagueness of the early mind of man. This view is reinforced by a consideration of the third use of the verb-root, namely as the third person singular of the aorist indicative.

---

[1] The process of change of meaning from 'a throw' to 'a missile' is common in language – see *post*, p. 177.

CHAPTER ELEVEN

The Third Person Singular of the Aorist Indicative

The typical example of the use of the verb-root as the third person singular of the aorist indicative is afforded by that most conservative of all families of languages, the Semitic. In Hebrew, for example, the word qaṭal – note the two vowels 'a' – signifies the third person singular masculine of the aorist (or, as it is sometimes called in Semitic grammar, the 'perfective') of the verb 'kill'. This use has no necessary relation with time – it may be used to signify past, present or future, and it is often difficult to see which of the three is in fact meant. The contrast is with the imperfective (third person singular masculine yqeṭōl or yqeṭál). The former signifies a simple action, and therefore a complete action, at any time. The imperfective signifies action in progress and not completed, past, present or future. Accordingly the latter bears a more elaborate and precise meaning than the former. Also the latter is more commonly used for the future, because future action is incomplete, whereas the former is commonly used for the past, because past action is generally complete. But this is not always so. For example, in Assyrian – as in many languages of other groups – it is commonly used as the present. This reminds us of several uses of the English 'present' – for example, 'I reach my office at eight o'clock', meaning 'I have done so in the recent past, I do so in the present and shall be doing so in the near future'; or the use of the 'historic present': 'He then ups and hits me in the jaw'. The time element in the 'tenses' of all verbs is subtle and evanescent, and intermixed with non-temporal elements and relations. In Semitic there are, properly speaking, no tenses in the sense of *time forms*. But in Hebrew qaṭal[1] normally means

[1] In Hebrew, unlike Arabic, the accent is on the second syllable, but originally seems to have been on the first (see, Wright, p. 170). Accordingly the difference in Hebrew between qeṭốl or qeṭál (imperative); qáṭōl or qeṭốl (construct) infinitive; and qáṭal (aorist) is a mere matter of accent. The change from the accent on the last syllable in the imperative to the accent on the 1st syllable in the aorist is frequent in language (cf. classical Greek and Hausa).

'he killed'. For the other persons, abbreviated pronouns are suffixed to the root.

In Eastern Europe and Asia the Finno-Ugrian family provides equally striking examples. Here, until the other day, all the tenses indicated aspect, not time; and now in Finnish and Hungarian the verb-stem indicates the third person present (Finnish: *tuo-n*, formerly *tuo-m*, I bring; *tuo-t*, thou bringest; *tuo*, he brings. Hungarian: *var-ok*, for *var-om-ke*, I sow; *var-sz*, thou sowest; *var*, he sows – imperative *varj!*). Similarly in Samoyed, in the indefinite indicative, denoting simple, complete, momentary action, first person singular *madâ-dm*, second person singular, *madâ-n*, third person singular *madâ*, he cut – imperative *madaʼ*, infinitive *madâ*). The additions in the first and second persons are pronominal. In the Turkish-Mongolian-Tungusian languages the position is very similar.

In the Indo-European family we see this feature in one of the most conservative of these languages, namely the Greek. βαλε (bălĕ) is the root of the verb meaning 'throw', and the imperative is βαλέ, throw! In Homer, βάλε is also the third person singular of the aorist indicative,[1] which (as in Semitic) is independent of time, but was usually employed as a past tense or preterite, for it denoted simple and therefore complete action. In Homer we find an alternative form in which a prefixed short syllable (ĕ-, known to grammar-books as the 'augment') is in use as a means of distinguishing the third person singular aorist from the imperative. This is not altogether surprising, for Greek had a fondness for introducing a short syllable to words beginning with a consonant without alteration of meaning,[2] and the same augment was also (though less commonly) in use in the Indo-Iranian languages and Armenian[3] for the same purpose. In Greek literature the use of the augment gradually spreads until it becomes regular in Attic prose in all three persons, where it applies to all past tenses in the indicative (and in the indicative alone); but there remained a few old, familiar verbs which

---

[1] Cf. the Slav aorist, e.g. *pade* (he fell) = Greek πέτε later πέσε.
[2] I take the following neat set of examples from a letter of Max Müller to W. E. Gladstone dated 7 Sept. 1862:

Sanskrit naman, name – Greek ὄνομα
" nakha, nail – " ὄνυξ
" bhrû, brow – " ὀφρύς
" navan, nine – " ἐννέα
" rudhira, red – " ἐρυθρός
" laghu, light – " ἐλαχύς
" star, star – " ἀστήρ

(Latin stella = sterula, diminutive of ster.)

[3] In Armenian, however, it is not employed except with monosyllables of the 3rd person (e.g. *e-ber*, he bore).

never acquired it.[1] Abbreviated personal pronouns were suffixed to the root to form the first and second persons (a nasal for the first person and dental for the second, in singular and plural, as in Semitic) but never to the third singular. In all verbs showing this 'strong' aorist the root vowel is short (usually *a*, *e* or *o*) and the vowel *a* predominates.

In Greek, from the aorist, by lengthening the word – either by lengthening the vowel in some way or by reduplicating a consonant – arose at some time the tenses signifying repeated, continuous, uncompleted action, the present, imperfect and perfect. As the time element in the tenses became more pronounced, and the speaker became more self-conscious, the first person singular of the present tense became (as in Modern English and Classical Latin) a new centre from which expanded a more modern verb, its conjugation more suited to the needs of modern man. From it, from early times, was developed a new form of aorist, known in grammars as the 'weak' aorist, shaped from the present tense, usually by adding a dental consonant (*s* in the active and middle voices and *th* in the passive).[2] All the later-formed Greek verbs had the new form of aorist, and no later verbs had the old. Consequently, in the history of Greek, the proportion of verbs with the new aorist steadily increased, and the verbs with 'strong' aorists are still the old, familiar, verbs of every day.[3]

If we now turn to the Germanic group of languages, we see a good deal of evidence of the same history. There is a strong aorist, now used as a preterite tense, in which the simplest and shortest form is the third person singular, which is also the verb-root and commonly has the vowel a. The verbs possessing the strong aorist are old, familiar verbs in everyday use. So in O.E. typical examples are bītan (to bite), preterite bāt; fleōgan (to flee), preterite fleāh; findan (to find), preterite fand; helpan (to help), preterite healp; weorpan (to throw), preterite wearp; feohtan (to fight), preterite feaht; brecan (to break), preterite braěc; and so forth. In Modern English the verbs with strong aorists are still the old, everyday words – eat, ate; run, ran; begin, began; drink, drank; sing, sang; swim, swam; sink, sank; get, gat (now got); speak, spake (now spoke); break, broke; drive, drove; see, saw. But the newer verbs have always a weak preterite, formed from the present

[1] E.g. ἔδον, I ate (Latin edo, I eat; Skt. admi).
[2] The middle and passive voices now emerging.
[3] Examples, κάμε, πόρε, ἵκε-το, τέκε, βάλε, γένε-το, φύγε, ἴδε, πίθε, ἕλε, μάθε, θάνε, λάθε, πάθε, λάβε, λίπε, θόρε, μόλε, πέσε (from πέτε), τύχε, πύθε-το, κίχε. Note also the large proportion of plosive consonants. I have omitted in the above sketch verbs of the type ἵστημι (aorist στῆ, ἔστη); they are comparatively few, but the same observations apply.

by the addition of a dental consonant d or t (so Modern English walk, walkt, corresponds to Classical Greek λύε, ἔλυσε). It is not difficult to recognize one important reason why this change has taken place in the Greek and Germanic grammars. It follows from the advance of these peoples towards civilization and the consequent increase in vocabulary. In the early history of language, if we suppose that verb-roots were mainly monosyllables of the form CVC, and the vowel was everywhere much the same, it was possible to express a variation in the tense of each verb by a regular variation in the vowel. But in the Indo-European languages, when the vocabulary increased the verb-roots largely remained monosyllabic, and where they did so the increase in vocabulary was effected by change in the vowel between one verb and another. It then became impossible any longer to express variations of function in the same verb by a uniform variation of vowel, and this purpose was achieved by the usual method of lengthening the word; in the case of the aorist by an added dental consonant. This change of method never became necessary in the Semitic languages. They lengthened their roots by an added consonant, retaining the same vowel. But the change of method in the Indo-European languages must have started more than 4,000 years ago, for it shows itself in these different groups of the family. Moreover, it commenced in an age of CVC verbs.

The Greek and Germanic aorist are unlike in one respect. In the Greek aorist it is only the third person singular that is represented by the mere verb-stem, and so βάλε can only mean 'he threw'. But in O.E. and German both the third and the first person are represented by the old stem, and they can only be distinguished by the subject noun or pronoun – in M.H.G. er kam = he came, and ich kam = I came. This is a situation very common in language: though the third person singular of the aorist is often alone represented by the verb-stem, in many languages that simplicity is shared with another person or even with both the other persons, and the pronoun is needed to express the difference. It remains true that the form of the third person is the simplest form after that of the imperative. As we said, to appreciate the simplicity of the form of the third person of the aorist, we must look more widely than when we considered the imperative, for here language has departed from its central function.

Sumerian shows a similar phenomenon. The stem of the verb signifies the first or third person singular of the aorist, but it is preceded in both cases by a pronominal prefix. Yet, so far as is known, one or other of various forms of pronominal prefix may be used, no matter which person is intended. So *du* is the root, *build*, and in-du signifies 'I have built', or 'I built', or equally 'he has built' or 'he built'; and we could equally use one of a number of other prefixes in place of 'in' for either purpose, and the meaning would appear from the context.

When we turn to the Bantu languages we find throughout a somewhat similar phenomenon, which is common in language. Among the many tenses with which these tongues are endowed is an aorist indicative which in many grammars (as in grammars of North American and other languages) is called an 'indefinite present'. This, in all persons, consists of the stem or root of the verb preceded by a pronoun. For example in Ila (where *bona* is the root and the imperative of the verb 'see'), nda bona = I saw[1]; wa bona = he saw. But it remains true that the third person singular of the aorist (wa bona) and the infinitive (ku bona) are the simplest form of the verb after the imperative (bona). So that whereas the first and third persons singular are of the same form in Sumerian and German, and the first, second and third persons in many Bantu languages and Modern English, and the third person stands alone in Greek, Semitic, Finno-Ugrian and Turkish, it still remains true that in all these languages the third person singular of the aorist is the simplest form (after the imperative) though other persons and the infinitive *may* be equally simple.

Throughout Africa the distinction between the perfective and imperfective is the dominant feature of the verb.[2] Throughout the Hamitic and Sudanic languages of Africa we see the same general picture as that described above. In Old Egyptian the indefinite present is expressed by the root followed by a subject-suffix, and the simplest form is the third person singular. In Somali the first and third person singular of the verb are in all its parts the simplest in form; and in the aorist are the simplest of all after the imperative – so, sheg! tell!; aorist, first person shèga, second person shegta; third person masculine shèga. In Hausa, in all persons, the aorist is the root preceded by the subject-pronoun.[3]

Much the same applies to the Sudanic tongues. Here there is an 'indefinite present' or 'aorist' tense signifying simple action irrespective of time, and it is generally expressed by the infinitive (that is, the stem)

---

[1] The tense can equally indicate a past, present or future meaning.
[2] Homburger, p. 136.
[3] Na zo, I came (have come, had come), ka zo (2nd person sing. masc.), kin zo (fem.), ya zo (3rd person sing. masc.), ta zo (fem.).

with the pronominal prefix in all persons.[1] But in some of these languages the third person alone (sometimes third singular, sometimes singular and plural) has no pronominal prefix.[2]

In the Bushman languages the indefinite present is expressed by the root preceded by a pronoun.

So with other Asiatic families of languages beyond those already mentioned. In Siamese the present indicative is formed by the verb alone (the verb is an invariable word) preceded by the personal pronoun – xan ma, I come; thàn ma, thou comest; khao ma, he comes. The other tenses are indicated by the addition of a particle. In the same language the infinitive is expressed by the verb alone – ma, to come. and the imperative can also be expressed by the verb alone when the sense is sufficiently clear. In Ainu the verb-root signifies the third person present indicative as well as the second person singular of the imperative.

The position is not very different in the Malayo-Polynesian languages. Looking, for example, at the most backward of these peoples, the Melanesians, we find that, as in the Germanic words of Modern English but to an even greater degree, the distinction between noun and verb is expressed by usage and context rather than form; so that the root, without any addition, expresses the infinitive or verbal noun. It also expresses the second person of the imperative, though in most languages some separate particle of emphasis may be added or omitted at will. Separate particles (varying from language to language) also express the distinctions between the tenses; but in most of these languages the root can be used with no added word except an abbreviated personal pronoun, and in such case it represents an indefinite or aorist tense of the indicative which can be loosely used at will to signify the present or past. But in some of these languages there is a simple, added particle to represent even the aorist tense, and yet in such case the pronoun is usually omitted in the third person singular.[3]

Generally, in spite of the complexity of the grammar of North America, the picture there is much the same as elsewhere. In many languages the simplest form of the verb is expressed by the third person singular of the indefinite present. In Zuñi, for example, in many verbs, the simple stem indicates both the imperative and the third person

---

[1] E.g. in West Africa, Nupe: u bé, he came; u wo, he hears; Ewe: yi, to go; meyi, I go I went, I shall go; eyi, he goes, he went. So, too, E. Africa, Bari, Lango, Masai.
[2] So e.g. Nandi (which retains older grammar better than Masai: a-mwe, I run away; i-mwe, you (sing.) run away; mwe, he, she or they run away. So also Acholi.
[3] See, in regard to these various languages, Ray (1926).

singular of the present indicative completive (that is to say, the expression of a single, complete action) – so ita = 'eat!' and also 'he eats'; alu = 'go about!' or 'he goes about'. Other stems require suffixes also. In Coos the third person singular has no pronominal prefix but is expressed by the mere stem (with or without the article). In Sioux the verb alone may be used as well for the more or less abstract idea of verbal action as for the third person of the indicative.[1] In Sioux, indeed, as in Latin and Greek and many other of the world's languages, there are pronouns of the first and second person but none of the third.[2] In Blackfoot the third person singular is the simplest form of the verb after the imperative.

These examples must suffice to present the general picture as we see it in the world's languages. A phenomenon which is so widespread must have been created by world-wide and fundamental causes. What are they?

We have, in this chapter, been solely concerned with statements – our sentences of Type 2 – and the overwhelming bulk of all statements in language are in the third person. Compared with their number, statements in the first and second persons are very few. As regards the second person, there are few occasions when it is important to tell a hearer facts about himself. Statements in the first person form even in modern times a small minority, and we need not doubt that in earlier days, before man was so self-regarding and introspective as he has increasingly become, they were rarer and rarer. We have seen more than once that what is commonest in language tends to be the briefest and simplest in form – or, in other words, tends to be expressed by a stem or root – and it would follow from this that the statement in the third person, that is to say the third person of the indicative verb, would be shorter and simpler in form than that in the first or second person. But it is quite rarely that we find the statement of the third person plural (or dual), as well as the singular, to be of the shortest and simplest form. We noticed this in the two kindred languages of the Masai and Nandi, and there are a few others, like Ainu, but generally the phenomenon we are considering is confined to the third person singular. We might not have realized, without examining the forms of language, that the statement in the third person singular is much more common than that in the third person plural. But there can be no question about it, and we need feel little doubt that this is an important

---

[1] H.A.I.L., part I, Introduction by Fr. Boas, p. 42.
[2] H.A.I.L., part I, p. 908, i.e. there are pronouns for 'I', 'thou' and 'I and thou'.

reason for the brevity of the third person singular of the verb.[1] Moreover, we have noticed a good number of languages in which there is no true personal pronoun of the third person, and particularly of the third person singular, or where, if there is, it is commonly omitted. And wherever we can recognize the meaning of that part of the indicative verb which is added to the root, it is generally pronominal – either a separate pronoun (as in Modern English or Bantu) or an abbreviated version forming a suffix (or less commonly, a prefix) as in Indo-European, Semitic, Bantu, Finno-Ugrian, Turkish, Sudanic and other families of languages. So there are obviously good reasons for saying that the brevity of the statement in the third person singular is due, at least in part, to its familiarity.

But it would be untrue to say that in language generally the statement in the third person singular of *all tenses* of the indicative is in the form of a stem or root, or is shorter or simpler than the statement in the first or second person, True, there are a number of languages which we have noticed, and in which, throughout the tenses of the verb, the statement in the third person is briefer than that in the first or second. There was one African instance in Nandi, and striking instances in the Finno-Ugrian and Turkish families of languages. But these facts are exceptional in the languages of the world: in many or most tenses, in many or most languages, the statement in the third person is, to say the least of it, no shorter than the others. In language generally it is only in one tense that the third person singular is expressed by the shortest form. The nature of that tense varies but little from language to language and we may almost everywhere term it the aorist or indefinite present. It may be suggested, therefore, that the explanation of the simplicity in form of the third person singular of the aorist is its vagueness of meaning; it may be suggested that because of this vagueness it is expressed by the verb root or little more, and the precise applications of the verb are expressed by the various formal complements of the verb roots – prefixes, infixes, suffixes, variations of the vowel or tone, or added particles. An alternative explanation may be suggested – an explanation of the type that we have repeatedly

---

[1] As an example of early literature taken at random, I choose Homer's Iliad, and count the verbs in the first 245 lines of Book 1, as follows:

3rd person sing.	3rd person plur.	3rd person dual	1st person (sing. & plur.)	2nd person (sing. & plur.)
138	36	3	54	41
50%	13%	1%	20%	15%

This passage concerns a quarrel, and accordingly the proportion of statements in the first and second persons is unduly high.

tried and approved – namely that the statement in the aorist or indefinite present is the most frequent and familiar kind of statement. A third explanation may be suggested – of the type that we have more than once been driven to accept – namely that the third person of the aorist indicative is the original form of statement, from which all other statements have been derived. These three explanations are in truth one. The first of these explanations indicates that this 'vague' statement, with its vague and radical form, must historically have preceded the more precise applications of the verb, with formal complements to the stem. The second explanation, based on an assumption of the greater frequency of the aorist statement than of other statements, is only true of earlier and less developed languages, in which the aorist is in truth the commonest of tenses.

The true explanation, it is suggested, is that the Statement – the verb in sentences of Type 2 – originated as a third person singular of the aorist indicative. The process is well illumined by the light of history, for it is a somewhat later process than the others we have just examined. I do not think it is possible to look widely at the world's languages without seeing this origin. There are still great numbers of tongues which possess no tenses, in the sense of variations according to time. There are many other languages which, like the Finno-Ugrian group, have only evolved true tenses in very recent times. It is only a minority of languages, chiefly confined to peoples of the Modern Grade, which distinguish these functions of the verb according to time alone – as for example, classical Latin, which has lost its earlier conjugation of the verb and acquired a wholly modern apparatus. In a language like Greek, which retains old forms, we can watch the development. A language that has once achieved distinctions of time is unlikely to lose them, and there are probably no known instances of such an event. If the aorist betokens a vagueness of mind it is the vagueness of the mind of early man; but in truth what has produced the facts that we have instanced is not the vagueness of the aorist so much as its simplicity – the simplicity of the concrete as opposed to the elaboration and precision of abstract conceptions. Language takes its meaning from its physical context. The simplest statement records an action or movement of a third person, animal or thing. Accordingly it is a simple and complete action, and, though the statement is not concerned with time, it is an action present or recently past. Later comes the imperfective: again a photographic record of an action or movement, but in this case produced, as it were, by a larger lens, a more rapid shutter and more sensitive film. It records an action in progress and incomplete – again irrespective of time, but involving a more precise and elaborate conception of action. Out of it easily develops not merely the imperfect but the future (in the Semitic they are still the same) and a system of tense-relations based partly on differences of time. But it is the simple use of the verb as third person of the aorist that is the verb of the original statement, and it long continues to be the most frequent application of the verb. Hence it long continues to be expressed by the stem, or at least a form as near thereto as may be, bearing in mind the necessity of avoiding confusion with the imperative and the infinitive (or verbal noun). Accordingly, the explanation of the phenomena into which we are enquiring is the same that we have so often given. Language has in essence always been what it is now, except that it has gathered successive rings around the earliest growth, which has hence become the heartwood. What is old and familiar in language remains, as it were, its centre of gravity, or a fulcrum by which it operates. Out of the old and familiar uses develop the new uses, and the forms expressing the old and familiar uses are extended to express the new uses. In the history of language, the aorist performs a less and less important part and is less and less in use. These considerations explain, for example, the change in the form of the aorist in Greek. The third person singular of the aorist began as the verb (or stem of the verb) or something very close to it in form, because it was the most familiar use of the verb in the statement. In time it was less and less used, as other uses of the verb increased, especially the present, imperfect and future. Hence the aorist – for the conservatism of the Greek language retained an aorist – changed its form to a form expressed through the new fulcrum of the first person singular of the present tense. It can be seen, by comparing the earlier with the later Greek literature, that the use of the other tenses increased as time went on. Taking again as an instance the first book of the Iliad, lines 1 to 245, we see the aorist more used than any other tense of the verb. Of the verbs used (counting each verb and part of a verb every time it occurs), aorist words (strong or weak) are 37% of the whole.[1] In a number of sample passages from the first book of Thucydides I count the proportion of aorist verbs as only 26%. But this is merely another aspect of the development of the human mind. The third person of the aorist indicative is a wholly extrovert record or reflection of an event; from

[1] Counting such words as ἔφερε and ἔκλυε as imperfects. If they were counted as aorists the proportion would of course be increased.

it language expands to record the more and more introvert processes of the mind in which the first person singular of the verb is conceived to be the typical form of language and its centre of gravity. It stands in the centre of time, as a present tense, the past and future extending from it on either side and their forms derived from its form.

Lastly comes the important question – whence came the statement verb, the third person singular of the aorist indicative? This also is a process which unfolds itself in many places in the light of history. It comes from the infinitive or verbal noun.

Several linguists have observed the origin of the indicative verb as a verbal noun; and it is largely this observation that gave currency in and about the year 1880 to the error (oft repeated since) that the root in language was originally a noun – an error that has since then barred progress towards a history of language. Several Semitic scholars have observed that the vowels of the third person singular of the perfective – the type-form of the Semitic verb – are characteristic of a large group of old nouns. For example, Wright in the classic *Lectures on the Comparative Grammar of the Semitic Languages* (published posthumously from his papers in 1890) points to the type qaṭal (Hebrew) and qaṭala (Arabic), 'he killed', as one of 'the commonest nominal forms in the Semitic languages',[1] and expresses himself as 'inclined, after careful consideration, to acquiesce for the present in Stade's view, that we have here a simple noun, without any pronominal affix. . . . If so,' he says, it 'would be an ancient adjective signifying "killing", or, as verbal form, "he killed".'[2] Fick sought to show that the so-called persons of the Indo-European verb were merely old infinitives eked out by infixes.[3] Sayce in the preface to the second edition (1883) of his *Introduction to the Science of Language* reports various recent discoveries and ends: 'The third person, in fact, as in Turkish and so many other languages, was primarily a noun.' The truth of the matter is that, before the statement emerged, the verb had already come to signify an infinitive, which is both verb and noun, and so qaṭal signified 'to kill', or '(a) killing'. Accordingly the observer of a killing by another man, if he stated to a hearer 'Killing', would be clearly understood to mean '(There is) killing (over-there)' or 'He kills' (or *killed*, or *has killed*) or 'his killing'. Later, when he sought to say 'I killed', he would express this by 'Killing I', or (which is the same thing) 'My killing'; and for 'You (singular) killed' he would say 'Killing thou' or 'thy

---

[1] p. 161. [2] p. 165.
[3] In a review of a book in the Göttingen 'Gelehrte Anzeigen' (6 April 1881).

killing'. We see this everywhere. We see it in Semitic,[1] and it is plain in Old Egyptian, in the Finno-Ugrian group[2] and in Turkish and other languages.[3] There are indeed languages in which the construction of verbal noun and personal pronoun remains unchanged and never becomes in form an indicative verb. So, for example, in colloquial Tibetan, the equivalent of the English 'he is eating mutton' is khö luk-sha sa-ki-du, literally 'by him, as regards mutton, an eating is'; and one must translate 'the trader will arrive tomorrow' by tshong-pa té sang-nyi lép-yong, 'as regards the trader tomorrow an arriving will be'.[4] In the earliest times it was presumably not necessary to add a personal pronoun in the third person, for reasons that have been mentioned; but when the third person of the aorist ceased to hold its unique position, then by analogy with the first and second person of the aorist and all persons of the other tenses, the pronoun crept into the third person of the aorist too (as it did in the -t of the Sanskrit aorist though not in Greek or Slav or Armenian). These considerations also explain why in the Finno-Ugrian and Turkish languages, in all tenses generally, the third person singular is the simplest form – the reason is that the same relation remains between the persons as in the original aorist.

At this point, from the Request for Action (or sentence of Type 1, containing one term) has been formed, if we are right, the Statement (or Sentence of Type 2, containing two terms). A long age has been spent in the progress to this point, and from these beginnings grew the widely varying apparatus of the verb and noun.

[1] Where, for example, 'she killed' is the feminine-noun form of 'he killed'.
[2] E.g. Hungarian: varok (for varom-ke), I sow; varz, thou sowest; var, he sows; házam, my house; házad, thy house, háza, his house. Compare the following Samoyed languages, where the indefinite present is expressed in all persons by root and pronominal suffix – Yurak: lamba-u, my ski; lamba-r, thy ski; lamba-da, his ski; madä-u, I cut (my cutting); madä-r, thou cuttest; madä-da, he cuts. Yenissëi: l'ibe-bo, my eagle; l'ibe-lo, thy eagle; l'ibe-ra, his eagle; motä-bo, I cut; motä-lo, thou cuttest; motä-ra, he cuts.
[3] E.g. Nandi (see *ante*, p. 135).
[4] C. A. Bell, *Grammar of Colloquial Tibetan* (Calcutta, 2nd ed. 1919), p. 51.

CHAPTER TWELVE

Animal Behaviour

Examining various facets of language in the earlier chapters of this book, we thought we saw, in each separate facet, evidence of an origin of language in requests for action – or appeals for assistance. In the present chapter it is proposed to consider what can have been the factors in the realm of animal behaviour that led to this starting-point. To a large extent we must here be content to make conjectures.

But the nature of the human communities among which language first appeared is hardly a matter of conjecture. The most primitive method of subsistence, and the most primitive of the human communities known to us or imaginable, are those of the Food Gatherers, men who, like the animals, take their sustenance where they find it. All the societies of Food Gatherers known to us possess already a highly developed language with a mature and complex morphology and syntax. They also possess a stock of cultural ideas and a technology that, simple as they are, could not conceivably have evolved or been transmitted without the aid of the possession of speech over thousands of years. It cannot therefore be imagined that the earliest speakers were as advanced as these, and accordingly they must also have been Food Gatherers. They collected plant food, insects, vermin and shell-fish, and caught the smaller animals and fish. The bulk of the more backward Food Gatherers known to us (Bushman, Pygmies, Alacaluf, Yahgan, Ona, Guayaki and Tasmanians) lived in local groups of an average size of between 10 and 20 persons, and among the more forward Food Gatherers these groups tend to increase in size, as they have ever since increased in the history of man. Accordingly it is likely that the peoples we are considering lived in local groups no larger than these, if they were so large. They consisted (as they do among the peoples with whom we are comparing them) of no more than one or two families, except that they included, perhaps, one or two individuals closely related by blood. Their contacts with other local groups were infrequent and irregular. Humanity was rare, scattered and isolated.

These local groups were semi-nomadic, each group roving over one restricted territory of, say, 50 to 100 square miles, and the density of population was in general no higher than a rate of about one person to 7 square miles. There was no government or leadership except the influence of the older members of the family over the younger. There was no social organization, no clans and no totems. War – that is to say, organized inter-group violence – was unknown. Their weapons of the hunt (if indeed they possessed any) were digging-sticks and rough clubs of wood, and stone implements (if they had any) of the most primitive order.

Accordingly we must not (as some writers) think of these men as living in hordes, or as being hunters (except in this restricted sense) or as evolving language in the stress of warfare, or as learning to speak in opposing dangers met with when they descended from an arboreal life and took to the ground. We must, however, agree with the obvious truth that speech evolved when it was necessary, and not before, and that it evolved for the purposes for which it was necessary. Throughout its known life language has developed to express the needs of man in society, and those needs have moulded it. For this reason we cannot imagine speech – and it would be a baseless conjecture to assume its existence – until those needs required it, and we must believe that it appeared when needed.

When, then, and for what purpose was speech required? Not for the purposes of man as a member of his family. Not for the purposes of the relations between a man and his wife: woman is still wooed and wedded, and the spouses still cohabit, with hardly a word spoken. The same applies to the relations between parents and children as such. Physical sustenance and comfort, warning cries of alarm and visual example – these, not words, are the things most needed for the rearing of the family. For what, then, is speech necessary in so simple a community? There is only one thing left – to obtain an action by others which we cannot do for ourselves: to request action by our fellows.

This is plainly a daily need. It may arise between any two persons in the local group, on occasions of every kind, though it is also the spring of conduct that actuates every society, the cement that holds together every social structure. This is not Noiré's theory of the origin of language.[1] He saw that origin in the rhythmical cries or sounds made by a body of men in the course of a common work – such sounds as we hear from sailors hauling on a rope or pulling at an oar. But requests

[1] Ludwig Noiré, *Der Ursprung der Sprache* (1877).

for action must go infinitely further back in history, and are far more common and fundamental than these. For every request for action, addressed in a modern society to a plurality of persons, there are a thousand requests made to one. The intelligence required to appreciate the heightened power of joint effort; the social sense and solidarity and the precision of conduct and mind needed to cause a group of men each to labour for the others and at the same time; the economic progress necessary to enable this to be done in a sphere so far outside the normal activities of the family as common work – these are characteristics of advanced men in an advanced society, and it is impossible to imagine how they could have progressed so far as this without the aid of speech. Moreover, even in such a society such common work is an exceptional occurrence. An origin of speech, in so rare an event, is an unnecessary assumption and only increases the difficulty of imagining it.

But the facts of language alike belie it. In all languages ancient and modern, in all grades of economic advance, wherever the verb-root represents the imperative and wherever (as is usual) there are separate forms for singular and plural, the verb-root is the imperative singular. If there is anything in the reasoning contained in the preceding chapters of this book, the cause is that the fundamental use of speech, and (over the ages) the commonest use of speech, and the original use of speech, is the request for action addressed to one person. We may, however, also add here that in the few families of languages (such as the Semitic and Hamitic) which make this formal distinction, the verb-root is the masculine and not the feminine imperative. This serves to indicate by the same reasoning that the original addressees of requests for action were the males; and as the males are physically the stronger this need not surprise. We may also assume that the originators of speech were the males. The feminine sex are by repute fluent, but the males are the innovators, the originators. The females take, in this as in other activities, the normal, mean position – their speech, though fluent, is commonplace: the males are the orators, but they are also the aphasics and the almost speechless. Language, then, originated in requests (or appeals) for action between males, and, as we said, not between spouses nor the members of the family as such. It occurred on the fringe of family life, at the point where the family extends into the social organism, and instinctive action extends into social activity.

This was the purpose for which speech was required – to obtain an action by a fellow which a man could not do for himself. Can we, then, go still further and hazard a conjecture, for what kind of action?

The origin of language that we have arrived at, based, as it is, upon the common features of languages, may be explained by supposing that, among the innumerable sounds uttered by the members of such a community, there was a predominant usage of sounds of a distinct kind for this purpose – namely, as requests for action – and this usage ultimately defined and fixed in the mind the sounds of this character as having this meaning. For what type or types of action, then, would a request be predominantly, that is, most commonly and urgently, made? We have already in part suggested the answer – actions that a man could not do for himself. No doubt the circumstances of the requests would be innumerable, but among all others one circumstance, in particular, would be recurrent – namely, that the asker was not strong enough to do the act for himself. Accordingly, we may conjecture that the actions suggested were actions requiring the maximum of bodily effort – requests to smash, break, cut, crush, kill, destroy. Break it! Kill it! The common feature of all these is the act of striking with maximum effort, and a breaking or cutting.

We cannot view this process in operation: societies so primitive have long passed away. They are perhaps as far removed from modern man that followed them as from the highest animals that preceded. But what were the psychological factors surrounding the origin of language as requests for action; how can they be assumed to have operated; and could they have facilitated the origin that we have imagined?

Animal life is manifested and characterized by actions or movements. The dead alone is utterly still. At the heart of the behaviour of animals and man is that which is known as instinct or instinctive behaviour. It is the name given to the tendency of a particular species to perform actions of a certain type in given circumstances, which actions are directed to some end fundamental to the existence of the species – for example, to feeding, reproduction, rearing of the young, flight from danger. Instinctive actions are not learned, and the actor may be wholly unconscious of the end to which they are directed. On the one hand, they are closely linked with physiological factors. For example, the nest-building or mating instinct may be seen developing in a maturing animal, or in the physiological changes accompanying the onset of the breeding season. On the other hand, instinctive behaviour is closely linked with intelligence, namely the capacity to learn from experience. Though a bird of a given species constructs a nest of a particular shape from a limited range of materials in a limited number of types of localities, it learns from trial and error to vary and adapt the nest within certain limits to the available locality and materials. In all the intelligent behaviour of man can be seen the operation of instinct – for example, the instinct to make a home – of which he may be as little conscious as the other animals. Instinct is a necessary basis for the acquisition of learning.

Instinct is a system or linkage the elements of which are an affection (or feeling), and a consequent conation (or striving), leading to an action. The system may be touched off or released by a change of bodily condition which causes the affection and striving, or, more commonly, by a cognition (or impression derived by the senses) of something external, giving rise to the affection. So, the search for mate or food may arise, first, through some inner bodily change causing an affection, conation and action, and, in the next instant, as the animal catches sight, or receives scent or sound, of mate or prey, the affection may be further stimulated, the conation intensified and action continued. Similarly the behaviourist analyses all behaviour into stimulus and response, of which the stimulus may come from an external impression or internal bodily change.

Of the affections of another animal we must judge mainly by its action – sudden flight betokens fear, and when the flight ceases we may conclude that the fear has subsided. As the animal rises in the scale of evolution there is great development in the variety of its actions. Few are the movements of an amoeba: the dog has a far greater variety of actions: the man infinitely more. At the other end of the chain perception (or external cognition) develops. It remains, from various aspects, part of the same linkage: for example, an animal or thing may not be noticed, although it is visible, in the absence of a relevant affection producing attention – a prey will not be noticed in the absence of hunger, or a mate in the absence of the appropriate affection and conation. Action, too, remains in various aspects part of the same linkage, for perception depends largely upon action as well as action upon perception. The mate may not be found except by wandering in search of her; the perception of the features of a thing may not be gained except by handling or tasting it. But, above all, the story of evolution is the advance of perception, which seems to gain upon action. The lowest form of behaviour may be movement in a uniform environment, stimulated, perhaps by little more than bodily changes: in the highest stage perception may be of great variety, brought about by a vast versatility and variety of cognition, which may, indeed, lead to no action but only the storing of impressions.

Needless to say, cognitions – impressions by the senses – are quite distinct from the things in nature from which they are derived; and it is the cognitions with which we are directly concerned, not the things in nature. In some species of animals perceptions are mainly by one sense, in some species by another. All animals have perception by touch. In the lower animals perception is chiefly by touch or smell. The world of spiders is a tactile world; the world of dogs is chiefly a world of smells, and their sight is weak. The world of man is chiefly a world of sight. Even among the apes smell has become of lesser importance, and throughout the history of ape and man the sense of smell has continued to diminish, and sight to improve. After sight, man's world is one of sound. So, too, with the apes. There is general agreement that among the chimpanzees sight is more important than sound as a means of cognition[1] and far more important than smell. In all these respects man and ape are nearer to the birds than other animals, for the birds, too, derived these characters in the trees. On the whole, the sight of birds is only a little better than man's, their hearing about the same and their sense of smell even less.

It is plain that the development of sight as a means of perception has contributed vastly to the progress of man. The whole world, as far as the horizon, lies open to his mind. The limits of a tactile world are the animal's reach: the world of smell can hardly extend far beyond the realm of instinct and its horizon is narrow indeed.

Next to sight, we said, man, like the apes, obtains his cognitions mainly by sound. Like sight, it lays open to him a wide country. He is extremely sensitive to sound. It has been shown, for example, by J. B. Watson how potent a source of fear to human infants is a loud noise.

Yet though so wide an area is open to sight and sound, little (as we said) will be noticed except where there is attention, and that depends on affection. Little will be noticed that is not being sought, that does not serve to fulfil men's strivings and practical uses. In the lower animals this need hardly be stated: where (as among the birds) action is chiefly instinctive, there will be few cognitions except those relevant to instinctive behaviour. Yet it is fundamental throughout human life. We see examples in languages of the simpler peoples, where there are no words for uninteresting natural objects and a variety of terms for those of practical use.

But though attention is produced by an affection, it can be caught

[1] See R. M. Yerkes, *Chimpanzees* (1945), p. 92.

and held by external factors. The chief of such factors is movement. It can be caught and held by something seen, but especially if that something is moving. Of this there is more evidence than our observations: there is the physiology and behaviour of animals. There is, firstly, the instinct of a vast number of animals to 'freeze' at the approach of danger, and this is because nature, whose observations are more reliable than ours, has selected this as a factor favourable to survival. She has done so because the rest of animal life will notice a moving object when a still object would escape them. Much of the natural camouflage also bears evidence of the same fact: it chiefly protects its possessor if he is motionless. Among apes and man the attraction of movement is even plainer, for to other animals sight is less important than touch and smell, and it is to the organs of sight that movement is chiefly apparent. Movement is the one common characteristic of animal life and the animal is sensitive to it and appreciative of it. The birds will take no notice of an object which is irrelevant to their instincts unless it moves,[1] and they will take little notice even of a human being near them if he remains still for long enough. Their interest flags and they may finally disregard his presence.

This is the perpetual psychological foundation to the structure of language – namely, that perception is especially the perception not of animals and things but of moving animals and things. To an extent this foundation has existed from the beginnings of animal life, but it is firmer now in the life of the apes and early man as the reliance on smell has diminished. Language would never have been requisite for the operation of mere instinct. But the behaviour of apes and man (though instinct is still at its heart) has branched out ever more and more widely, and outside the cognitions that form part of the chain of instinct – the smell or touch or sight of the mate or prey of the species, and so forth – and to a large extent even within that chain, perception is especially derived from movement. To turn from the proposition that perception is especially the perception of movement to the proposition that language begins with words signifying actions, is merely to turn from that perennial psychological foundation to the linguistic structure that has reared itself upon it. It is on the same foundation that developed languages have been based, in which every sentence contains a verb.

---

[1] This can easily be tested upon the robin that stands watching the gardener a few feet away in winter. He takes no notice of a shout or a whistle; but a slight movement and he darts away, if only for a few feet, before he can stop himself.

But attention can be caught and held by a sound no less than by something seen to move. That is another reason why a great number of animals 'freeze' at the approach of danger. The young nestling or the young peewit on the ground 'freezes' to escape hearing as well as sight. To what sounds, then, is the animal chiefly sensitive?

The ear of the animal has trained itself to be most acute in discrimination of pitch for those sounds which are of greatest importance to it. These are the sounds produced by fellow-members of the species, on whom it relies for cries of alarm, comforting calls and the like, and so the ear has adapted itself to hear the particular sounds produced by the species. Certainly the human ear is most sensitive to pitch discrimination within the range of the human voice, and particularly the narrow range employed in ordinary conversation. To differences of volume or intensity it is less sensitive.[1] It seems similarly likely (though less susceptible of proof) that the animals relying on sight are most sensitive to differences of movement on the part of members of the same species. This is another relation that gives a permanent psychological foundation to the structure of language, namely the special sensitivity of man to the sounds and movements of fellow-men.

Among the apes this linguistic structure has not yet been begun; but everywhere among the apes, and sometimes among animals (such as the birds) below them in the scale of evolution, appeals for action are commonly to be seen. If they were expressed in language they would necessarily be 'imperative' verbs, but they are chiefly expressed in gesture and inarticulate cries. Among the lower animals one animal will often push against another knowing or expecting that it will move aside and desiring it to do so. The male robin or warbler at the approach of a strange male of the same species into his 'territory' flies at him with eager beak to drive him away. He first did so, no doubt, through instinctive irritation at the stranger's presence so near; but now, in addition, he knows from experience and expects that if he does so the interloper will flee; and almost invariably he does flee. Two young herring-gulls compete for the remains of a fish lying on the shore. One opens his wings to their full height and span and menacingly moves a step towards the other, who retreats and leaves him in possession. The first time he made that gesture he may have done so by instinct in anger, but he now knows from experience that the other will recoil, and he does it in that expectation, The fat fledgling blackbird, following his parent on the lawn, shrieks for food: the repeated

[1] Negus, chap. IX.

sound almost drives his parent frantic, and he desperately stuffs worms into the gaping bill. When the fledgling was newly hatched, he no doubt cried by instinct as the parent bird reached the nest, and by instinct the parent pushed the worm into his yellow gape; but now it is plain that the fledgling (like a human baby) has learned that his yell is followed by food, and he yells with an expectant eye on his parent and his parent's bill. In the higher animals, developing in intelligence, requests or appeals for action are more and more recognizable as action becomes more varied and the intention of the animal plainer. The plaintive requests of a dog for action of some kind by a human are too familiar and unmistakable to need a mention. In the apes they cannot be counted. In the words of Köhler,[1] referring to chimpanzees: 'It may be taken as positively proved that their gamut of *phonetics* is entirely "subjective", and can only express emotions, never designate or describe objects'; and he quotes Bühler for the proposition that 'their gestures of face and body, like their expression in sound, never designate or "describe" objects'. 'But,' he goes on, 'their range of expression by gesture and action is very wide and varied, and, beyond all comparison, superior, not only to that of the lower apes, but also to the orang-utan's. Much is easily comprehensible to us human beings – for example, rage, terror, despair, grief, pleading, desire, and also playfulness and pleasure. . . .'[2] Chimpanzees understand "between themselves", not only the expression of *subjective moods* and emotional states, but also of definite desires and urges, whether directed towards another of the same species, or towards other creatures or objects. . . . A considerable proportion of all desires is naturally shown by direct imitation of the actions which are desired. Thus, one chimpanzee who wishes to be accompanied by another, gives the latter a nudge, or pulls his hand, looking at him and making the movements of "walking" in the direction desired. One who wishes to receive bananas from another, imitates the movement of snatching or grasping, accompanied by intensely pleading glances and pouts. The summoning of another animal from a considerable distance is often accompanied by a beckoning very human in character. Human beings are often the recipients of invitations by a gesture of what the animals want done; thus, Rana, when she wished to be petted, stretched her hand out towards us, and at the same time clumsily stroked and patted herself, while gazing with eager pleading. Another obvious method of invitation is for an ape to assume or indicate in his own person whatever movements he would

---

[1] Kohler, p. 317. [2] p. 319 f.

perform in the activity he wishes the other to undertake, in the same way that a dog invites us to play with him, by leaping and running, and then looking back towards us.'

This is the beginning of the erection of the linguistic structure upon that psychological foundation that we spoke of. Let us see to what point we have now reached, and by what steps.

Looking generally at these examples we see that between the lower animals and the apes everything has changed in some degree. But one fact to be noticed is that the request for action develops out of simple action and is itself an action. We start with an animal making an action – for example, pushing another animal so that it moves out of the way – and then in a later stage making a threatening gesture which causes it to move out of the way. We end with an entreaty by gesture to an animal to take one of many different actions. The analysis of the behaviour remains the same – perception-affection-conation-action. A child sees an apple hanging on a tree. The sight rouses in him an affection, a desire to eat it. He stretches his hand towards it, but the apple is too high to reach; nevertheless the gesture serves to communicate the affection to the father, who picks the apple and gives it to the child. Similarly an ape sees a banana and desires it and reaches unavailingly for it, but the same gesture is employed to obtain it through a fellow-creature. We have only to compare the request for action with the 'statement' of later times to appreciate the difference in the behaviour and the change that has taken place. The request for action is itself an action: the statement is an expression of a cognition. In the former case the ape sees something, feels an affection, makes a conation and the fellow-creature seeing and understanding completes the action. In the latter case, in the simplest form of the statement, the speaker sees something, feels perhaps an affection and speaks. There is hardly a recognizable conation. This behaviour presupposes a condition in which language is so well-established as to be itself a species of action. The behaviour ends there, and nothing further is done. In such a group as that of the apes the statement would serve no useful purpose – only that of drawing attention to what is happening under the nose of the addressee. The animal cry is sufficient for that.

The second fact to be noticed is the development of a social sense and solidarity which we see later developing in mankind throughout his history – a social cement which ultimately builds up political societies whose population is numbered in hundreds of millions. The request for action is the basis of all human society, and human society is the basis of all language. The lower animal pushing his fellow, so that for comfort he moves out of the way, effects his end by force. The robin or warbler and the young herring-gull get their way by threat of force, which is usually sufficient. The young blackbird (like the human child desiring the apple) gets his food through the parental instinct and affection. But the chimpanzee obtains his end by the mutual understanding between members of the same small local group. Of this mutual understanding and solidarity there is abundant evidence. For example the same author tells us[1] that when a member of a group of chimpanzees is punished with a blow, the whole group will set up a howl as with one voice. Not through fear: on the contrary, they try to reach the place of punishment – if necessary, by a detour; and one of them (little weak Consul) would run up excitedly and with a pleading countenance stretch out his arm to the taller man who was administering the punishment, or try to hold the latter's arm, or even hit out at him. Then there is the custom of the mutual inspection by two chimpanzees of one another's skin, hair and hind quarters, a pursuit followed with the greatest eagerness and attention and common pleasure; and this, says Köhler is a distinctively social event, for no chimpanzee shows so much interest in his own body, if he is alone.[2] Still more significant is their pleasure in paying attention to one another's hurts and wounds, not merely through motives of mutual aid, but in the pleasure of squeezing an abscess or removing a splinter or the like.[3] Köhler indeed tells us that 'it is hardly an exaggeration to say that a chimpanzee kept in solitude is not a real chimpanzee at all. That certain special characteristic qualities of this species of animal only appear when they are in a group, is simply because the behaviour of his comrades constitutes for each separate animal the only incentive which will bring about a variety of different behaviour, and observation of many peculiarities of the chimpanzee will only be clearly intelligible when the behaviour and counter-behaviour of the individuals and the group are considered as a whole.'[4] But there is never any common work: two apes may be similarly engaged, following a similar pursuit, in close proximity – like a tea party of human children two years old, sitting with their backs to one another, playing quite independently with their host's toys – but there is nothing more as yet.[5]

---

[1] Köhler, p. 297.
[2] Köhler, p. 321.
[3] See Köhler, p. 322.
[4] Köhler, p. 293.
[5] See Köhler, pp. 172-6, and photograph at p. 174. Compare p. 293 f.

The third fact to be noticed is the effort that must be invested in a request for action if it is to bring in a return. It is different in a modern human society, where a person in authority may have only to indicate his desire – by giving a 'command' or by his mere behaviour – for it to be observed and obeyed. Among the apes – and we may be sure it was so among the earliest men – it is not enough to make a recognizable gesture: the affection must be intense and its intensity communicated, and it must be accompanied by an intense conation, more than proportionate to the desired result, if it is to make the desired impression. If one may use the expression, the supply of requests is greater than the demand for them, and this is a factor operating throughout the history of language, with results of the highest importance in the history of meaning. The conation is intensified by a kind of frustration – by the need to overcome the obstacle to fulfilment of the animal's desire; but it is also an outflow of the excitement that is the affection, and as affection is to be measured by the force of the action to which it gives rise, so the affection and conation will be the more intense the more violent is the action which belongs to them. But this conation and frustration does not vent itself merely in gesture but also in vocal sound: hence not merely the pleading gestures but also the pleading tones of dog and ape.[1]

Fourthly, it is to be noticed that the meaning of the request – like the meaning of language – is given partly by the environment. It is not given by words, for there is as yet no articulate speech; but it is given by affective tones, and it is given much more by gesture (of which we shall have more to say) and by the environment, for example the presence of a banana, lying out of reach, which the animal points to or stretches towards.

Lastly, it is to be noted how much development of intelligence is required in order to reach the present stage. There is involved the feasibility of communicating an affection (in this case a desire); but this presents no difficulty between members of the same homogeneous group of animals. There is involved also the perception by the addressee of the gesture of the asker, and of its purpose, and still more a certain consciousness by the asker of what he is doing and what he desires, and an application of mind to the problem how to communicate his intention. The communication is subjective – a communication of an affection, in this case a desire; but it is also objective – namely, the communication of a desire for a particular and definite

---

[1] The dog's are for his master, the ape's for his fellows.

action by the addressee. Here, then, is the first of the missing links we seek – the connexion between the communication of affection, so common between the members of a local homogeneous group of animals, and effected by environment, movement and animal cries; and the communication of an objective reference, effected by environment, gesture and language. It remains later to trace the parallel connecting-link between the animal cry and articulate speech.

The movements and gestures of ape and man, the consciousness of which (as we said) is required for the emergence of language, are of increasing variety. Man has in the hand evolved an organ of high precision, capable of a vast variety of discriminated and discriminatory actions. One cannot read a book like Köhler's *Mentality of Apes*, with its account of the use by chimpanzees of digging-sticks (the chief implement of Food Gatherers and early Agriculturists), and of sticks employed to reach something beyond their grasp – and how they pile one box upon another, and squeeze a splinter out of a fellow-animal's hand – without appreciating that it is only an animal possessing a hand that could perform such functions. Not only is it capable of many distinct actions, but it has given to man a greater variety of perceptions. This has occurred mainly in two ways. Firstly, he has not only learned these uses of the hands, but he has learned to recognize them (as we have seen in regard to the ape) when employed by others as gestures, so that they have been the means of communication of requests for action. Secondly, he has by moving and handling become familiar with the possible uses and functions of a great variety of objects. This has occurred chiefly in his striving after food – the instinct that has undergone the greatest development of all. The innumerable inanimate objects of nature would have been merely part of the static, unnoticed, unmeaning background, but this affection and conation has impelled him to notice and recognize not merely articles of food but objects lying ready to hand for use as implements – sticks and stones capable of use for the purpose of the same conation. It is as part of their use that he has improved them and so made them.

Instances of these facts are conspicuous in the books of those who have written of the intelligent behaviour of the apes and especially of the chimpanzee. For example, in Köhler's classic work, so often referred to above, we read of an experiment performed upon an adult chimpanzee Tschego. Her sleeping-quarters contained no movable objects except straw and her blanket. In a previous test she was let out of her sleeping-place into a barred cage in which she spent her waking hours. In a stockade outside the cage, and beyond the reach of her long arms, a bunch of bananas had been placed. Within the cage, a little to one side but near the bars, were several sticks. Tschego made efforts to reach the fruit by stretching out her hand between the bars, but failed each time after attempts extending over half an hour, and lay down and took no further interest. But now some younger chimpanzees, disporting themselves in the stockade outside, began to notice the bananas and gradually approached them. Suddenly Tschego leapt to her feet, seized a stick and quite adroitly placing it on the farther side of the bananas pulled them in till they were within reach, using first one arm and then the other, and frequently changing arms. She had, therefore, under stress of circumstances learnt to use the stick in this way, thereby lengthening her arm. In a second experiment the following morning, two sticks were placed inside the cage, but about $1\frac{1}{2}$ metres away from the bars. Tschego, when let into the cage, at first stretched her arm through the bars towards the bananas; then, as the youngsters approached them she caught up some lengths of straw and angled with them fruitlessly. Only after a considerable time, as the young apes approached dangerously close to the fruit, she had recourse to the sticks and secured it with one of them.

In the further test which took place on the same day, the sticks were put against the wall of her cage on the opposite side from the objective and 4 metres away from the bars. After vain efforts to reach the bananas with her hand, she jumped up and went quickly into her sleeping-place, which opened into the cage, and returned at once with her blanket. This she pushed between the bars, flapping it at the bananas, and so beat them towards her.[1] When one of them rolled on to the tip of the blanket, she immediately changed her tactics, and drew the blanket with the banana upon it gently towards the bars. But a blanket is a clumsy implement, and the next banana could not be caught like the first. Tschego looked blank. The experimenter used every means at his disposal to attract her attention to the sticks, which were behind her as she stood at the bars and looked towards the bananas; and she in fact turned and looked straight at them, turning her back on the bananas as she did so; but she showed not the slightest interest in them. Another stick was now thrust through the bars, diagonally opposite to the objective, and Tschego at once took and used it.[2]

This and a number of similar experiments in the books illustrate several truths in regard to the psychology of the apes – for example,

[1] Compare Hobhouse, p. 272.   [2] Köhler, pp. 30-35.

that the ape's appreciation of the significant relation of one object to another depends in part on the relation of the two in space. In particular, the relation is less likely to be perceived if they are not seen in one field of view: in other words, the conation towards an object involves attention to objects seen at the same time. But the relevance of this experiment to our present purpose is that, the sticks and the blanket being both out of sight when Tschego looked at the coveted bananas, and though she turned and glanced at the sticks, whose use to obtain the bananas she had already learnt, she took no notice of them. They were merely background, and her mind turned to the blanket that she had so often manipulated and used. But if the stick had been moved in her sight, it would have been detached from the background: her attention would have been drawn to it, and she would, no doubt, have used it.[1] As the ape becomes more habituated to manipulate the stick – that is to say, learns more and more its function – it is more likely to be used though it is not in the same field of view. The hand and its fingers, capable, as they are, of fine, precise, varied and complicated movements, make possible a general development in behaviour and mind. The ape – like the human child before and after the appearance of language – obtains perception of the functions and properties of objects by its own manipulation of them. For indeed, in this way, several means of perception are employed at the same time – sight, and often taste, and smell, and touch, and the varieties of manipulation. In substance these means of perception are all by movements – movements of the object perceived and movements of the hand. Thus we glimpse from another angle the same psychological foundation to the structure of language. To turn from the proposition that the knowledge of objects is chiefly derived from movements, to the proposition that in language nouns are chiefly formed from verbs, is merely to turn from the same psychological foundation to a second stage in the linguistic structure that has been reared upon it.

But though the movements and gestures of ape and man are of this increasing variety and fineness, the emergence of language postulates (we thought) that a certain type of vocal sound must be associated with a plainly observable result in the form of action by another individual – that is to say, a type of movement or gesture plainly distinguishable by sight and hearing from others, so that this vocal sound might bear the same meaning to all. Moreover, in the earlier chapters of this book we thought we saw evidence everywhere leading

[1] See Köhler, p. 40.

back to languages containing a smaller and smaller vocabulary and consisting of a trivial number of word-sentences with the meaning of verbs, namely requests for human action. Can we then hazard a conjecture, for what type of human action these requests of earliest man were made? It is suggested that we can: that such action would be the most noticeable type of early-human manipulation. It would therefore be an action, as large as possible, as sharp and sudden as possible, as violent as possible and as noisy as possible. These qualities would be best represented in an action of breaking, cutting, striking, smashing, crushing: in other words, the same type of action that we figured to ourselves in the last chapter, when we were proceeding along a different path of exploration.

We have not far to look for evidence of such behaviour among the apes. The same author, Köhler, referring again to the chimpanzee, accentuates 'the tearing, smashing and demolishing tendencies of the species'.[1] Human children present a similar picture. They have not the strength of adults, but their tendency (and particularly the tendency of the males) to learn the properties of objects especially by breaking them or taking them to pieces is too familiar to need instances.

We have noticed, too, that in the request or appeal for action the force of the operative affection and conation must always be proportionate to the force of the action requested. Indeed, we can only measure the intensity of affection in any animal by the force of the conation and action to which it gives rise. We measure the intensity of rage and anger by the violence of the actions which immediately ensue. Affection is, in greater or less degree, consciousness; and in early man we can safely conjecture that (outside the realm of instinctive action) the most intense affection and consciousness, and therefore the greatest opportunity for conditioning and learning on the part of the actor, and the greatest opportunity for impressing the mind of the beholder, will be associated with the largest and sharpest and most forcible acts of which man is capable. Here we find ourselves again at the same junction between the communication of an affection and the communication of an objective reference: and this junction is a request (that is, the communication of a desire) for a certain kind of action. A violent, smashing action by a fellow-animal, prompted, for example, by a passion of rage, will make a greater impression on a beholder than any other type of action; and will thereby so imprint the action on his mind – or, shall we say, condition him to it – that he will be most

[1] Köhler, p. 324.

likely to recognize again that action, or the imitative gesture of a fellow-animal, expressing such an affection, requesting such an action, and being itself of the like violent kind.

The request is communicated by gesture and environment, as well as by sound. Now there is a difference between the gestures of apes and modern man. The gestures of apes are not a self-conscious, isolated movement of one limb or feature, calculated to eke out or illustrate a passage of speech. In the chimpanzee an affection is not differentiated from other bodily or mental activity: in excitement the gesture is of the whole body. 'His whole body is agitated and not merely his facial muscles. He jumps up and down both in joyful anticipation and in impatient annoyance and anger; and in extreme despair – which develops under very slight provocation – flings himself on his back and rolls wildly to and fro. He also swings and waves his arms about above his head in a fantastic manner as a sign of disappointment and dejection.'[1]

We can see that the gesture expressing a request for an action o cutting, breaking, tearing, smashing, crushing, must have been the largest, sharpest and most violent of all gestures – as violent, at least, as the action it called for; an outflow of the excited affection that prompted the request, accompanied by an intense consciousness on the part of the asker, and unmistakable even to the dull receiving mind. We begin to see how speech originated. It was necessary, in order to create language, that there should be a separate type of human action, recognizably distinct from others, and, associated with it, a type of vocal sound on the part of the actor, distinct from others, so that this sound and action, appearing together during untold millennia, might be impressed upon the dull, nascent intelligence of actor and beholder as one phenomenon, each suggesting the other, and so deeply and irremovably imprinted by process of long conditioning as to form a firm starting-point for language. It was also necessary, in order that this type of action might be communicated by a full gesture of maximum sharpness and force – the most recognizable of all gestures – that gesture and action should involve the same movement as well as the same vocal sound. These conditions, in these folk, could be provided by a type of action of maximum force and speed, using the whole arm and hand, and its accompanying type of vocal sound. What that sound was, we shall consider in a later chapter. Then, in the succeeding millennia, as intelligence and consciousness developed, the affection

[1] Köhler, p. 318.

and gestures diminished[1] and ceased to be necessary concomitants of the vocal sounds, and the latter stood out more and more in isolation and gained an independent value as meaningful words – and all the while innumerable other words and meanings developed from them.

But early man was not a mere destroyer – even the ape is not a mere destroyer. The facts we have envisaged accompany progress in intelligence. Can, then, the stage of intelligence reached at the beginning of language be further defined or described in any way? Only that man alone uses language. It is the continuity of mental development from his predecessors that prevents further definition. Man is often defined as a tool-using animal, but this does not mark a new stage in the progress of intelligence. Many animals use tools: the conation forming part of some instinct – the striving after food, the building of a home – enables them to notice natural objects suitable for the purpose. Some ammophilas use small pebbles to beat down the earth where they have made a nest. Thrushes use stones to break the shells of snails. Another of the birds (*Camarhynchus pallidus* of the Galapagos Islands) uses a cactus spine or a twig to poke into holes in the trees and dislodge the insects on which it feeds. The nest-building instinct of birds and apes and a thousand other creatures employs materials found in nature. Among the apes the use of tools shows much increase. Chimpanzees and other apes in a state of nature use stones to crack nuts, and they and other apes use objects at hand as missiles. Darwin, in the third chapter of his *Descent of Man*, quotes Wallace[2] for the statement that on three occasions he saw female orangs, accompanied by their young, 'breaking off branches and the great spiny fruit of the Durian tree, with every appearance of rage; causing such a shower of missiles as effectually kept us from approaching too near the tree'. Several writers (including one quoted by Darwin in the same chapter) have watched chimpanzees using a stick to lever up the lid of a box[3]; and their use of digging-sticks is well authenticated. This growing use of tools is part of the process by which instinctive action is more and more diversified among the higher animals, and by which they wield a growing control over their environment.

Alternatively, it has often been suggested that if man is not the first

---

[1] According to Rothmann and Teuber, *Einzelausgabe aus der Anthropoidenstation auf Teneriffa*, 1. Abh. Preuss. Akad. Wiss., Berlin 1-20 (1915), pp. 13-14, vocal sounds are less important, and bodily attitude and gestures more important, among chimpanzees than in man. The same impression is to be derived from other accounts of the chimpanzee.

[2] *The Malay Archipelago*, vol. i (1869), p. 87.

[3] See e.g. Hobhouse, p. 283.

tool-user, at least he is the first tool-maker. Certainly this process shows further development of mental powers, and ultimately, when a man fashions an implement, not having in sight the objective for which he intends it, his progress has been great, for he recollects or imagines that objective and therefore has to some extent conception, and not mere perception of it. But tool-making with the end in sight can be observed among the apes. In a sense, indeed, every time a bird breaks a straw to build its nest it is making a tool. Chimpanzees and other apes are spoken of by many authors as breaking the branches of a tree to form a tool. Improving a natural object, available for use as a tool, is a common way of making a tool among apes and men. When a chimpanzee with his teeth breaks pieces from a stick so as to obtain a splinter, or to narrow the whole so that it may be inserted in a place which it could not otherwise enter,[1] or when Köhler's chimpanzees break up shoe-scrapers made of iron bars to use as tools,[2] this is the fashioning of tools just as much as when primitive man broke or flaked a flint and later ground it.

It would not, therefore, be accurate to speak of man as the first tool-maker, though tool-making had progressed only a little way before his time. We may perhaps, with rough truth, describe him as the first manufacturer, but in saying so we must notice one important fact. In the world of the ape and (we may be sure) in the world of early man when language first appears, the process of tool-making or manufacture is by breaking and cutting and tearing. At this stage, making is by breaking one thing into two. This is shown in every example cited above, and we cannot suppose much further progress by early man. Manufacture by *joining* two things together is as yet substantially impossible. An impression to the contrary may be derived from a unique experiment of Köhler, which is perhaps the most celebrated of all experiments conducted with chimpanzees.[3] Sultan (a highly gifted young ape) is presented with two firm but hollow bamboo sticks, one much smaller than the other, so that it can be pushed in easily at either end. The desired fruit is outside his cage, beyond the bars, and too far to be reached with either stick. He tries for an hour, pushing one stick with the other towards the fruit, then abandons the task. Later, while playing with the two sticks, he finds himself holding one in each hand in line with the other, and he pushes the thinner one a little way into

---

[1] See Köhler, pp. 136-8, and other authors; for example, Hobhouse, p. 320, where Consul made a key for himself by biting a piece of wood till it would fit into a square keyhole.
[2] Köhler, pp. 105-7.
[3] Köhler, p. 130.

the wider opening, and so has learned the trick.[1] This is a rare event, made possible by man. Manufacture by joining two things together is a task for an advanced mind, involving as a rule the collection of at least three elements and a skilful manual operation, and it must have been exceptional even in the days of earliest man. Here, then, we arrive again at the action of breaking, cutting and tearing as the chief and most important action in human work, and the one for which request was most likely to be made in the days when language first appeared, in the early days of human intelligence.

There is one further prerequisite of speech. The apes have no language. Those highest in intelligence are the chimpanzee, orang-utan and gorilla, but of these the last two are by repute taciturn, and the chimpanzee, though vocal and generally the most advanced of all in intelligence, gives no sign of producing speech. Why is this? It is generally agreed that 'in the structure of the organs of respiration, of the tongue and larynx, there does not appear any reason why the (chimpanzee) should not speak . . .; yet this animal, according to the best evidence, has never been known to make any attempt at articulate sounds'.[2] Furniss tried persistently for 5 years to teach a chimpanzee to say 'Mama', but acknowledged failure. R. M. Yerkes conducted a series of elaborate and carefully conceived experiments to interest a chimpanzee 'in human speech and the production of sounds', but without avail.[3] It is generally agreed that 'they have so many phonetic elements which are also common to human languages, that their lack of articulate speech cannot be ascribed to secondary (glosso-labial) limitations'.[4] The chimpanzee produces sounds which vary greatly in quality and intensity.[5] Yerkes and Learned produce a list of 32 'words or elements of speech' used by two chimpanzees, which they have reduced without apparent difficulty to an alphabetic record. It is, therefore, generally agreed that, in the words of Traill, their deficiency in this respect is to be referred not to corporeal but to mental limitations – namely that they cannot be induced to imitate sounds. Their imitative tendency seems to be controlled chiefly by visual stimuli.[6]

---

[1] See also Nueva's constructive achievement, Köhler, p. 324, which the author describes as amazing. She tied a woollen rag to a stick.
[2] T. S. Traill, *Observations on the Anatomy of the Orang Outang* (1821). By this name the author referred to the chimpanzee. Compare Köhler, p. 75; Yerkes and Learned, p. 53; Yerkes, *The Great Apes*, p. 306.
[3] Yerkes, *The Great Apes*, p. 307.
[4] Köhler, p. 317.
[5] Yerkes, *The Great Apes*, p. 307.
[6] Yerkes and Learned, pp. 53-6; see also Yerkes, *The Great Apes*, pp. 306-7.

CHAPTER THIRTEEN

The History of Meaning

We must now leave apes and primitive men and return to language as we know it, and look at language in a light in which we have not previously regarded it in this book.

Some of the earlier chapters of this book, in which we sought to describe the process of development of language, might suggest that language is an independent entity which creates its own universal history. First we examined the proportions of the different parts of speech, and noticed a regular increase in the nouns and then in the adjectives, the proportion of verbs diminishing in a constant ratio with the progress of civilization. Then we looked at vocabularies of languages, and saw the regular transfer of individual words from the one part of speech to the other in the same set order of events. These and other developments that we noticed might seem to indicate that language advances along these paths because of its inherent nature. But this is not so: the effective cause is the advance of man from one stage of material and mental progress to another: the changes in language are the results. In so far as those changes are regular it is because a language is the means of communication between all the members of a language-community, and must therefore serve the uses of the whole community, and not merely the special needs or habits of individuals. It is the means whereby the aid of fellow-members is enlisted, and therefore all must understand its uses. It is true that speech has in turn been an instrument by which mind has advanced, for without it the discoveries of man could not have been retained or communicated. But language is but the vocal sounds uttered by man, and it would be erroneous to regard it as a biological or physical entity containing the seeds or laws of its own development. The soft wax of language records the mental and material history of man, but it is the imprint of that history upon it that created the record. This will become clear in the present chapter, where a different aspect of language is considered, and the most important and characteristic of all – namely, the changes in the meanings of words.

Let us begin to illustrate this theme with one or two simple examples. The English word 'house' (O.E. *hus*) is an old word. In Anglo-Saxon times it would mean to most men a one-roomed hut of wattle and daub or wood, used for their habitation and that of their families and some domestic animals. But houses have changed since then, and so to a modern Englishman the word means something different. There is still an objective resemblance: the thing still stands on the ground, has walls, roof and door and holes for windows and chimney, and the same general shape. There is a closer functional resemblance. It does much the same things for him and he does much the same to it: he still occupies it with his family (and possibly a dog or cat). There is a still closer affective resemblance: he still feels for it as a home. The retention of the name for the altered thing has been assisted by the fact that the changes have been gradual and therefore the change of meaning has been unintentional. Much the same considerations apply to the words 'shoe' (O.E. *sceo*), 'ship' (*scip*) and 'to shoot' (*sceotan*). All these words have, of course, also undergone some change of form, but we are not considering it here. If the change in form had proceeded far enough we could not have made the comparison of meaning.

Now let us take a few significant examples of economic and legal interest, because law and economics are closely allied and show a history of stages of progress which can be instanced from widely sundered ages and places.

The English word to 'sell' signified in O.E. (*sellan*) 'to hand over'. In modern English *to sell* signifies to agree to transfer the ownership of a thing for a sum of money, and also to perform the agreement. So when two gentlemen in Mincing Lane conduct a conversation on the telephone and follow it up with a note 'Sold to you 1,000 tons of Indian groundnut oil' or some other commodity 'at so much per ton', this does not mean that anything has been handed over. On the contrary, the thing they contemplate may not yet exist. It means that the parties have agreed that, in some form or other, on the one side the ownership of a quantity of goods of a certain description will be transferred and on the other side a certain payment will be made. This change in the meaning of 'sold' has nothing to do with linguistics: the explanation is to be found in the history of commerce. The parent of sale is barter, which was a contemporaneous exchange of goods for goods, each party handing over and receiving, and nothing remaining to be done. By degrees a particular commodity, because it was in great demand and imperishable and usable for a variety of purposes, came to figure more and more frequently on one side of the transaction, and this commodity became money. So barter was turned into sale; but in the Anglo-Saxon period sale was still a cash transaction. On the one side goods were handed over, and on the other side money, and generally speaking you had to be content with what you got. It was not an agreement but a mutual transfer. There was no preceding agreement to sell – at any rate none to which importance was attached or which the law would enforce, because no one would lose if it were not performed. Market prices were fairly stable and indeed traditional, and men did not need to trust one another to carry out such agreements. But by Elizabeth's time the preceding agreement became enforceable. Traders relied on it, and on the faith of it entered into agreements to resell or to buy; market prices were rising rapidly and a man stood to lose or gain if the agreement were not performed. Finally sale takes its place in the public mind among other transactions, and the common characteristic of all is singled out and stressed, namely that they are agreements, completed or not completed. Hence the change in the meaning of the word 'sell': originally it referred to any handing-over of goods, and therefore especially barter or cash sale, which were the chief of such transactions, and it continues to refer to sale though sale has changed its nature. The community still regards it as the same transaction, but it has changed in character and so the meaning of the word has changed. This is a world-wide development, where trade has sufficiently advanced. For example, in classical Latin 'emere' was 'to buy', but its earlier meaning was 'to take'; and 'vendere' signified 'to hand over for the price'. Similarly in the Babylonian tablets the purchaser still 'took for the price', and sale was regarded as a cash transaction.[1]

Let us take another example. In modern England the 'ownership' of property is a familiar notion, simple in outline. But it is a developed and technical conception, difficult to define. The owner of property has generally the right to hold it to the exclusion of anyone else; but he may have parted with his rights or part of his rights, for a period. So, the owner of a motor car may have let it on hire, and the owner of land may have let it on lease for a term of years or even for his life. In English and Roman law one man may be the legal owner, and another may be the owner according to a different set of rules (equity in England and the praetorian law in Rome). It need not be said that

---

[1] Old Babylonian *ṣabâtu* (Neo-babylonian and Assyrian *leqû* or *abâku* or *nadânu*) *ana šîmi* or *ana kaspi*. See *Primitive Law*, p. 411 f.; *Evolution of Law and Order*, chap. viii.

the simpler societies have no such technical conception. It evolves in comparatively complex economic systems, in which two or more persons share the enjoyment of property, and it enables their respective rights to be defined, In the simpler societies the nearest relation to this is the relation between a man and the chattel which he holds and which is considered his. In England the word 'own' has a corresponding history. 'To own' is found with the meaning of 'to take' as early as A.D. 888, and with the meaning of 'to hold as one's thing' from A.D. 1000, but 'ownership' is not found till 1583.[1] We see then that out of the notion that the person who holds a thing is the person entitled to hold it (because that which normally occurs ought to occur and is right) is developed the technical conception of ownership, and the development is shaped by economic changes. A like English word, though not so precise and technical, is the word 'belong', which is found with the meaning of 'accompany', 'be with' and 'relate to' from 1340, and with the meaning of 'to be the property of' not before 1393. Words meaning 'to hold', 'to be with' or 'accompany' are everywhere to be seen in Africa in a slow process of change from one stage to the other according to the economic progress of the people.[2]

These examples, because of their precise character and widespread history, illustrate the truth that changes in meaning are not created by language, but by mental progress largely shaped and accompanied by economic advance. This indeed follows from what we have previously said – namely that, from the first emergence of speech, words derive their meaning from the circumstances in which they are used and the use to which they are put. Language, in its most important and characteristic aspect, is the reverse of what it is generally supposed to be. Instead of consisting of a bundle of labels which name the thing to which they are attached, it rather consists of labels which obtain their meaning from the things to which they are attached; and these things, like all else in the world, are forever changing, and with them changes the meaning of the labels. In all these cases there is, as before an objective resemblance between the old and new meanings – for example, the physical relation between person and object; a closer functional resemblance, in that the relation still serves much the same purposes; and also a still closer affective resemblance, which, though it may seem small, has widespread relations with the whole of a man's general way of life and what it means to him.

[1] See Oxford Dictionary 'ownership', and *Primitive Law*, p. 261.
[2] See *Primitive Law* (1935), p. 26; Homburger (1949), p. 152.

So far we have been speaking of one aspect of the process of change of meaning, namely, where the changes are gradual and unintentional. But there is a further aspect, where words are transferred to new things. This transfer on the part of the speaker, and the understanding of this use on the part of the hearer, come about, as before, because of the resemblance between the new thing and the old, but the new is a separate thing from the old. As before, the resemblance must be apparent to the whole mind, and must therefore appeal to the affective and conative-active as well as the cognitive elements of mind – that is to say, it must be affective and functional as well as objective. This is what is meant by saying that the transfer is a 'metaphor'. Sometimes the transfer is wide, and the metaphor seems (according to circumstances) poetical or far-fetched. For every such a one there are a thousand that are not readily recognized as metaphors because the extension is too slight to be noticed or because it was made too long ago; but the process is the same, and it is of the very essence of language and mind. It is because the extension appeals to the affective as well as the other elements of mind that metaphor is the very stuff of poetry. It speaks to the heart because it is in the heart of language and mind. When we read the lines

> *I could a tale unfold whose lightest word*
> *Would harrow up thy soul, freeze thy young blood*

or

> *Full many a glorious morning have I seen*
> *Flatter the mountain-tops with sovereign eye*

we easily recognize that 'unfold', 'lightest', 'harrow', 'freeze', 'glorious', 'flatter', 'sovereign' and 'eye' are the metaphors of a poet; but in all probability all or most of these words are metaphors, though in some the allusion has been lost. And who shall say where metaphor begins and ends in this? –

> *The heavens relate the glory of God*
>   *And the firmament telleth his handiwork.*
> *Day unto day poureth out speech*
>   *And night unto night imparteth knowledge.*
> *There is no speech nor language –*
>   *No voice of theirs is heard –*
> *But their voice is gone forth through all the earth*
> *And their words to the ends of the world.*

But poetry also has its commoner metaphors, full of the gentle, moving quality – at least, moving to simple minds – of quiet, homely associations and the occupations of every day.

> O gentle son
> Upon the heat and flame of thy distemper
> Sprinkle cool patience!

And still quieter and less moving are those of prose. 'Poetry', said Milton, 'is simple, sensuous, passionate.' Prose is less simple and less passionate, but the metaphors are of the same character. We speak of the 'foot' of a staircase or a mountain, of an 'arm' of the sea or of the law; and in England innumerable juts of land are called a 'cape' or a 'head', just as the juts of North Africa are called by the Semitic *ras*, 'a head', and so in a hundred other languages. To 'comprehend', in Latin and English, is by origin 'to hold together, to grasp'; just as we use 'grasp' itself for the same purpose, and just as in Egyptian *am* was to grasp and also to understand, and so in many other languages. To be 'in suspense' is originally to be 'hung up', just as we repeat the metaphor when we speak of 'hanging' on another's words. To be 'afflicted' was originally to be crushed or broken; and we use 'crushed' and 'broken' in the same sense. When we use the word to 'decide', we are using the Latin de-cido, which bore the same meaning as the English, but originally meant to 'cut off' or 'cut in two'. The German expresses the same idea and metaphor in the word ent-scheiden. The Greek κρίνω and the Latin cerno, 'to decide', originally meant 'to separate'. The Assyrian *parâṣu* was *to break* and also *to decide*, and *baru* had the same two meanings. In the Hebrew Old Testament *gaẓar* was 'to cut, to divide', and in Job and Late Hebrew and Aramaic had come to mean 'to determine'. The Hebrew *ḥaraṣ* was originally 'to cut', and so 'to decide', and similarly the Assyrian *ḥarâṣu*, to cut, dig, decide. The Hebrew root *ḥatak* was to divide and determine; the Hebrew root *qaṣah* was to *cut off* and *to decree*; and so in a hundred other languages. We speak of 'cutting' an acquaintance, and similarly to 'contemn' was originally 'to cut' (Latin and Greek *temno*, *to cut*), and in Latin had already come to mean 'to despise'. So in Hebrew *baẓa'* was 'to cut' and *baẓah* 'to despise'. To 'spurn' was originally to 'kick away'; to 'bore' (to weary) originally meant 'to pierce' (as Latin foro), and it still bears the same meaning. The words *right*, *recht*, *droit* are 'straight', 'direct', as well as 'customary'; and *wrong* is 'twisted' or 'crooked'. 'Straight' and 'crooked' are still used in the same senses. These same metaphors are to a large extent found in all languages and ages, wherever a similar mental advance allows it, for they are concerned with fundamental behaviour of the speech community and the human mind; and for the same reason the same metaphors are forever repeating themselves, moving, as it were, along the channels of the mind cut in the distant past with the force of language. Of such metaphors language is full. Most of them can be descried and even the affective values felt; the rest were also metaphors once. But sooner or later, having been generally accepted in the new sense, the old words become the ordinary terms for the new ideas, and the sense of metaphor fades. 'Every language', said Richter long ago, 'is a dictionary of faded metaphors.'

The first aspect of change, which we illustrated by *house, shoe, ship,* and *to shoot* – what Stern calls 'substitution' – shows us meanings of language changing gradually and insensibly with changes in man's environment, so that it continues to serve his changing needs. It lays stress on the changing object and the viewpoint of the hearer. The second aspect – illustrated by transfers by metaphor – shows us the process viewed rather from the speaker's end, and lays stress on his intention rather than on the thing meant, and on the discontinuous rather than the gradual and insensible change. Yet the difference is largely a matter of degree and innumerable instances lie between. For example, when the French *plume* (feather) came to mean (among other things) a steel pen, we may say that there was merely a process of *substitution*, the writing-instrument changing from feather to steel, or that it was a process of *transfer*, the three-fold similarity between the two making possible the change of meaning. The same would apply to the change of meaning of 'horns', from horn-shaped to other instruments of similar materials and timbre. And the same would apply to some cases of 'to shoot'.

The affective element shows itself in varying intensity and in various ways. Sometimes it is hardly to be noticed, or is reduced to the level of mere interest or attraction. But there would indeed be no speech at all without affect, for speech is an action and affect is necessary for action, and it is affect that chooses the metaphors and renders them expressive and appealing. For example, it is the affective associations of the sea for a sea-faring community that causes *adripare* (to reach the shore) to be used for *arriving* at a destination, or the top of a staircase to be called the *landing* (cf. Spanish *arriba*, upstairs); and the passion for golf that induces the expression *stymied* or *bunkered* for 'hindered', and the affective associations of everyday occupations that cause *cut in two* to signify *decide*, or *penser* (from *pensare, to hang*, and so *to weigh*) to mean *think*; and fear of a thing that causes it to be named by an evasive name, as *brown* for *bear*, or Euxine (hospitable) for the Black Sea.

There are innumerable details by which the above general picture can be filled in. For example, when one word undergoes a certain change of meaning, a word of similar meaning may undergo a similar change by 'analogy'. Or a meaning may be acquired by a word because of its resemblance to another word of that meaning – as now in French, St Genou (Genulphus) is the patron saint of those suffering from gout, owing to the resemblance to *genou* (knee). Or, as words change their form – for example, by shortening – the meaning of a word may consequently change – as when the expression 'the red ball' at billiards may be shortened to the 'red', and thereby the meaning of the word 'red' may change. Or the name of a part may be used as sufficiently indicating the whole (as *forty sail* for *forty ships*) or the whole for the part (as *Whitehall* or the Quai d'Orsay, for those who work there). These details will not help us to find the broad highway along which the meaning of words has travelled.

Change in the meaning of words is facilitated by the nature of the meaning of words. Words, as we said, name, in the first place, not things or actions but their characters or aspects, and classes and not members of classes, and these aspects and classes are apparent to memory, the senses, opinion and affect, and are accordingly vague and subjective, and their outlines shift and are irregular. Words have characteristically more than one meaning, and there are often some common features of resemblance between certain of the meanings of a word, and different common features between other meanings of the same word. It is this vagueness of meaning and its irregular outline that, above all else, make possible the changes of meaning. We have already illustrated this in the language of children, Let us look again at children's speech[1] and see what light it casts on the history and beginnings of meaning.

It is obvious that the meanings of children's words must in some respects be remotely different from those of the earliest men. The two

[1] The main study and standard work in this field was that of the Sterns—Stern, C. and W., *Die Kindersprache* (1907), 4te Aufl., 1928. In England of recent years has appeared Dr M. M. Lewis' valuable *Infant Speech* (1936), and the equally useful chap. XX of Dr C. W. Valentine's *The Psychology of Early Childhood* (3rd ed., 1946). For useful bibliographies, see *Infant Speech* (*supra*) and Arnold Gesell, *The First Five Years of Life*.

environments have little in common. In the one case meaning was to be derived from the needs of primitive adults taking each step forward for the first time: in the other case from the needs of modern infants, learning established words and meanings from their parents and supplied with whatever they call for. But the changes of meaning in the language of infants are of the same general character as the changes that continue in the known history of the languages of men, and there is no reason to think that changes of the same general character did not occur in the earliest days of speech.[1]

As Meumann observed as long ago as 1902, the language of children is at its beginning mainly 'affective – volitional', and becomes increasingly objective thereafter. The earliest vocal sounds uttered by children express overwhelmingly affect and conation, but by degrees these sounds are used more and more in reference to particular classes of situations, and there is a continuous increase of objective reference to these situations. The changes reflect changes in their mental processes.

We begin with the inarticulate cries of babies and very young infants, which mainly express bodily condition and affect-conation. In the next stage, either the child produces its first articulate sound – such as dă or dădă – or the parents induce it to imitate a word of theirs, and in either case condition the child to give it a particular meaning.[2]

A good illustration of the earlier stage is to be found in the remarkable experiment of J. B. Watson upon the unfortunate Albert. Albert was 11 months of age. 'He was a wonderfully "good" baby. In all the months we worked with him,' says Watson, 'we never saw him cry until after our experiments were made!' He had no fear responses to any objects, and everything coming within 12 inches of him was reached for and manipulated. But a loud sound will call out the fear

[1] It is not, however, possible to obtain light upon the history of the proportions of the parts of speech from the language of very young children. The reason is that while parents endeavour to teach the children mainly through nouns, most words used by infants are sentence-words, and most express *desires* for objects. Dewey points out the necessity for keeping in mind 'the extent to which the formal noun "ball" has really an active sense. "Ball" is "to throw" just as much as it is the round thing' (J. Dewey, *Psychology of Infant Language*, Psych. Rev. I (1894)). Tracy pointed out long ago (*The Psychology of Childhood*, by F. Tracy and J. Stimpfl, 7th ed., 1909, pp. 144-9) from information collected from various sources, that the vocabulary of children from two to three years of age contained 20% verbs. C. W. Valentine, op. cit., p. 420, shows similar figures for the same age from another source. These figures cannot be relied upon, for the reasons given above. Tracy was right in pointing out the importance of ideas of actions rather than objects in the language of infants, but his argument from figures was unfounded. There has been inconclusive work in this field in America.

[2] For example, by producing a particular person or a particular object when a particular sound is used.

reaction in any child quickly and easily, and the object of the experiment was to condition a fear response to a white rat. On the first day, the white rat which he had played with for weeks was presented to Albert, and he reached for it, but at that moment a steel bar was struck loudly just behind him. He jumped violently and fell forward, burying his face in the mattress. The experiment was repeated with the same result, and he also began to whimper. At the close of the series of experiments the rat was shown to him, and the bar was not struck, and he immediately began to cry, turned sharply, fell over and then crawled rapidly away. He was now, therefore, afraid of the white rat. Before the experiments, he had been playing for weeks with rabbits, fur muffs, the hair of the attendants and false faces. After the experiments, when a rabbit was placed in front of him his fear reaction was very similar to that in regard to the white rat. A dog produced a similar, but not so violent a reaction, and so did a fur coat. His fear reaction to cotton wool was marked, but only for a short time, and he also refused to play with the hair of Watson, who conducted the experiments, though he played with the hair of the other attendants. Watson concludes by saying that there was therefore a convincing proof of spread or transfer. In other words, human behaviour in a child of that age being mainly affective-conative and to a small degree cognitive, the fear reaction was not directed merely to the white rat, or to the class of white rats, but to things forming a class of vague outline, each member of which through some feature of resemblance impressed the child's mind in a somewhat similar way. But the common feature was not necessarily the same in the case of each member of the class. For example, the fur coat produced the same reaction as the white rat and to some extent so did the cotton wool, but the hair of a human head only if it was the head of the person associated with the experiment.[1]

Another example of the earliest stage is that of C. W. Valentine's boy B, who, at the age of 1 year 2 months (in the example given in an earlier chapter)[2] having often seen pictures of dogs and barked at them, now barked at pictures other than those of dogs. There is also the example of M. M. Lewis' boy, who at the age of 1; 4 having said *ahaaa* on smelling a handkerchief scented with lavender, also said *aaa* on seeing and smelling jonquils growing in a bowl.[3]

As examples of the beginning of the later stage – that of early articulate speech – there are the instances, given earlier, of the use of

[1] *Behaviorism*, pp. 158-63.   [2] *Ante*, p. 94.   [3] Lewis, p. 192.

kuk-kuk and Dada by the same boy B, at the age of 1 year 6 months,[1] and Romanes' account of the remarkably forward child in his first year, who, having been taught to use the word 'quack' for a duck, called 'quack' to an eagle on a coin, and then to coins in general.

Looking at these and the innumerable other examples contained in the books, we see the growth of the cognitive element – these words become directed to an increasing number of classes of situations. We see also that these classes are combined according to features of resemblance in the members. Firstly, there is in these cases – and probably in all cases – an affective resemblance: that is to say, that situations are classed together which evoke a similar affection. This was the case, for example, with Albert and his fear. Secondly, there is a resemblance of function, as for example M. M. Lewis' boy uttering *aa* when smelling a handkerchief and smelling flowers. Thirdly, there is an objective resemblance – for example, between the coin with an eagle upon it and the coin without; or the pinafore with a bird upon it and the pinafore without. We are encouraged to think that these three types of resemblance are fundamental because they are due to the fact that instinctive behaviour can be analysed into cognition, affect and conation-action. We must also remember the corresponding differences, which reject other situations from these classes. We are not considering here the forms of sounds, but it is also obvious that there can be little development of objective reference to situations till vocal sounds become articulate, so that by the increase in the number of available sounds, and the increased possibility of distinguishing them because they are articulate, each sound can be applied to a different perceived situation.

[1] See *ante*, p. 94.

CHAPTER FOURTEEN

The History of Meaning
(continued)

What, then, is the path that meaning has taken in the changes that it has undergone since the emergence of speech? The chief lines of change, seen in the facts described in the previous chapter, are three.

First, the meanings of words have become less vague and more precise.[1] This important process can be seen from several aspects. There is always a lack of correspondence and a contradiction between language and mind, on the one hand, and the objects of the physical world on the other. The mental processes and language are necessarily general, being partly (though decreasingly) affective. A slow, progressive precision of meaning results from application to specific situations. Mind sees only aspects, and language expresses only impressions; and the application of speech is necessarily the naming of a situation in terms of one impression or aspect of it. It recognizes and names the situation as resembling some other situations objectively or functionally or as evoking the same feelings. But as soon as this recognition and naming is made and generally felt and accepted by the community, the process of origin is forgotten and the name of that general aspect or impression becomes the usual symbol for the situation. By a continuation of the same process it becomes the usual symbol for a diminishing part of the situation. In terms of the behaviourist the process may be described as a repeated conditioning. For example, if a dog has been conditioned to the tone of a bell of pitch x by hearing it whenever meat is brought, that tone will call out the salivary response just as does the meat. But so will any other tone of a bell. Yet within the limits of the dog's capacity to distinguish tones, if we now proceed to feed him only when pitch x is sounded, and not others, he will

---

[1] Or, as expressed in the metaphors 'vague' and 'precise', less *wandering* and more *cut off*. The large number of metaphors contained in this paragraph exemplify what occurs in the attempt to apply old terms to new conceptions.

finally respond only to *x*. Experiments of this general type have been conducted with some success upon apes and other animals. So with language; when a term A has been adopted as the name of a situation, and a term B as the name of another situation, repeated applications of the same or similar terms to new situations in which some only of the features are the same, will result in the adoption of names whose meaning is progressively limited and defined by the narrowing context.

This process is closely allied to and often accompanied by a phonetic process. Words vary and change in their form as well as in their meaning, and public approval singles out one or more forms for survival as it narrows and singles out a group of meanings for survival. So, when the combined process has gone a little way it may be seen that an earlier word has divided into two forms and two meanings, and one meaning is approved and limited to the one form, and one to the other. So the words 'one' and 'an' are both derived from the same O.E. original, and so are 'of' and 'off', 'as' and 'also', 'outer' and 'utter'; and in the course of a longer history, travelling through more than one country, the Modern English descendants of the Greek 'diskos' are *discus*, *disc* (or *disk*), *desk* and *dish*, each with its own particular meaning. For this purpose, of course, articulate speech is necessary.

This process of the growing precision of meaning marks also, as we have seen, the whole process of development of intelligence from infant to adult. Articulate words (being of much the same meaning as the inarticulate cries that preceded them) have at first broad fields of meaning, of vague position and outline, readily extensible; but the process of development of mind is the breaking up of the partly emotive field into an increasing number of shrinking areas of objective reference; the outlines become clearer, and any shifting is slower and more difficult. In the child's use of *Dada* and *Gaga* and *Quack*, extensions may take place almost from day to day; but many of the metaphors we have spoken of are several thousand years old and still recognizable.

Looked at more narrowly, as a functional-linguistic process, this is a process of the same nature as that fundamental advance when a word changes from verb to noun. An object is named by that more general expression, a verb, which hits upon some characteristic action or movement of the object – so the moon (lu-na from luc-na) is called a 'shin-er'; a cessation of movement is called a 'break'; and by a metaphor, the affective value of which is recalled by Tennyson's

> *Break, break, break*
> *On thy cold grey stones, O sea!*

waves of the sea are called 'breakers'. Bréal, indeed, attributes the existence of this whole process to the application of verbs to describe objects. 'Elle vient,' he says, 'de ce que le verbe est la partie essentielle et capitale de nos langues, celle qui sert à faire des substantifs et des adjectifs. Or, le verbe, par nature, a une signification générale, puisqu'il marque une action prise en elle-même, sane autre détermination d'aucune sorte. En combinant ce verbe avec un suffixe, on peut bien attacher l'idée verbale à un être agissant, ou à un objet qui subit l'action, ou à un objet qui est le produit ou l'instrument de l'action, mais cette action gardant sa signification générale, le substantif ou l'adjectif ainsi formé sera lui-même de sens général. Il faudra que par l'usage on le limite.'[1]

Bréal calls the process 'La restriction du sens' (the restriction of meaning, a term which Whitney had used before him).[2] Both point out that restriction of meaning is the normal course of the history of language, but that the converse process of extension of meaning is also found, though to a lesser degree; and that, where is it is found, it is generally due to historical accident. There is, first, as we have seen, the 'expansion of meaning' treated of by so many writers on the language of children. The term is best regarded as a misnomer. An adult teaches a child the conventional name for an object (for example, 'quack' for a duck) and the child calls 'quack' to an eagle on a coin, and then to coins in general. The important feature is the affective-conational nature of meaning in the child's mind: it is not a case of the extension of the boundary of meaning so much as the wandering of the cloud of meaning. A large number of the extensions of meaning in the language of adults are due to changes in the form of property by economic advance. So the O.E. feoh (cattle) in the later form of 'fee', came to include land (held e.g. in 'fee simple') and money; and this was because cattle was at first the main form and measure of a man's wealth. Later, as a metal currency superseded cattle as a means of payment, and in feudal England the extent of a man's holding of land measured his status, and from the beginning of the 14th century a regular market in land appeared in England, land and money became the measure of wealth. In Latin *pecus* (= O.E. *feoh*) in the form of *pecunia* underwent a similar development. Similarly in France *gagner*

---

[1] *Essai de Sémantique*, pp. 119-20.   [2] Whitney, L. G. (1896), p. 84.

was originally to feed flocks, and a *gagneur* was a farmer, and *gain* was the harvest; and *gain* too became extended to any property. In England a *book* need no longer be made of *beech* nor *paper* of *papyrus*, nor need a *volume* be a *roll*. A *butterfly* need not be yellow. *Graeci*, the name by which the Hellenes were called in Italy, was originally the name of a group of northern Hellenic settlers, and the Italians called by the same name all subsequent Hellenes whom they met; and we now call them by the same name, *Greeks*. For similar reasons the Hebrews called a Greek a *yawan* (Greek *Ἴων*, an Ionian), and the Arabs called the Western Europeans *Franks*. These are details. The whole process is not so much a restriction of meaning (with exceptional extensions): it is rather a growing precision of meaning.

This first process of change of meaning continues throughout the history of language, but it is especially characteristic of the earlier stages. It is, for example, as Bréal said, the process by which verbs change to nouns. A second process of change runs also throughout the history of language, but is specially characteristic of the later stages.

We might hastily describe it as a movement from the concrete towards the abstract. In the functional-linguistic aspect it is, above all, the process by which concrete nouns change to adjectives (e.g. 'wood' as a noun to 'wood', 'wooden' or 'woody' as an adjective), adjectives to abstract nouns ('woody' to 'woodiness'), demonstratives to definite articles,[1] and independent verbs to auxiliary verbs (e.g. 'have', meaning 'hold', changing to 'have' in the sentence 'I have done'). But to define the change as being from the concrete to the abstract is to forget the affective aspect of metaphor. Moreover, 'concrete' connotes too much precision: the contrasted epithets of 'concrete' and 'abstract' are both characteristic only of developed modern thought. Mind can only take impressions from the concrete by the senses: it cannot absorb or photograph the concrete.

This second process is more accurately defined as the change-over from impressions derived from actions and objects to abstract conceptions. The philosopher Locke described it in the following celebrated passage:

'It may also lead us a little toward the original of all our notions and knowledge, if we remark, how great a dependence our words have on common sensible ideas; and how those, which are made use of to stand for actions and notions quite removed from sense, have their rise from

[1] See *post*, p. 183.

thence, and, from obvious sensible ideas, are transferred to more abstruse significations, and made to stand for ideas that come not under the cognisance of our senses: e.g. to imagine, apprehend, comprehend, adhere, conceive, instil, disgust, disturbance, tranquillity, etc., are all words taken from the operations of sensible things, and applied to certain modes of thinking. Spirit, in its primary signification, is breath; angel, a messenger; and I doubt not, but if we could trace them to their sources, we should find, in all languages, the names which stand for things that fall not under our senses, to have had their first rise from sensible ideas. By which we may give some kind of guess, what kind of notions they were and whence derived, which filled their minds, who were the first beginners of languages.'[1]

A number of instances of the process have been given in this and the previous chapter. Max Müller described it as the process by which 'all words expressive of immaterial conceptions are derived by metaphor from words expressive of sensible ideas'.[2] In the words of Dwight Whitney: 'There is a movement in the whole vocabulary of language from the designation of what is coarser, gross, more material, to the designation of what is finer, more abstract and conceptional, more formal. Considered with reference to the ends rather than the methods of expression, there is no grander phenomenon than this in all language-history.'[3]

Yet Bréal does not mention this phenomenon. On the contrary, he devotes a chapter to a process which is almost the converse of this, and which he calls the Concretion of Meaning (L'Épaississement du Sens).[4] He points to the large number of cases where an abstract noun becomes a concrete noun. We might cite from Modern English 'a sensation', meaning a sensational event; a 'mansion' (French *maison*), originally a Latin abstract noun meaning 'staying, remaining', and the similar case of a 'residence'; an 'association', meaning not the tie but the institution and the persons composing it. *Bedes* (prayers) become the *beads* that are counted. But, properly speaking, these are detailed applications[5] of our first process; for that process, as we said, though perhaps especially characteristic of the early stages, continues throughout the life of language, and even an abstract noun, like any other general expression, being used in reference to a particular situation,

---

[1] Locke, *On the Human Understanding*, iii, 4, 3.
[2] Max Müller, vol. ii, p. 372.
[3] Whitney, L. G. (1896). p. 89.
[4] Bréal, chap. XIII.
[5] Another example.

will tend to be limited to it. It is, in Bréal's phraseology, an example of 'restriction of meaning'.

While, therefore, in our first process of change, we observed meaning becoming more and more precise, the cognitive slowly and partly freeing itself from the affective element in mind, in our second law of change we see the meaning of words moving from impressions of the material to the abstract, from the sensual to the non-sensual, from perception to conception, from the cognitive to the intellectual. Looking at the change as a formal, linguistic process, we can see the results for ourselves, and confirm some propositions adduced in this book, by comparing the meanings of the verbal 'roots', to which language can be reduced, with the meanings of modern language. Looking at the change as an advance of mind, we see it on an immeasurably grander scale – the mind turning from observation of what is in sight to what was in the past and what will be in the future, to the esoteric world, to the modern study of the mind and the modern introspective novel and poem.

There is an equally important, or even more important, third process of change of meaning. I propose to call it the law of wearing-out. It is hinted at by Dwight Whitney, where he calls it 'an attenuation, a fading-out, a complete formalizing, of what was before solid, positive, substantial'.[1] It is rarely, if ever, spoken to by other linguists. It is akin to the second rule of change.

We speak to impress the minds of others. Directly and fundamentally, we do so in the request for action; but indirectly this is the whole purpose of language, and indeed all language is a request for help. As we said earlier, for this purpose the intensity of the speaker's desire and affect must be communicated, and an effort proportionate to (or indeed greater than) the desired result must be expended if it is to bring in a return. In the result there is a universal tendency to exaggeration and overemphasis: the metaphors are more striking than the situations to which they are applied; the language and its contents are more emotional, the facts are overstated, the whole picture tends to be overdrawn and overcoloured. And then, because linguistic labels take their meaning from the things to which they are attached, and words their meaning from the context to which they are directed, these powerful words and phrases – that is to say the whole of language – tend ever to lose their force. Put differently, there is a loss of power in the transmission from speaker to hearer. We see this process in

[1] Whitney, L. G. (1896), p. 90. He speaks of it as a branch of our second process.

operation in all languages and all ages. We see it more clearly in some literatures, as where, for example, the forced expressions of Silver Latin succeed to the directness of the Augustan age, in an attempt to attract a jaded attention. In our own civilization we see the over-emphasis particularly among those of us who, for their livelihood, (like advertisers and commission-agents) must quickly make an impression beyond the merits of their subject-matter, and it is typical of 'journalese'. 'They literally tore him limb from limb' signifies that he had a warm reception. 'Literally', from meaning 'true in every letter' is sinking to the level of 'almost'. 'They were soundly thrashed' indicates that they lost by two tries. News is no longer spread but 'revealed'. Other examples, taken from the language at large, have been given earlier.

If we now look back at these three processes of the change of meaning, we shall easily recognize that they are but one – the three dimensions of the waters of one mighty river. First we said that meaning becomes more and more precise, the cognitive element beginning, as it were, to free itself from the affective-conative.[1] Secondly we said that sensual impressions from concrete objects and persons, moving or still, give place to the abstract and the conceptual. This, too, must mean that (in terms of the first process) meaning grows more precise. Impressions upon the senses from objects in nature are necessarily less precise than the abstract and the conceptional. Since language and thought are impressionist, impressions from the concrete cannot be more than imperfect, at the best. Any concrete object possesses an unlimited number of aspects. We can call the moon or the sun a 'shiner', but they are more than that: they have position and movement and size and colour and many other aspects. Language can only be complete and accurate when it names the purely conceptual, the thing that has no existence save in the mind of the speaker and hearer, for then there is no conflict or contradiction between physical reality and mental impression. The third process, we said, was one of wearing-out – a loss of force, 'an attenuation, a fading out, a complete formalizing of what was before solid, positive, substantial', and, we may add, powerfully moving. This must, in any event, occur when language ceases to express sensual impressions from concrete objects and actions.

If now we trace back language in our imagination along this three-

[1] We may add that in the course of this process the semantic load of each word grows heavier – the number of its meanings must progressively increase.

fold path, to what origin does it ultimately tend? Surely to the origin that we described in Chapter 12. It leads back to a language whose few articulate words possess meanings overwhelmingly affective-conative, and only to a small degree cognitive; to a language of few words each of which covers so vague and unlimited a field of meaning that each word bears practically the same meaning; to a language whose few words express impressions derived by the senses from human action and concrete objects – that is to say, from human beings in action; to a language whose few words express a maximum of force – that is to say, all signify human actions of maximum physical force.

If now we look back to the earlier chapters of this book, we shall see that to this origin every fact that we have noticed, every process of change that we have observed, continuously, harmoniously and unmistakably tends. First we examined the history of the proportions of the parts of speech. The latest parts of speech are the prepositions and conjunctions; before them the adverbs; before the bulk of them the adjectives; previously the nouns; before them the verbs; and the earliest form of the verb was the request for action; and the earliest form of request was that for action of maximum human force. This succession marks a progressive diminution, from the beginnings of speech, in the expression of human force. The latest parts of speech, the prepositions and conjunctions, are words mainly of grammatical or syntactical significance, and of no physical force or affective power or sensual significance. Many languages of the simpler peoples have substantially neither of these parts of speech. When the Common Indo-European was breaking up into Sanskrit, Greek, Latin and the other ancient languages or groups of languages, there was not a single real preposition or conjunction; at any rate none has left a trace in the succeeding languages. Before the prepositions and conjunctions came the bulk of the adverbs, and indeed from them the bulk of our prepositions have been formed, for the latter were originally adverbs, and are still mainly adverbs in some Indo-European languages, notably ancient Greek. The adverbs connote more of physical force than the prepositions and conjunctions. In many languages, as we have seen, there are hardly any adverbs, and in the Indo-European languages they are one of the most recent parts of speech: for example they show no common inflexions characteristic of this part of speech, and must have acquired their inflexions since, for Indo-European was very much an inflecting tongue. The adverbs originate in the main from the adjectives (though also from noun and verb) and there is no great difference in physical substance and force between adjective and adverb. Most of the adjectives originate from the nouns, names of concrete objects and persons, solid and substantial though not expressing physical movement or force. The nouns are mainly derived from verbs, which are nothing if not the expression of physical force, and especially does this apply to the request for action, by which, through a fellow-being, the speaker wields physical force. Behind it are the first verbs, expressing maximum, human, physical force.

This was the course of history that we traced in the earlier chapters of this book; and in the present and the previous chapter it has become apparent that the succession of the parts of speech is a mere series of incidents in a history of meaning betokening a progressive loss of force.

Let us end this chapter with two examples of this loss of force in language. They are of particular interest because they can be instanced from people in far-flung continents and ages, and illustrate in how wide a sense this phrase 'loss of force' must be understood.

The first example illustrates the history of the 'copula' – the verb 'to be'; so called because to many grammarians it is a mere 'link' between the subject and predicate of a sentence. 'George is fast.' It has a special interest because of the place it occupies in our three types of sentences. It has also a certain special interest because of an ancient controversy. Locke's observation of the change of meaning from sensible to immaterial ideas was much controverted by some succeeding writers, and among others by Victor Cousin in his *Lectures on the History of Philosophy during the Eighteenth Century*.[1] He there describes the verb être (to be) as something not to be reduced, not to be decomposed, primitive and intellectual, expressing no sensible idea, representing nothing but the meaning which the mind attaches to it, a pure and true sign without any reference to any sensible idea. 'I know of no language', he says, 'in which the French verb être is rendered by a corresponding word that expresses a sensible idea; and therefore it is not true that all the roots of language, in their last analysis, are signs of sensible ideas.'[2]

In an earlier chapter we divided sentences into three types. Type 1 ('Look!') the request for action, consists in its simple form of one term, a verb. Type 2, which we called the statement ('George runs') consists in its simple form of two terms, a noun and a verb, and therefore the verb is now only half the sentence, and has itself lost

[1] Paris, 1841.   [2] Op. cit., vol. ii, p. 274.

force, being no longer a command but a mere statement (or description) of an action. Type 3, which we called the description-statement, contains three terms – verb, noun and adjective ('George is fast'). It is a description of the noun. The verb is now reduced to one-third of the sentence. In addition, the verb has further lost force: it is now the verb 'to be' and contains a minimum of action. Sentences of the third type are so recent that we can watch their development out of sentences of the second type in the languages of the simpler peoples. For example, in our instances of languages taken from peoples of the First Agricultural Grade and the lower half of the Hunters (of North America) the place of the second and third terms of the description-statement (that is to say, copula and adjective) is generally taken by a single verb. So, in Natick, womónat = to love, be kind to, womonausu = he is kind to; ônouwussu = he is lean; ashkoshki = it is green; missi or mishe = it is great. But as, with progress, description of objects becomes more common, language isolates and specializes an adjective-form, and a verb 'to be' which can be conveniently used with any adjective. The adjective, as we have seen, is originally a noun in most cases, but sometimes a verb. In many early languages the verb 'to be' has not yet been evolved, or, if it has, only in certain uses, and commonly not in the simplest case, namely the third person aorist or historic present, where it can easily be implied. Even in the classical languages it is very commonly omitted in the third person present – always in Hebrew (which has no such form), usually in Greek, and sometimes in Latin.[1]

But various verbs of stronger force are commonly applied to the purpose, and lose their force by that use. In many languages it is the verb 'to eat' which, diminishing in strength, comes to mean 'to live' and 'to be' (*he eats well* = he lives well, he is well; *he eats over there* = he is over there). For example, in Bini, a Sudanic language, the language of the Edo of Southern Nigeria, possessing five or six tones, the same word [e,[2] with the same high tone, signifies 'to eat' and 'to be'. Throughout the Bantu tongues we see the next stage. The use of the verb 'to be' is more common than that of the verb 'to eat', and accordingly, as a copula, the word is slightly abbreviated; and also (being familiar, and not, therefore, needing the aid of grammar), becomes

[1] E.g. Ashrē ha'ish 'asher lo halak ba'atsat resha'im (Happy (is) the man who walketh not in the counsel of the wicked – Psalm l, 1). Ariston men hydor (Best, indeed, (is) water, Pindar, Ol. i, 1). Felix qui potuit rerum cognoscere causas (Happy (is) he who has been able to learn the causes of things, Virg. G. 2, 490).
[2] [= a liquid consonant, between r and l, a flapped variety of l.

irregular and defective. So in Buluba Lulua, dia = to eat, and the defective verb di = to be; in Luganda lya = 'to eat', and also sometimes 'to be'.[1] and the defective verb li = 'to be'; in Herero – ria = 'to eat', and the defective verb -ri = to be; in Kikuyu -rîa = to eat, and the defective verb -ri = to be; and in South Kikuyu there is a further weakened form -i (instead of -ri) = to be.

The same phenomena are to be seen in the Indo-European languages. In the Common Indo-European, the root 'ed' signified originally (and continues to signify) 'to eat', and in a somewhat weakened, abbreviated irregular and defective form, 'to be'. *Edmi** was 'I eat' and 'I am'; *edsi** or *edti** was 'he eats' and 'he is'. The 'd' was weakened to 's' in the verb 'to be', and often also in the verb 'to eat'. So Sanskrit, admi = I eat; asmi = I am; and in Homeric Greek edo = I eat; edménai = to eat, and the abbreviated eînai = to be, and eimi = I am. In Latin *est* means 'he is' and 'he eats', *es* = 'you are' and 'you eat'; *esse* = 'to eat' and 'to be'. Modern German *iszt* and *ist* = 'he eats' and 'he is'. Modern English '*eats*' and '*is*'.

In other languages other verbs are employed – in the Semitic a verb meaning 'to live': so in Hebrew ḥayah = he lived, and hayah = he was. In the Indo-European a verb apparently meaning 'grow' is also employed. The root was 'bhu' – Sanskrit *bhavami*, Greek *phuo*, Latin *fui*, O.H.G. *bim*, Mod. German *bin*, English *be*. In Modern French the Low Latin word for 'stand' is also employed – so être (= *estĕrĕ* from *stārĕ*, to stand) to be; était (from regularized Low Latin perfect *stavit*, he stood) he was; Mod. Greek estathē.

The other example we shall give of this loss of force in language is the example of the demonstratives.

In the Romance languages there is a definite article (il, le, la, etc.) which is an abbreviated form of the Latin demonstrative ille, illa (that). This demonstrative has a physical significance, for it indicates a man or object standing yonder in a particular place. As a definite article in Romance it has lost that physical force, for its meaning is purely grammatical. It signifies usually the man or object previously referred to, as distinct from any unspecified member of the class 'men' or 'objects'. In some usages, however, the definite article undergoes further loss of force and has no meaning whatsoever. In French, le beurre = butter, and l'éléphant can mean merely 'an elephant'.

This process of change from demonstrative to definite article is world-wide. In English, for example, the definite article 'the' is arrived

[1] So, *ali'de obwāmi* = he – has – become a – chief.

at by a mere phonetic weakening (namely, loss of the final consonant) of the demonstrative 'that' (Mod. German *das* still has both meanings), and in the final stage we find in English, as in French, a complete loss of meaning: 'The elephant never forgets' = 'an elephant never forgets'. Classical Latin did not evolve a definite article. Greek begins with a demonstrative (ὅς or ὅ, ἥ, ὅ or τό) which (except in a few usages) ceases to be a demonstrative and becomes a definite article.

In some languages the demonstrative pronoun also becomes the third person pronoun (as in the Romance languages); in some (as in Greek and English) a relative pronoun or conjunction (e.g. 'I know that the man has gone' = 'I know that (neut. demonstrative) – namely, the man has gone').

This weakening of the demonstrative is widespread also in the Semitic languages. So, for example, Arabic has the demonstrative hā, which is slightly abbreviated into the definite article hă in Hebrew, Phoenician and Moabite; and in Hebrew is on the verge of becoming a relative pronoun. The h which is practically universal throughout the Semitic languages in the personal pronouns of the third person, has, it is suggested, the same origin. So, too, the demonstrative 'la' in Arabic becomes an article,[1] and occasionally a relative pronoun.

We see the process also in North America. For example, in Hupa, 'hai' is in process of change from demonstrative to definite article.[2]

In Africa the same phenomena are very manifest, and visible far and wide. In some languages demonstratives are used as definite articles; in some as pronouns of the third person. A good example is furnished by Masai. This language has several demonstratives – elle (fem. enna), elde (fem. enda), illo (fem. inna), lello (fem. nenna). It will be seen that these are all variations of a demonstrative *el* (fem. *en*). They survive as the definite article in Masai – masc. *ol* (plur. *il*) fem. *en* (plur. *in*).

This article has travelled even further than the French definite article, and in most cases its employment is compulsory; it is pronounced as one with its noun, and has no meaning, and if it were omitted the text would not be understood. For example, if one wished to say in Masai 'Once upon a time there was man who had three children – two girls and a boy', it would be:

E – tii   opa   ol –   paiyan,   n – e – i – u
'He-is – there formerly   the - - - old-man,   and-he-begets

---

[1] Wright, *Arabic Gr.*, I, 269 B.   [2] Fr. Boaz in H.A.I.L., p. 148.

'n – gera   uni, 'n – doiye are, o   ol – ayōni ōbo
the – children three, the – girls two, and the – boy one.'[1]

So, when the demonstrative pronoun is joined to a substantive it takes the place of the article – e.g. elle – tuñgani = this man; enda-kerai = that child.

There is also a relative pronoun, masc. sing. ō, fem. na; or (when the negative *me* is combined with the relative) le-me is used for masc. and ne-me for fem.

So   Ol – tuñgani   o – ra   sapuk
      'The – man   who – is big'

      Ol – tuñgani le-me-ra   sapuk
      'The – man   who-not-is big.'[2]

It is obvious, therefore, that the relatives (masc. *O* and *le*; fem. *na* and *ne*) are all weakened forms of the same demonstratives, just as are the definite articles *ol* and *en*.

[1] Hollis, *The Masai*, p. 117.   [2] Hollis, op. cit., pp. 11, 43.

CHAPTER FIFTEEN

The Earliest Words

There remains one great facet of language, whose nature and recorded history we have hardly looked at – namely, the physiology of speech. This is of high importance to us, for its shows some clear evidence of a succession of changes and a path leading back towards the origins of language. The subject divides itself with difficulty into two branches: the first, the forms of the words, and the second, the human physiology that shaped them. In the present chapter we shall consider mainly the forms of words, and here we have evidence as precise as any that we have hitherto found.

We have said little so far of the forms of speech-sounds. It was pointed out in an earlier chapter[1] that the vocabularies of languages have grown larger in the course of man's advance, and that, so far as concerns the forms of words, this has involved a tendency to increase their length. We went on to analyse the vocabularies of a number of languages, and found words or word-parts common to many words in the language and of constant meaning, and we called them 'radical words' or 'roots'. It was found that they generally bore the meanings of verbs, and we came to the conclusion that they were nothing more nor less than the old verbs (or the consonants of the old verbs) out of which those vocabularies had been expanded. Still more important for our purpose, it was noticed that those old verbs were predominantly of one group of forms, namely CV or CVC or CVCV – where C is any consonant and V any vowel – and it was found that the forms CVC and CVCV (between which it was difficult to distinguish) much outnumbered the rest. These roots, then, or radical words, began with a consonant, and the bulk ended in a vowel, and they contained a succession of consonant and vowel, no two consonants being found together. It was also noticed that the vowels were generally short, and that among them the vowel A predominated. Were these word-forms and these meanings mere skeletons of words and ghosts of meanings,

[1] Chap. 6.

arrived at by a process of analysis and abstraction, or were they the original vocabulary that survived as a nucleus in the expanded and developed language? We thought that the truth lay in the latter proposition; and we shall see in this and the following chapters strong reasons that corroborate this opinion.

The sounds that constitute speech are received by a series of rhythmical pressures of air on the ear-drum of a listener – very gentle but very rapid pressures, of a frequency within the range of human hearing. Air is of an elastic nature, and these pressures – or rather

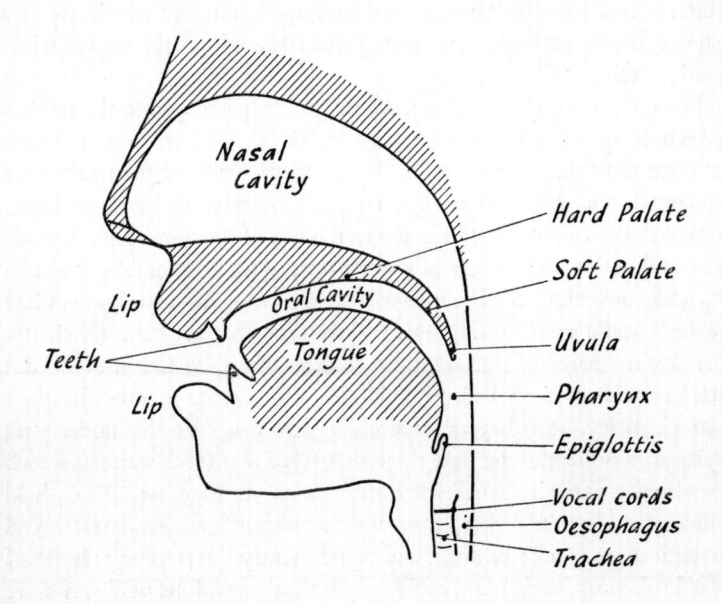

variations of pressure – are caused by a rhythmical disturbance of air at some point from which the sound originates. Vocal sound is caused by interference with a column of air passing from the speaker's lungs, up along the trachea (or wind-pipe), through the larynx (or 'Adam's apple'), along the chamber known as the pharynx; and from there out over the tongue and through the mouth, or behind the veil of the soft palate and through the nose. Some few sounds in some few languages are pronounced by intake of breath,[1] but this is so rare a phenomenon that it need not be considered here. The lungs perform the function

[1] For example the 'click' by which a driver starts his horse, and the consonantal clicks of Bushman, Zulu and other South African languages, and Fulbe and Hausa in West Africa.

of bellows: in the vocal process their part is merely to supply the column of air, which is emitted at a controlled rate and pressure. The lungs are filled by a muscular effort, and their normal condition is to be relaxed, and as they relax, air is expired without effort. A column of air enclosed, or partially enclosed, in the vocal cavity between larynx and mouth and nose, being of this elastic nature, will, when interfered with, oscillate back and forth, air going out, smaller quantities returning, still smaller quantities going out, and so forth, until equilibrium is finally regained. So are caused the rhythmical variations of pressure which travel through the air, and impinge upon the ear-drum of a listener, much as ripples are created and travel along the water[1] when it is interfered with.

The column of air, pressed from the lungs, passes along the trachea (or wind-pipe) to the larynx, where the sides of the trachea are much flattened until they can meet. At this point the walls of the trachea are thickened, and supplied with a complex of muscles and cartilages, known as the larynx. In effect, across the top of the wind-pipe (known here as the glottis) is a pair of mobile lips, lying horizontally fore and aft, and consisting of elastic tissue, fat and mucous membrane. They are the 'vocal cords'. During normal breathing they are held sufficiently apart by the force of the outgoing column of air, so that they do not interfere with it; but when not held apart, they close together by their own elasticity, for they are merely a covering for the underlying thyro-arytenoid muscle, and they also form a smooth surface which fits with the opposite 'cord' when the two come together. When held sufficiently close together, they vibrate like a reed as air is forced through them from the lungs; and consequently the passing column of air is broken up, and sharp, rapid, rhythmical variations of air pressure result, which produce a note at the ear-drum of the listener. The volume (or loudness) of the note varies with the air pressure from the lungs and the consequent greater or lesser amplitude of each vibration. The pitch of the note varies with the rapidity of the vibrations – the more frequent the vibrations, the higher the note; and this rapidity varies with the length, breadth and thickness of the vocal cords. If the pitch is constant the result is a singing note, but if there is a series of gliding pitches the result is speech-sounds. The human ear has evolved with the voice, and the ear's chief range of audibility corresponds with the range of frequencies of normal conversation.

[1] The water does not travel, of course, nor does the air, but only the vibration. The same applies to the waves of the sea.

The note thus produced by the larynx does not consist of one pitch: there are at the same time several pitches – that is to say, several series of vibrations of different rates. The laryngeal note is a complex of a fundamental and a number of softer overtones (or partials), together giving the quality of the 'tone'. But, in addition, the laryngeal note is affected by resonators. There is little, if any, resonance in the thorax and trachea: the resonance is chiefly derived from the vocal cavity between larynx and lips and nose. It is affected by altering the size (and to some extent the shape) of the vocal cavity, particularly by movement of the tongue, lips, lower jaw and soft palate, and also by altering the size of the orifice at the lips. The resonators do not affect the fundamental so much as the partials, which they may intensify or absorb. But in some positions a second, subsidiary note (in addition to the laryngeal note) may be created in the mouth (for example, in the sounds [i] or [s], between tongue and hard palate). So far we have been speaking of what occurs when the vocal cords (or, more accurately, the membraneous part of the vocal cords) are caused to vibrate, thereby producing a laryngeal note and voiced speech. But there are also whispered (or unvoiced) sounds when no note is produced at the larynx, and there is then a variation in the width and shape of the opening of the glottis, and there is vibration of the outgoing air caused by contact with the walls of the glottis, the palate, tongue, teeth and lips.

But whether the vocal cords are vibrating or not, the column of air which has passed them can be affected in the speech-cavity in one of two ways. The first is by a stoppage of the air at some point in the cavity, with a vocal result, as soon as the outflow is resumed, which is known as a consonant – for example the consonant [t]; the second is by altering the size and shape of the cavity and the oral orifice, and thereby producing one of a number of vowels while this position of the organs continues. For example, in producing the high vowel [i:], as in 'feet', the buccal cavity is reduced to a narrow space between the roof of the mouth and the tongue, which is held against it in a shape allowing a channel down the middle for the passage of the air.

The first of these types of interference with the air shades into the second, and we can think of the two as forming a continuous line or series. At one end is the sound made when the interference is at the minimum: the mouth is opened from the closed position by dropping the lower jaw, but the tongue remains at rest, the vocal cords do or do not vibrate, and there is little obstruction to the column of air passing out at the mouth. The short vowel-sound thus produced is one of the 'middle' group of vowels – either the 'neutral' vowel [ə] (as the English a in *above*) or the vowel [ʌ] (as the S.E. English u in *hut*) or the vowel [a] (as the French a in *la*), or the vowel [ɑ] (as in the English *far*). It requires the finest and most delicate adjustment of the mouth and tongue to distinguish between the four, and I shall use the sign A to indicate any vowel of this group. At the other end of the series are the sounds made when the interference with the outgoing column of air is at its maximum – that is to say, when there is a complete stoppage, and, as the stop is taken off and the breath released, the 'plosive' consonants are sounded. These are chiefly p and b, t and d, k and g, and the corresponding three nasals (or, as I propose to call them, 'nasal plosives') m, n and ng [ŋ]. The bulk of the other vowels and consonants are brought about by the partial stoppage of the outgoing breath, or the narrowing of the oral cavity, in varying degree and at different places.

First, then, the stops or plosives. They are effected, in the main, in three areas of the oral cavity. One is in the labial region, and the stoppage is effected by closing the lips – and thereby forming (as the breath is again released) the voiced labial b when the chords vibrate, and the unvoiced labial p when they do not. The second is in the dental (or alveolar) region, where the stoppage is effected between tongue and hard palate at or near the front teeth, thereby forming the voiced dental (or alveolar) d and the unvoiced t. The third is in the region of the veil of the soft palate, where the closure is made between it and the upper surface of the tongue, forming the voiced velar consonant g and the unvoiced k. In addition to these three stoppages, the veil of the soft palate may be lowered, allowing the air from the pharynx to pass behind it and out through the nostrils, with the result that the voiced plosives become nasal plosives – b becoming m, and d becoming n, and g becoming ng [ŋ].

Next comes the partial stoppages, also known as the fricatives. In these cases the stoppages are not complete: the two organs come close together and are held close together, but do not quite meet, and the friction is heard of the column of air passing between. Thus the voiced labial b becomes v, and the unvoiced p becomes f;[1] the dental d becomes [ð] and [z] and [ʒ], and t becomes [θ] and s and sh; and the velar k becomes [x] (as Scottish ch in *loch*) and English h. Intermediate

---

[1] Though in English v and f are not bi-labials, but are formed between the upper front teeth and lower lip.

between the two groups are the liquid (or lateral) l, and the liquid (or fricative) r.

Next come sounds which are half consonant and half vowel – w (the vowel u becoming a semi-plosive consonant and semi-vowel) and y (as in *young*; the vowel [i] also becoming a semi-plosive consonant and semi-vowel). All other sounds in English are vowels.

Now let us approach the same point of junction between consonants and vowels from the opposite, the vowel, end.

There is first the group of middle vowels already mentioned, and symbolized as A, and we might also add the S.E. English [æ] (as in *hat*). All these, [ə], [ʌ], [ɑ], [a] and [æ], are distinguished from each other by fine and delicate adjustments in the oral cavity.

By somewhat wider adjustments of tongue and lips and lower jaw we arrive at two series of vowels, one of front vowels – so called because the tongue is forward and high – and the other of back vowels, in which it is lowered and retracted. The former series starts with [æ], and then comes [ɛ] (as in *bear*) then [e] (as in *bet*), and then short [i] (as in *bit*) and long [i:] (as in *beat*); and here we reach the semi-vowel y [j], already mentioned. In the back series we find [a], then [ɔ] (as in *hot*), [o] (as in *November*), [u] (as in hood) and here again we meet the semi-vowel w.

We may then set out the English consonants and vowels in the series shown on p. 192.[1]

But though there is this continuous physiological and acoustic series, including consonants and vowels, there are appreciable differences between the two groups. The distinction between one vowel and another is effected, as we said, by a much finer adjustment of the speech-organs than the distinction between consonants. This difference is often exemplified in the speech of two individuals, who, though they appear to pronounce their consonants alike, may be markedly unlike in their vowels. One may say 'nice' [nais] and the other 'naice' [neis]; one may say 'either' [aiðə] and the other "eether' [i:ðə]; and consequently, as dialects form, the first differences to be noticed are those between the vowels, though the consonants are generally pronounced alike. So there are many English dialects showing no appreciable difference in the pronunciation of the consonants and a wide variation in pronunciation of vowels. Looking further we see but an extension of the same process. So, in the history of English, the pronunciation

[1] See also Whitney, L. G. (1896), p. 62, and Prof. Daniel Jones, *An Outline of English Phonetics* (introduction).

of vowels has changed almost century by century, though the consonants show little alteration. And we may see languages formed by dialectic variation from one parent language, and note an extension of the same feature. So, for example, the Indo-European languages show changes in consonants which can be expressed in terms of rules, whereas the changes in the vowels are such that it is far more difficult to see any regular process.

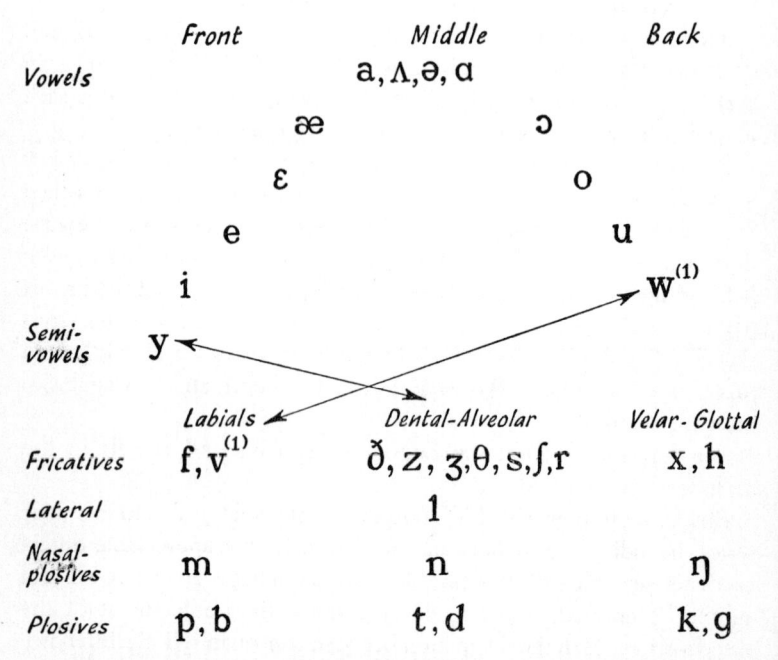

	Front	Middle	Back
Vowels		a, ʌ, ə, ɑ	
		æ ɔ	
		ɛ o	
	e		u
	i		w[1]
Semi-vowels	y		
	Labials	Dental-Alveolar	Velar-Glottal
Fricatives	f, v[1]	ð, z, ʒ, θ, s, ʃ, r	x, h
Lateral		l	
Nasal-plosives	m	n	ŋ
Plosives	p, b	t, d	k, g

[1] The semi-plosive w is a labial, like f and v, being formed with tongue low and back, but pursed lips; hence the back vowel u in the next stage becomes a front consonant, and the wheel turns full circle.

There is only one explanation that will fit so widespread a series of phenomena, namely the one already given – that precision in pronouncing a vowel is more difficult than in pronouncing a consonant, and that it has always been so, as far back as we can reach. Now it must always be remembered, in considering the phonetic aspect of language, that speech is a partnership between speaker and hearer. It is this partnership, existing for many millions of years before language emerged, that has evolved the correspondence between the range of frequencies of human conversation and the range audible to the human ear. What creates communication is not only the intention of the speaker but also, and more so, the sounds received by the hearer. Language demands a remarkable constancy in the sounds that it employs, and it is this that gives to words an appearance of an unchanging personality. It demands that its speech-sounds should be such as the speaker can repeat at will and the hearer can always recognize and imitate – not a *tour de force* which can be brought off with varying success. Accordingly if a certain sound is sufficiently difficult for the speech-community to produce and recognize, it will not appear in the language; or (which is the same thing) if it is uttered – for the variations of speech-sound are infinite – the language will not rely on it for purposes of communication.

We said that it was more difficult to achieve precision and constancy in vowels than in consonants. Now we can aver with confidence that man found all speech-sounds more and more difficult to achieve, the nearer we penetrate back to the beginnings of language. There was a time before men could speak, and the anthropoid apes and human babes cannot speak. The capacity to pronounce and distinguish with precision and constancy sounds previously unnecessary to utter or recognize for any purpose, can only have grown slowly and painfully over the long millennia, while nature selected and handed on, as a factor favourable to survival, a developing capacity of fine adjustment between one vocal organ and another, and a growing fineness of appreciation by ear. If, then, the vowels have always been more difficult to pronounce than the consonants, and if all speech sounds become more difficult to articulate, the nearer we penetrate to the beginnings of language, we approach a situation, as we penetrate back, in which language relied on the consonants for communication: a situation in which few speech sounds could be pronounced and distinguished with precision and constancy, and no vowels. And as vowels are necessary for speech, this path leads back to a point of origin in which there was one indistinct nondescript vowel and a small number of comparatively precise consonants. Startling as this may seem, it is one of the few fundamental facts in language. It is the primary fact in the phonetic history of speech, just as the regular diminution in the proportion of the verbs is the outstanding phenomenon in the history of the parts of speech, and the origin as a request for action is the crucial fact in the functional history of language.

This prominence of the consonants and concentration upon them has but slowly diminished. In the classical languages we still see it plainly. It survives to this day, almost as strongly as ever, in the most conservative of all languages – namely, the Semitic – in which each radical verb consists of three unvarying consonants, conjugated mainly by variation of the vowels but also by the addition of new consonants. If we are right in drawing this deduction from the Greek, it was originally so some thousands of years ago in the Indo-European languages; and it was certainly so in the Hamitic; and the Bantu tongues give evidence of the same situation at some time in the past. In some languages, like the Polynesian, where the consonants are decaying on all sides, we can see a faster movement in the same direction. But even in modern languages where the consonants are less important (for the vowel has developed many varieties of resonance and length) it is still the consonants rather than the vowels that give meaning. Vowels are too few, as compared with the consonants. We may, for example, easily recognize the beginning of Mark Antony's speech in the following passage from which the vowels have been removed:

   Frnds! Rmns! cntrmn! lnd m yr rs
   . cm t br Csr, nt t prs hm.
   Th vl tht mn d lvs ftr thm.

but not where the consonants are missing:

   ie oa ouye e e ou ea.
   I oe o uy aea o o aie i.
   e ei a e o ie ae e.

Accordingly what we are imagining at the beginnings of speech is merely that the vowels retained much the same relation to the consonants as now, so that there were, as now, far fewer articulate vowels than consonants, but there were fewer of both.

Which consonants, then, were they, and what vowel was it, that appeared in the language at the beginnings of speech? The answer must surely be: such articulate consonants and such vowel as could and can be pronounced without the aid of the physiological adaptations and capacities that have evolved for the purposes of speech.

When the mouth is closed and the organs of speech are at rest, the jaws are shut always in the same position in relation to one another, the lower jaw not unduly forward or back, and the tongue neither backward nor forward, low nor high, but at rest in the mouth. The lips touch one another; the tip and front upper part of the tongue is in touch with the hard palate and the back of the front teeth; and the back of the tongue lies in close proximity to the soft palate. The outflow of breath through the mouth is stopped, and any breathing is through the nose. The more so (if there was any difference) was it through the nose in primitive man, for he relied more on scent than do his descendants. The pressure of the breath is rather outwards than in, for the natural position of the lungs is to be relaxed and so to press out air; and especially when great physical effort is made, the movement of air to and from the lungs by the nose alone is insufficient. Accordingly, as we well know, in such circumstances, sooner or later, the mouth will be opened to release an outgoing column of air, which is always discharged with more or less of a spurt or gasp. As it is released, two sounds are usually made. First there is a plosive sound – the sound of a plosive consonant: as the lips break contact with one another, the front of the tongue breaks contact with the hard palate, and perhaps the back of the tongue with the soft palate. If the opening of the mouth is entirely without purpose of speech, it is a matter of chance, or at least uncertainty, whether the consonant will be heard as a labial, dental or palatal. It depends on which speech-organs break contact last, but it will be a plosive, with the precision of a plosive – that is to say, a release following a complete closure. There is no local continuity between the areas of the oral cavity where labial and dental consonants are produced, and no real continuity between dental and palatal. It must be one of the three groups of plosives. And it will be voiced or unvoiced according as the vocal chords are vibrating or not, and a nasal or simple plosive according as the outflow of breath is or is not accompanied by a lowering of the veil of the soft palate. As for the vowel, there will only be a slight, short vowel sound, but, such as it is, it will be a middle or neutral vowel, something between the a in *above*, or u in S.E. English *hut*, or short a in *far*, or a in French *la* – our vowel A. Here, then, we have a possible total of some nine plosive consonants, and only one short middle vowel, forming bă, pă or mă; dă, tă or nă; and (less often) gă, kă or ngă – and the most likely of all is dă. These are the simplest of sounds to produce, for none involve the aid of any adaptation for speech. These were the earliest speech-sounds.

The plosive consonants and the middle vowel are at the opposite ends of our continuous series of speech-sounds. The middle of the series consists of later refinements and combinations. The plosives are the most consonantal of the consonants. The rest are mainly fricatives.

They are more difficult to pronounce than the plosives, for the plosives may be articulated merely by breaking contact, whereas the fricatives require that two organs be placed close enough together to cause vibration of one or both organs and of the column of air passing between, but not too far apart to cause vibration, and not near enough to close the gap. They are effected by a long-developed adaptation for speech.

This unique position of the plosives, as the earliest and simplest of the consonants, is corroborated by considerations similar to those we adduced for the consonants generally. As the plosives are simpler to pronounce than other consonants, so there is less difference between one individual and another in their pronunciation. Between one dialect and another there is less variation. Different men and different dialects in England may pronounce an s as th, or z, or sh; th may be pronounced as v or a glottal stop; v may be pronounced as w, r as a liquid of various kinds or as a w (and in many languages it is not found, and in others it exchanges readily with l) and aspirates may be dropped. But throughout the history of English the pronunciation of the plosives has hardly varied; and among languages descending from a common parent-tongue, the plosives are the last to exhibit change.

If, for example, we look first at the Semitic languages – the slowest to change of all known tongues – we find that because they have altered so little they are still very close together. The plosives are constant between one Semitic language and another. The only shift in the consonants is, in effect, confined to one group of fricatives, namely the sibilants.

In the Indo-European tongues change has been more rapid, and between one language and another there are many shifts of the consonants. The phonetic correspondence (or *lautverschiebung*) between the languages has been studied in great detail for over a century. It is commonly known in England, after a linguist and man of genius, as Grimm's Law. He set out the changes in the consonants between one language and another: the changes in the vowels are more obscure. Whatever version of Grimm's Law one may examine, it is plain how much closer is the correspondence between the plosives than between the other consonants. A version, for example, contained in Rhys, *Lectures on Welsh Philology*, p. 17, tables the changes between 13 languages (Sanskrit, Zend, Greek, Latin, Oscan and Umbrian, Gothic, English, Modern High German, Lithuanian, Church Slavonic, Gaulish, Old Irish and Old Welsh). We can get a fair idea of the matter by counting, for each consonant, the number of languages in which it remains unchanged[1]:

N	is constant in	13 languages
M	" "	11½ "
Ng	" "	11 "
T	" "	10 "
D	" "	9½ "
Dh	" "	9 "
B	" "	9 "
S	" "	7½ "
P	" "	7 "
G	" "	6 "

It is noticeable that at the top of the table were the three nasals, then the other dental and labial plosives. There is really only one non-plosive, the sibilant S. R interchanges with L.

The Polynesian affords an example of a family of languages undergoing yet more rapid change, but still showing correspondences of the consonants between tongues descended from a common parent. A table of the changes of consonants between 10 Polynesian languages[2] shows the following figures:

E. and I. D Andrews (modified from Tregar)				Hale[3]
M	is constant in	10	languages	8
N	"	10	"	8
P (or B)	"	10	"	8
T (or D)	"	9	"	7½
V	"	8	"	6
Ng (or nasalized G)	"	8	"	5½
K (or G)	"	7	"	5

Here, again, highest in the table come the nasals, then the other labial and dental plosives. There is only one non-plosive in the list, namely V. R interchanges with L.

The languages of Africa present in some respects a somewhat different picture. Here the shift of consonants between one language

[1] Allowing half a point where the particular consonant occurs as well as another.
[2] In E. and I. D. Andrews', *A Comparative Dictionary of the Tahitian Language* (Chicago, 1944), p. xv. The 10 languages are Tahitian, Maori, Hawaian, Samoan, Tuaumotu, Tongan, Marquesan, Manga Reva, Rarotongan, Easter Island.
[3] Cited in L. Andrews, *A Dictionary of the Hawaiian Language* (1865), p. xiv. This is a table of 8 languages: Fakaafo, Samoan, Tongan, Maori, Rarotongan, Tahitian, Hawaian, Marquesan.

and another may be violent though regular. For example, n often corresponds with d; d and t regularly correspond with l and r[1]; and l often turns to n, as well as initial t to k, and p to t. Yet a similar comparison produces similar results. For example, an old table by Bleek[2] of the correspondences in 7 Bantu languages shows:

M is constant in 7 languages
N " " 7 "
Ng " " 6 "
K " " 5 "
T " " $4\frac{1}{2}$ "
F " " $4\frac{1}{2}$ "
P " " $3\frac{1}{2}$ "
ND " " 3 "
S " " 3 "
Z " " $2\frac{1}{2}$ "

Again, then, the nasals head the list, followed by the other plosives and, lastly, the fricatives. R interchanges with L.

These examples must suffice. It will be seen that in all these cases the nasals head the list; next come the other plosives and lastly the fricatives. So much for the consonants.

If we now turn to the vowels, we see, in brief, that in all the above families of languages the vowel A is almost as unchanging as the nasals. It is constant as the vowel of the Semitic roots. It is almost constant in the Indo-European languages[3] and generally in Polynesian and Bantu.[4] The rest of the vowels fall far behind. The nearest are the semi-vowels u(w) and i(y): the other vowels undergo unlimited change.

All these considerations, therefore, support the view, expressed above, that the simplest and also the earliest speech-sounds are the plosive consonants and the vowel A. But there are further considerations that support the same conclusion. These speech-sounds (as has often been suggested in this book) represented the release of a stoppage, and a short outward spurt or gasp of breath. The vowel, therefore, was a short vowel. Now, it is important to notice how much simpler it was and is to pronounce with precision a short, rather than

---

[1] Compare the instances given above, p. 183. See also e.g. Johnston, vol. ii, chap. viii; Homburger, pp. 48-72.
[2] Cited, Sayce, vol. 1, p. 327. The 7 languages are 'Kafir', Setshuana, Herero, Kisuahili, Kinika, Mpongwe and Bunda.
[3] See, e.g. the version of Grimm's Law in Sayce, vol. 1, p. 305.
[4] See Johnston, vol. ii, p. 221.

a long, vowel. To sustain with accuracy an unchanging resonance requires considerable adaptation of the organs for speech. We see this in the whole history of speech sounds. First it is to be noted that a vowel cannot usually be lengthened at all without change of quality and resonance. The vowel [a], for example, (as in French *la*) changes its quality when lengthened, and becomes [ɑ:]. The vowel [i:] (as in *beat*) is not merely a lengthening of [i] (as in *bit*). The lengthening of the vowel [u] (as in *put*) produces the quite different vowel [u:] (as in *rule*). The results are plainly to be seen in the history of English. The long vowels have been transformed during the centuries, while the short vowels have remained practically constant. So the short [a] [ɑ] and [æ] in English have hardly changed, while the long 'a' of M.E. is generally no longer [a:] (as in *father*) but [ɛ:] (as in *cake*). Similarly the short 'i' is practically unchanged, while the long 'i' is no longer [i:] (as in *cheese*) but [ay] (as in *kite*). So, the short 'e' remains the same (as in *bet*), but the long 'e' is no longer [ɛ:] (as in *bear*) but [i:] (as in *cheese*). So, too, with 'o' (*cot* and *cote* [kout]) and even with 'u' (*cut* and *cute* [kiu:t]). This shows us that when the first step forward was taken in the development of the vowels, and the nondescript vowel A became differentiated into a number of separate vowels, they must still have been short vowels. Long vowels would still be impossible to pronounce precisely enough to add new speech-sounds to the language.

There is another important consideration that firmly corroborates our view that the plosives, and particularly the nasals, were the simplest and earliest of consonants, and have changed the least in the history of language. One of the most remarkable of the phenomena listed in this book is that in practically all known languages of the past and present the consonant M, or N, or (somewhat less commonly) NG, has always signified the personal pronoun of the first person singular. We came to the conclusion[1] that the only explanation to fit the facts was that M signified this pronoun at the time when its meaning first appeared in the language of man. That the same speech-sound should have retained the same meaning throughout man's history from that early time, demands at least two requisites. First, the meaning must be unique and unchanging; for otherwise the same speech-sound would acquire a different meaning, or rather a number of different meanings, varying from language to language. And it is easy to see that to any speaker his person is unique. The second requisite is that the speech-sound must be unchanging: and we have indeed concluded

[1] *Supra*, chap. 7.

in this chapter that of all speech-sounds the nasals have changed the least, and that this was because they are and were the simplest to pronounce.

This phenomenon reminds us of another kindred fact of lesser importance but equally instructive. In a large number of the world's languages the consonant M or N or (less often) NG signifies the negative. This is so, for example, in our Indo-European languages (Greek mē, Latin ne and non, English ne), and in Sumerian (where the usual negative is nu). It is also found in many Semitic uses (later Northern Arabic ma, Abyssinian -m; and also Hebrew and Abyssinian 'en, Arabic 'in). It is common also in the Sudanic languages of Africa –for example Nandi and Suk (me), Masai (m – mi before m and k), Ewe (me). It is not found in Bantu though it is found in Semi-Bantu (n or m) and in many other languages. This phenomenon is less common than that in relation to the first person pronoun, because the meaning is not unique; but it is widespread because the nasal plosives are so resistant to change.

There is another series of phenomena that firmly corroborate the conclusions expressed in this chapter, but they are so important that they must be considered separately and in some detail.

CHAPTER SIXTEEN

The Earliest Words of Children

The conclusions arrived at in previous chapters as to the forms of the earliest words of man are strongly corroborated and confirmed by the data relating to the speech of infants.

Children's speech has now been closely studied for over fifty years by many skilled and learned observers, and much material has been collected. Its relevance to a study of the origins of language is a matter on which few have ventured to express an opinion. It is obvious that some aspects of the speech of infants have no significance for our present enquiry. Above all we can be confident that the meanings of children's earliest words are not the meanings of the earliest words of man. The meanings of words are derived from their uses, and the speech-sounds of infants are used by them – or, more accurately, used by their parents – for quite different purposes from those for which adult man can be supposed to have spoken in the past. But the matter stands quite otherwise when we turn from meanings to the forms of words. The forms of the first speech-sounds depend wholly on physiological facts, and we who are familiar with the biological doctrine that the history of man is largely repeated in the development of foetus and child, might reasonably expect to find that the first speech-sounds of children are the first speech-sounds of man. Children – like primitive man – are born wholly without the power of speech, and they must learn by degrees to co-ordinate and adjust the vocal organs for the production of speech and language.

The earliest speech-sounds of children are inarticulate cries. By this I mean that either they contain no consonants, or their consonants are obscure and cannot be repeated without great difficulty.

At the very outset there are substantially no consonants, and the cries are therefore vowel-sounds of a sort. Throughout the first year the vowel A predominates. I calculate the following percentages of the vowels from data recorded by a considerable number of observers of the spontaneous utterances of infants:

A – 64%. Of these, the overwhelming majority are apparently [a], but some are [ɑ], and only a very small proportion (about 3%) are recorded as [æ].
E – 17%, including [e] about 6%, [ɛ] 8% and [ə] 3%.
O – 8%.
U – 6%.
I – 2%.

These figures, however, cannot pretend to any accuracy. Most observers use no phonetic notation, but the above table gives a fair picture of the facts.

As regards consonants, during the first 6 months of life these are largely inarticulate when they do appear. They are mainly back-consonants. They include [x] and r, but also m, n, ng, g and l. They also include a number of consonantal sounds that can with difficulty be recorded even by a phonetician, and cannot be repeated by the infant or anyone else.

Between the 3rd and 9th month the first articulate word is usually pronounced by the infant – dă, mă, nă, bă, gă or wă. The first articulate word of my daughter J. was dă at 0; 5, 17, and the first articulate word of my daughter S. was dă. The first articulate word of Charles Darwin's boy was dă at the age of $5\frac{1}{2}$ months.[1] None of these 'words' bore any meaning.

In the second 6 months of life (which is the period of the rise of imitation) the consonants – whether uttered spontaneously or in direct imitation of adult speech – become overwhelmingly plosives: – p, b, m, n, d, t, g, k and also h; and s occasionally appears. The guttural sounds form now a much smaller proportion of the whole, and the consonants are now to a large degree articulate. At the same time there appears towards the end of the year (as we have seen in earlier chapters) one or two instances of vague meanings being attached to these sounds, other than the meaning of mere bodily comfort or discomfort. There is evidence enough to satisfy the bulk of observers that in a state of discomfort and strain the vowels and consonants of the infant are more nasal than those uttered in comfort.

In the overwhelming majority of cases (say 90%) the 'words' begin with a consonant, and only in about 10% with a vowel. In the vast majority of cases they end in a vowel. They are practically all either monosyllables or reduplications; that is to say, they are either of the

[1] *Mind*, 7 (July 1877); and see Sayce, vol. 2, p. 313.

type dă, mă, bă, or dădă, mămă, băbă, but a good many are of the type mǎm or mămăm. This is the state of affairs at the beginning of the second year, and the average child then possesses about 5 of such meaningful words. But there is great variety between one child and another. Of the words of infants at or about the end of the first year, recorded by many observers, I estimate that approximately 47% are of the form CVCV, 10% CVC and 22% CV – that is to say that these three types are 79% of the whole – and about 8% are of the form VCV. Words including two successive consonants are practically unknown.[1] In the words of types CVCV and CVC the two consonants of a word, as we have said, are nearly always the same. This is of course to be expected. If the position or 'set' of the vocal organs remains the same, it is not difficult to repeat the sound; but to change the 'set' of the organs at the present stage in the course of a word would involve an adjustment far more rapid than any child could achieve. Indeed, reduplication is hardly more difficult than a single utterance – and there is no particular reason why a child should stop there. In fact, infants repeat their new-found words again and again, and enjoy their triumph.

The data are still of the same general character at and around the age of 1; 6, which appears from the psychological development of children and chimpanzees and the linguistic data of children to be the mental age at which man first began to speak. The great difficulty experienced by children in their second year, in changing the set of the vocal organs and pronouncing a word of two different consonants, is best shown by their failure even to reproduce such words when they continually hear them. There are innumerable instances of such cases in the books – for example, tătă for café and tasse (Deville's daughter); didda for tic-tac (Stern and also Sander); gogi for doggie; baba for vater: faffaf and awa for wasser; go-go for Gordon (C. W. Valentine's boy B); Rasmussen's mama for mad (Danish = food); papô for drapeau and tatò for gâteau (Deville's daughter); goga for chocolate and fa for flower (M. M. Lewis' boy K); ba for blanc. To a lesser degree there is an objection to ending a word with a consonant – so Hilde Stern's fu for fuss, Deville's daughter's ta for Charles (French): didda for tic-tac; see [si:] for sleep; and other examples given above. All these instances are taken from the speech of children within a few weeks before and after the age of 1; 6.

The difficulty of children about this age in pronouncing fricatives

[1] But Hilde Stern is said to have pronounced her own name (Hildĕ) accurately at 0; 11.

is of some significance. Dr C. W. Valentine conducted two interesting experiments with his boy B. The first was at 1; 4½.[1]

Sound pronounced by C. W. V.   *B's imitation*

bow	baa
cow	gĕ
dow	dŭ (between dĕ and dow)
fow	(refused: later shook head)
gow	ge
how	(breathed roughly – almost h sound)
jow	ge
low	(no success)
mow	m (with lips closed)
now	awă
ow	(no response)
pow	ba
quow	? (some attempt)
wow	wow: wa
vow	bow-we (or vow-we? No reply at first till C. W. V. held out yellow pencil as reward)

No attempt, therefore, was made by the child at f or l, and j was pronounced as a plosive. No attempt was made at ow (the one word beginning with a vowel). The vowel sound 'ow' gave some difficulty in all cases, and produced an assortment of vowels, but all short except in one case (baa) and all middle vowels.

The second experiment was at 1; 9½.[2]

C. W. V.	B.	C. W. V.	B.
bow	bow	now	dĕ
cow	că	pow	bāā
dow	dă	qow	ga
fow	ŏ	row	oa(r)
gow	gār	sow	oa(r)
how	ŏ	tow	toa(r)
jow	oŭ	vow	ŏ
kow	kă	wow	ŏ
low	oa(r)	xow	ŏ
mow	mă(w)	zow	ŏ

[1] Valentine, p. 390.   [2] Valentine, p. 404.

This result is even clearer than in the former experiment. There is a complete failure to reproduce any consonants except the plosives – that is to say, to reproduce f, h, j, l, r, s, v, x or z. The attempt to reproduce the diphthong 'ow' has hardly progressed. The results are practically all short vowels, with a tendency to substitute the short ă.

These characters of children's earliest speech – namely the initial nasal or other plosive consonant followed by the vowel A and commonly reduplicated – are not confined to Europe or the modern world. This has been the earliest speech of children in all lands and all millennia, wherever we can penetrate. There is nothing in language better authenticated. Jespersen puts the matter well.[1] 'In the nurseries of all countries,' he says, 'a little comedy has in all ages been played – the baby lies and babbles his "mamama" or "amama" or "papapa" or "apapa" or "bababa" or "ababab"[2] without associating the slightest meaning with his mouth-games, and his grown-up friends, in their joy over the precious child, assign to these syllables a rational sense, accustomed as they are themselves to the fact of an uttered sound having a content, a thought, an idea, corresponding to it. So we get a whole class of words, distinguished by a simplicity of sound-formation – never two consonants together, generally the same consonant repeated with an *a* between, frequently also with an *a* at the end – words found in many languages, often in different forms, but with essentially the same meaning.'

These earliest speech-sounds of children, 'papa' and 'mama' and the rest, originating in this way, become the recognized words of adults in the world's languages of the present and the past, all signifying persons and things in the entourage of the child. It would be an easy display of learning to cite hundreds or even thousands of examples.[3]

Accordingly, first and foremost, they are the words for 'father' and 'mother'. For example, the latter two English words (like the Greek păter, mēter; Latin păter, māter; Sanskrit pita (pitri), mâta; O.H.G. fater, muotar; M.H.G. vater, mutter, were in Common Indo-European păter* and māter*; and these words were but the child's *pa* and *ma*, furnished with a familiar Indo-European noun-actor ending

---

[1] Jespersen, pp. 154-5.
[2] Jespersen, however, fails to do justice to the predominance of the forms ma, mama, da, dada, etc. They are as predominant in children's speech as in the world's languages. Such a form, for example, as 'ababab' is rare indeed in the nursery and elsewhere.
[3] See for a number of examples, skilfully arranged, Jespersen, op. cit., pp. 155-8.

(-ter), which turned them into nouns of familiar and declinable form.[1] But such a formal addition to the child's words is unusual: most languages have little or nothing of case-endings and adopt the words without alteration. In the overwhelming majority of languages (as in the speech of the great majority of individual children) these words begin with the consonant; but in a small minority of languages we find the reverse. This is so, for example, in the Sumerian[2] and Semitic[3] tongues, in the languages of some Bushman tribes,[4] and elsewhere.[5] With the vast majority of individual children the nasal consonant m or n signifies the mother, and the non-nasal plosive (p or b, t or d, and occasionally k or g) the father. We have already seen the explanation: the nasal appears in the straining cry of hunger and discomfort, when the teeth and perhaps the lips are closed, and the veil of the soft palate is lowered. It is the mother who fulfils the wants of the child in its distress, and hence the call *ma* is taken to refer to her, and later does refer to her. The child calls contentedly to his father in play, but should he cry he is handed over willingly or unwillingly to the mother. But a small minority of individual children use *mama* for the father, and *baba* for the mother; and similarly in a small minority of languages (chiefly in North America[6] and the South Seas,[7] but also elsewhere)[8] we find the same phenomenon, The semi-vowels are also in use for the same purpose.[9] Words of similar forms also indicate other family relationships,[10] and other persons and things in the entourage of the

[1] The difference between the two words in the length and character of the first vowel is created by the difference between the two consonants *p* and *m*. So, English *daddy* and *mummy*; and Sumerian and Semitic examples, below.
[2] Sumerian: abba, ama and umma.
[3] Assyrian abu, ummu; Hebrew 'ab, 'ēm.
[4] I take the following examples from the languages of a number of South (S), Central (C) and Northern (N) Bushman tribes (see D. F. Bleek, *Comparative Vocabularies of Bushman Languages*). *Father*: – S.1: ibo, bobo, tata. S.3: ba, ba. S.6: tata. N.1, N.2, N.3: -ba. N.3: -pa. C.2: aba. H: dadab. *Mother*: – S.1, S.6, H: Mama. C.1: mæ. *Father's mother*: – N.1: mama. C.1: mæ. C.2: mamasa. *Elder brother*: – C.1: tata.
[5] E.g. Indo-European; so from *aba*, Latin *avus* (grandfather), diminutive *avunculus*, English *uncle*; O.N. afi; Gothic avo, grandmother. From *ama*, Albanian ama=mother; Latin *amita*, English *aunt*. So *Ama*, the mother goddess of the Jukun of Nigeria, etc.
[6] E.g. Chinook: māma, father; qacqac, grandfather; tata, uncle. Zuni: nána, grandfather, grandchild; pāpa, elder brother; kuku, aunt; käkä, uncle; tātcu, father; tsita, mother: wowo, paternal grandmother.
[7] Mama=father in several Melanesian languages (such as Mota), and also in Indonesian. Maori: kōkā, mother.
[8] E.g. Slavonic baba, mother (also grandmother, old woman, etc.); tata, father. Buluba Lulua: baba, mother; also mamu, mother; tatu, father; kaku, grandparent. But baba generally means father, as e.g. in Turkish, Bulgarian, etc. In Hausa bāba means paternal aunt'.
[9] E.g. Zuni: wowo=paternal grandmother. Masai: papa, father; yeyo, mother. Kongo: tata, father; yaya, mother.
[10] See the examples given in previous footnotes, and also e.g. Greek pappos, grandfather; nennos, uncle: nanna, aunt.

child.[1] They do not name persons outside the child's circle – never, for example, 'husband' and 'wife'. But from these beginnings the meanings often travel far. So from *nonna*, grandmother, comes the English *nun*; and from *papa* comes French *pape* and English *pope*. From the Aramaic abba, father, comes the Greek abbas, and English abbot and abbey. Innumerable other words (like English *uncle*) have changed form and meaning beyond recognition. In the languages of modern peoples the same words often begin life afresh as the language of children, and live side by side with the old, now adult forms,[2] and they may themselves be accepted into the dictionary with a new form and meaning. Sometimes there is an intimate, midway meaning.[3]

These, then, are the forms of the speech-sounds at the beginnings of children's speech, and these were their forms in all lands and all ages, as far back as we can reach. And because the forms of speech are shaped by physiological facts, these are the forms we would expect to find at the beginnings of the speech of man. These, too, are the original forms which we inferred in the last chapter, assuming, as we did, that speech originated when man's vocal organs had scarcely been adapted for speech, and these, too, were the original forms which we inferred from the relations between vowels and consonants. These also are the chief forms of the radical words or roots which we found everywhere in language – CV, CVC or CVCV, the vowel being predominantly A, no two consonants together, and most words ending in a vowel. In these roots, however, the number of consonants had by now increased, and words contained more than one consonant; and we could not usually tell from their forms whether the consonants had originally been plosives. But looking back we now see how likely this was, for in these roots there are, as we said, rarely two successive consonants. Now it is a characteristic of plosive consonants that generally two successive plosives cannot be pronounced, at least at the beginning of a word or syllable. If, therefore, language originated with plosives, the roots, though they came to include consonants other than

---

[1] E.g. nana and nanny, nurse. See also Latin mamma=the nipple of the breast, and the corresponding English pap, teat and tit. Pap also=milky or watery food. See also pupa, poupée and puppet (doll); pupil and puppy. Also Greek nanos, Latin nanus, dwarf; and English ninny. And we must not forget the infant himself, bébé and babe.
[2] So in English, beside father and mother, are papa and mamma; and daddy and mummy. In Greek beside pắter and mắter, are pappas (vocative pappa, Hom. Od. 6, 57) and mamma or mammē. In Azande, buba (father) is only used by children; ba is very widespread in adult language, for example, as an honorific title or token of politeness. Mother is na, and nina=Eng. mamma. In Lango, 'baba' is 'father' in baby language.
[3] E.g. Bari: baba, my father; mama, my mother.

plosives, were merely retaining their original character in rejecting successive consonants.

It is not only the speech of children that supports our previous conclusions: we may go further back and see an approach to these phonetic forms in the recorded vocal sounds of chimpanzees, the nearest ape to man or at least the noisiest among the nearest apes to man. Yerkes, and Learned[1] made a list of 32 'words or elements of speech' used by one or other of the two apes which they studied. These sounds can barely be called articulate yet. The labials and dentals are missing. Gutturals still abound, as they do among human children during the first 9 months or so of life; and little meaning can be given to these noises. But here they are:

Commencing with the guttural g: gak, gahk, gah, gha, ghak, gho, ghoo, ga-ha.
Commencing with unvoiced guttural k: kah-kah, ko-ko, ku-ku.
Commencing with voiced k: ka-ka, ky-ah, kuoh, kah-hah, ka-ha-ha, kuh-huh, kha.
Commencing with h: ho-oh, hu-wha, whah, who-ah, hüh.
Commencing with labials and nasals: ngak, nghak, nkak, m.
Commencing with vowels: ah-oh-ah, ai, ae, ooh, ue.

We cannot say that man's predecessors made similar sounds. But it is significant that out of a total of 48 vowel-sounds here, no less than 26 are *a*, and a further 8 are *o*. Practically all these sounds begin with a consonant. There are practically no successive consonants, and there is a substantial number of reduplications.

But though the speech-sounds of children, described in this chapter, go back to the beginnings of language, as far as we can penetrate,[2] it is plain that their meanings do not go back to those beginnings. The meanings are not given by the children, but by the doting adults, and they are given by adults who are already so familiar with the phenomena of speech and meaning, that they attribute an objective significance to each of these noises – a reference to surrounding persons and objects. The consideration, then, of physiological facts has so far confirmed only our conclusions as to the original forms of words. Does it also confirm our views as to the original meanings of words? It is submitted that it does so powerfully, as we shall see in the following chapter.

[1] Yerkes and Learned, pp. 154-6.
[2] They go back to a period long before the introduction of the personal pronouns, which do not appear in children till about the age 2; 6 (see references in Tracy and Stimpfl, *The Psychology of Childhood*, 7th ed., 1909, p. 140; Valentine, p. 412).

CHAPTER SEVENTEEN

The Larynx

There is yet another aspect of the physiology of speech that we must take into account if we would give full weight to all the evidence of the origins of language. The survey of evidence that has been attempted in this book stresses the importance, in the rise of language, of the part played by the forceful use of the arms. The chief of the organs used in the production of speech is the larynx, and it remains to consider the important matter of the physiological relation between the use of the larynx and the forceful use of the arms.

Though crucial in the production of speech, the larynx did not evolve for the purposes of speech. It evolved long before and for other purposes, but was in the last resort made use of for speech also. The larynx has now been well studied, and particularly in the classic work of Sir Victor Negus, *The Mechanism of the Larynx*.[1]

The larynx first appeared in the animal kingdom when the lung evolved, making it possible to breathe air. At that stage a method became requisite for excluding all but air from the pulmonary air tract, and keeping it open as required for respiration. The larynx then evolved, at the upper end of the pulmonary air tract, for this purpose of excluding all but air (and particularly water and food) and protecting the passage for respiration. The purpose was effected at first by the creation of a sphincteric band of muscle around the glottis, which closed that opening as necessary, in the manner that a string closes the mouth of a bag.

This was the early form of the larynx, and all animals possessing a larynx can use such sphincteric action to a greater or less degree. But in the more advanced of the animals – in rats, dogs, bears, monkeys, anthropoid apes and man – the larynx evolves further as an inlet valve, which prevents the entry, at first of water, and then of air. The pre-

---

[1] (1929). Republished in abbreviated form as *Comparative Anatomy and Physiology of the Larynx* (1949).

vention of the entry of water was for the purpose of protecting the air tract. The inlet valve able to prevent the entry of air was evolved, as Sir Victor Negus shows, for quite a different purpose – not for speech but for the effective, independent use of the fore-limbs (or arms) 'for purposes other than locomotion, and particularly for grasping, climbing, hugging and striking with the fore-limbs'[1]; and this form of the larynx is found in almost all animals capable of independent use of the fore-limbs. The reasons were as follows, and we are considering particularly the arboreal monkeys and apes, among whom this organ is at its most perfect.

Such an animal jumps, for example, from tree to tree, catching hold of the branch, and supporting its body by its arms. Now the arms are fastened to the animal's trunk, and obtain their power and purchase, by a number of muscles, and particularly the pectoralis major, by which the arms are attached to the front of the body, and the latissimus dorsi, by which they are attached to the back. The latter muscle originates largely from the backbone, which serves as a firm and immobile point of origin, so that when the pectoral muscles contract there is a strong force tending to pull down the arm and thereby suspend the weight of the body as it hangs from the branch. But the pectoralis major runs mainly from the lower ribs to the humerus, and the ribs are mobile and rise with the intake of breath – and especially in man, whose breathing is less abdominal than among his predecessors and higher in the thorax. Accordingly, if the ribs are to form a firm base from which to contract the muscle, there must be some means to fix them. Such a purpose might have been served by more powerful abdominal muscles, with the expenditure of great muscular energy and some process of adjustment. In their absence, and with great economy of effort, the same end is attained by a temporary closure of the glottis and the prevention of entry of air. By this means, when the pectoral muscle contracts and tends to pull the lower ribs towards the humerus, the rise of the ribs by intake of breath is counteracted, and the stretch of the muscle is not shortened nor its force of contraction weakened. The exclusion of air is the purpose served by the valvular larynx. It is in the arboreal animals – monkeys, lemurs, gibbons and chimpanzees – that the inlet-valve larynx is at its most effective. In the more terrestrial animals, who have abandoned life in the trees, and do not demand such power from the arms, and whose arms have progressively shortened –

[1] Negus, p. 239.

the baboons, gorillas and man – this inlet-valve has somewhat degenerated. In man, for example, this valve – that is to say, the inferior thyro-arytenoid fold, or vocal cords – is somewhat less efficient, for the vocal cords are not so sharp-edged as in the lemurs and chimpanzees, and therefore not so effectively fashioned for excluding air.

But while the inlet-valve larynx resists the entry of air, it is easily opened by an outgoing column of air by way of the trachea, for the natural movement of the lung is to contract when relaxed and create such a column; but there is in apes and man a means of preventing this exit of air and raising in some measure the pressure within the thorax and abdomen, and further steadying the wall. The first end is served during arm-effort in the higher apes and man by the free ventricular bands (the superior thyro-arytenoid folds) which can come into apposition with one another to prevent the exit of air,[1] and in addition there is a certain effort at expiration, which compresses the retained air, steadies the thoracic wall and raises the abdominal pressure.

Now the arboreal animals, among whom the larynx of the inlet-valve type is at its most efficient, have also another outstanding characteristic. They are extremely vocal, and perhaps the most vocal of animals, for they have the greatest need of vocal sound for communication, living as they do among the leaves and branches. It follows from the physiological facts that have been mentioned, that vocal sounds must necessarily be greatly affected by the forceful effort of the arms and the accompanying closure of the glottis. Vocal sound must temporarily cease during such effort; but this is less important to our study. Silence will never produce speech. More important is what follows the effort. Vocal sounds, as we have seen, are almost always made by an outgoing, not incoming, column of air, and the temporary stoppage will be followed by a greater or lesser gasp of released breath as the tense cords are suddenly relaxed; and the greater the preceding effort the greater the need for a change of air. There is some difference of opinion between those who have written on this subject as to whether, as a rule, the lungs during such efforts are distended. Darwin, for example, was of that opinion. Negus thinks that the lungs are usually not full but partially empty. But however that may be, there would seem to be little doubt that, even if the lungs are partially empty, there is, during the forceful use of the arms, a certain effort at

[1] Negus, p. 263. He says, however, that they do not actually close in the majority of individuals, p. 264.

expiration and a raising of internal pressure; and when the cords are relaxed and the glottis opened, this cannot but add to the gasp of outgoing breath.

By and large, the same situation continues in man. The purposes of hugging and climbing have largely gone, but there remains the same closure of the glottis during forcible striking of the arms, and the more forcible the effort of the arms, the firmer is the closure. It is said, for example, that workmen, who have lost their larynx, are deprived of the ability to earn their living by manual labour. Nor is the closure of the glottis confined to cases of violent effort: during any difficult action which requires precise movement the breathing stops and the lips are generally closed, so as to produce a steadier hand and more accurate action of the arm. Darwin pointed this out in regard to man and the orang-utan. In woman there is said to be far less closure of the glottis during effort of the arm. Negus says it is exceptional; and it is clear that woman makes less violent muscular effort as a rule, and her arms are weaker. It is not surprising to find here further evidence that language arose with the male.

This outward gasp of breath upon release of the closure of the glottis may be by way of the mouth, or mouth and nostrils. It is suggested that expiration through the mouth has slowly and steadily increased throughout man's story. One prominent feature of his evolution has been an age-long development in the use of the mouth for breathing. In man's pre-arboreal ancestors the sense of smell was vastly more important than it is now, and sight far weaker. Those small terrestrial mammals, moving in the grass and undergrowth, could make no effective use of sight at any distance; but smell was vital for every purpose. And so as not to interfere with the scent of the ingoing colums of air, coming through the nostrils and along the naso-pharynx, it was important that the epiglottis (whose original function this was) should join with the soft palate in shutting off that column of air from the inlet through the mouth (except during the act of swallowing food and drink). But when man's ancestors took to the trees, and (as we saw) the sense of smell began to deteriorate and sight to improve, the epiglottis degenerated and became separated from the soft palate, and thereby allowed of buccal speech (that is to say, speech by a column of air going out through the mouth, affected by the shape and size of the oral cavity). Probably it was not till language first appeared that these conditions, conducive to speech, had been fully realized (for in the apes the junction between epiglottis and soft palate is still possible).

And so when speech first emerged, in all probability the laryngeal sounds were more nasal than now, as they are among babes than adults.

There was a further important difference – namely in the quality of the voice. When man's ancestors dwelt in the trees, and the vocal cords were sharp-edged and the closure of the glottis fierce and powerful, the tones of the voice were harsh and shrill. The trachea was also wider than it is now, and the voice was louder. As ape and man evolved and became more terrestrial, the trachea became narrower and the power of violent effort diminished. The vocal cords somewhat deteriorated and became more round-edged and fleshy and more capable of quick adjustment, and the tones of the voice more mellow and soft and variable. The laryngeal sounds escaping after violent effort of the arms became less harsh and loud.

If to these facts we add those that were mentioned in earlier chapters, when we considered the behaviour of apes and other animals, we see how inevitable was this accident of the production of speech. It is easy to imagine a modern European, in the course of his employment, dealing a steady series of heavy blows with a sledge-hammer or pickaxe, and silent before, during and after each effort – at any rate unless he taxes his strength to the uttermost, or begins to tire. It is not with such men, capable of such detachment of body and mind, that we are here concerned. Man at the beginning of speech was probably of a mental age of about $1\frac{1}{2}$ to 2 years. His excitements, movements and vocalizations were more of a unity, his moods spontaneous, superficial, uninhibited, changeable and extreme. He was perhaps more vocal than now, and certainly his voice was louder and harsher. He did not coo in the tones of a modern babe. If he made so intense an effort of the arm, it was in a mood of equally intense excitement, and he expressed his excitement by equally intense and loud cries. He was loudly vocal before the blow; as likely as not his lips and teeth as well as his glottis were tightly closed in the effort, and the following out-gasp or grunt was loud and excited, triumphant or despairing, and unmistakably different in sound, as well as in gesture, from the rest of his cries. According as his lips had been closed or not, and according to the tension and position of his tongue, as the closure was released the gasp was a bă, pă or mă, dă, tă, or nă, or kă, gă or ngă – always the same nondescript middle vowel and plosive consonant. Accordingly when, in the same mood of noisy and intense excitement, his fellow appealed for such an act, he mimicked by his gesture the act that he called for and this sound that usually accompanied it; for it was a sound that came to his mind with the thought of the act, and a sound that he himself was prone to produce as his own glottis closed in the effort of the gesture. Then, as man gained a growing control over his speech organs, and these gasps or grunts became more articulate (that is to say, the various plosive consonants grew more distinct and different), there was an opportunity – as there always is in language wherever there are synonyms – for one sound to acquire the meaning of one kind of violent action – say, a cutting – and another to acquire the meaning of a different action – say, a striking or crushing – and language had started on its high road of expansion.

There is one example of these earliest speech-noises that can still be heard and seen operating with a somewhat similar function and meaning. The glottis is also closed on another occasion – namely, during defaecation; and just as during violent arm-effort or absorbing manual work, there is a contraction of the abdominal muscles and an expiratory effort which compresses the air retained in the thorax. Consequently at the end of an effort at defaecation there tends to be a sudden release of the closure and a short gasp or grunt of expiration – usually an obscure velar plosive and neutral vowel, very audible in a young infant. The earliest occasion on which a mother needs to make a vocal request to her baby for action, is when she desires him to make such an effort. She cannot rely on a gesture, and she makes this grunt to him to suggest the effort that it commonly accompanies.

This is the kind of relationship between actor, action, vocal sound and request, that we must imagine to have occurred among earliest man in the remote days of the beginnings of speech. What was the history that followed? It was, above all, an addition of speech-sounds representing weaker actions of the vocal organs, together with less forceful bodily actions and less forceful meanings. Of this history of meanings we have said something in earlier chapters and will say more in the next. If we are right in thinking that the earliest speech accompanied and represented actions of maximum force, the added meanings of later language can only have been less forceful meanings. The same applies to the gestures, and also to the speech-sounds. When the glottis does not close of itself, as in manual effort, the pronunciation of plosives requires more force – that is to say, greater pressure of air – than the pronunciation of other consonants. The later consonants are arrived at simply by making less physical effort to pronounce them. The consonants have gone the way that we can see them going in the

Polynesian languages. Two organs must be joined firmly together to sound a plosive; in the fricative they are only set lightly together, so that the outgoing air escapes between, with consequent vibrations of the organs and the air, and the sound of friction between them. So b becomes v, and p becomes f, and d becomes z, and t becomes th or s, and k becomes ch [x] (as in loch), and so forth. But such a fricative sound can only have the constancy qualifying it for use as a distinct speech-sound with a distinct meaning, when men have acquired enough adaptation for speech and control of organs to pronounce it with ease. It is the law of minimum effort that we have seen before: men make no greater effort than is necessary to make themselves understood – or for any other purpose. From the stronger fricatives come the weaker, made as the contact diminishes. So the English *thank you* becomes in common speech '*hank you*', and in many languages a sibilant weakens to an aspirate. In the next stage, as the contact is wholly lost, the consonant weakens to a vowel. So, for example, in the Greek verb *to be* – where originally the root *ed* signified *to eat* – we see the plosive d or t weakening first to a fricative z or s, as in ἐσμέν (ĕsmĕn = we are), and then to the vowel *i*, as in εἰμί (eimi = I am). The 'i' is pronounced in the same part of the buccal cavity as the 's', with the whole cavity reduced to a narrow gap between tongue and hard palate; but in the one case a fricative contact is retained and an 's' is sounded, and in the other case the contact is wholly lost and in place of the consonant is the vowel 'i'. Thus we have moved from the plosives towards the middle of our continuous line of speech sounds. At the same time we have now formed a diphthong, ei.

From the vowel A, at the other end of the line, the process similarly moves towards the middle, as with advancing adaptation and control for speech a variety of short vowels can be enunciated and even a variety of distinct long vowels. And it is this growing capacity to pronounce distinctly these sounds of less effort, and the accompanying capacity of the ear to distinguish them, that enables a quieter language to be spoken and understood, and calls for and produces a voice softer and better modulated.

This weakening and disappearance of consonants is the most familiar milestone along the highway of phonetic history. Like most other processes in language it is forever repeating itself. It is this process that countervails the equally general process of the lengthening of words out of roots, and keeps them within manageable bounds. Let us take as an example the Indo-European word for 'night'. Probably its root was n-k, and it had acquired a suffix t. In Greek the word was nukt-, in Latin noct-, in Sanskrit nakt-. The vowel already varies so much in the classical languages that we cannot tell what the original vowel may have been, if indeed there was one common vowel in Indo-European. But two plosives in succession are not favoured in any language. In Italian the word is now notte – the k has become another t (a common transition). In M.H. German it is nacht: the plosive k has become a fricative, as in the O.E. night (pronounced much as in Scottish *nicht*). Now in both English and French it has gone, and in French the final t has almost gone; and all that survives in common in these two languages and their modern sister-tongues from the old Indo-European word is the initial nasal-plosive n. This, too, is not uncommon; we saw it, for example, in 'nationalization', from the old root 'gen', and we have seen how steadfast everywhere are the nasal-plosives.

But this phonetic decay and disappearance of consonants (and with them vowels) does not affect all parts of the word alike. Especially it affects the endings of words (as notably in French and Sumerian, but also in the other languages). For, firstly, words continue to be expressed by the pressure of a puff of outgoing breath, and the pressure is greatest at the commencement and quickly dies away as the lung contracts. And, again, men make no more effort than is necessary to be understood, and so, if the start of the word be clear, the end may be left to be gathered from the context. So Grimm's Law properly applies (as we said) to consonants and not to vowels; and among consonants, properly applies to the initial sounds of words rather than the rest. And again, in many words some parts are more prominent than others – because of stress or tone or length or quality of vowel or consonant; and in these cases if the more audible part is clear it seems unnecessary to take much trouble over the rest: it is likely to be understood from the context. This explains, for example, much popular usage – exáms for examinations, Bózzy for Bóswell, Nick for Nícholas, and also Claus for Nikoláus.

This, then, was the history of change of those earliest words – bă and băbă, nă and nănă, and the others. One of their outstanding characteristics was reduplication, and it has taken the whole life of man to witness its disappearance. If we arranged the languages known to us in the order of the economic development of the peoples who spoke them – as we did in an early chapter when we considered the proportions of the verbs – we should find that each successive stage witnessed a diminution in the amount of reduplication. Lord Avebury[1] long ago compared a number of primitive languages with Greek, French, English and German, and found between 20 and 80 times as much reduplication in languages of the first group as compared with the second group. In the classical Indo-European languages there are still substantial traces. It is made use of in the languages of man for a variety of purposes – often to form the plural of a noun; often to form a continuative tense of a verb by reduplication of the aorist (as in Greek to form the present and perfect from the 'strong' aorist); and similarly often to show repetition in the verb; and often to show intensive action or emphasis. In the most primitive languages it is commonly a reduplication of the whole of the short word; but as the roots and words grow longer, in the more advanced languages it is commonly a mere reduplication of one sound. So, in the Semitic *piel* voice, by reduplication of the second consonant, and in the Indo-European present or perfect tense by reduplication of the first.

One more important characteristic of the phonetic development must be mentioned. Those earliest words were mostly of the types bă and băbă or mă and mămă, and we have seen that among the changes that they underwent was the achievement of new vowels, and also the weakening of the plosives to form new consonants. But one of the earliest and most important advances was achieved when such words as bama and bata and kata and kaba and tasa and tara and other words of two different consonants appeared in the language. Bama (one of the earliest) may have come from baba by a phonetic weakening of the second consonant, and tasa from tata, and tara from tasa, by a similar process. To speak and hear the new sounds with precision involved (as we said) a new capacity of fine and rapid adjustment of vocal organs. With these various steps all the main phonetic advances had been made.

[1] *On the Origin of Civilisation*, pp. 403-5.

CHAPTER EIGHTEEN

The Origin of Language as displayed in Semitic and Bantu

In all the previous chapters of this book we have sought to trace the beginnings of language in each of the several facets of speech; and it has appeared in the course of that enquiry that every probe from every side leads towards the same beginning. The important question now presents itself: Is it possible that this origin of language, in speech-sounds and meanings of the kinds which we have inferred, can still be seen in any of the tongues of men?

It is, of course, mainly by the examination of the languages of men that we have pursued this enquiry. It is, for example, by this means that we noticed the changes in the proportions of the verb, and the origin from verbal roots of certain phonetic types. But the enquiry was pursued, to some extent, by grouping together the languages of the world and noting some general tendencies; and to some extent by following a course of reasoning, as when we saw a tendency for meanings to change from the physical to the non-physical and from the more forceful to the less forceful, and when we noted physical facts that would explain the origin and development which we inferred. We ended, however, by arriving at an origin of language in speech-sounds of a certain type, bearing the meaning of maximum human effort – cut! break! crush! and the like. Is there any language which still shows in its roots an origin from words of this type bearing meanings of this type? It is all that is needed to complete our enquiry. Above all it would shed a flood of light on the most important and the most fascinating of all aspects of the development of language and thought – namely, by what steps did words of these meanings reach the innumerable significances of modern speech? By what steps did man acquire the thoughts and ideas of maturity? Is it possible to find such a language?

If we are right in our conclusions, speech originated in this crude and vestigial form when man's mental age was little more than 1½ years, hundreds of thousands of years ago. Would it not be a miracle if traces of this beginning survived? We have seen so many languages changing during the short record of civilization. In Polynesia we have witnessed changes since the time of Captain Cook. In our own language, the changes produced in the last thousand years alone are immense. It would be impossible to infer, from Modern English alone, the characteristics of the Indo-European of only 4,000 years ago, of which it is but a changing dialect. Looking more widely at the world's languages, there are few tongues of North America which we would choose to examine in order to find the features of speech at its beginning. Old as are the written records of Chinese, we have hardly any knowledge of its speech-sounds of two millennia ago. Any language in which the same syllables have different meanings according to the tone in which they are uttered, is likely to present insuperable obstacles to an attempt to trace its history over many centuries. Remembering that the languages of primitive and modern communities, as we know them, are probably all of the same age, and in some respects of the same maturity, and that the peoples who speak them have had to apply the few speech-sounds that man's organs can readily produce, and the small vocabularies of these languages, to represent the innumerable ideas that they have acquired, while they have jettisoned a cargo of other notions since speech appeared, and with them words that expressed them – bearing in mind these things, and the evidence of phonetic change and decay on all sides, we are strongly impelled to the conclusion that such a survival would be a miracle and that it is not worth the trouble of a search.

But knowledge does not lie that way. In the first place, as all knowledge of human history and pre-history tells us, and as we have seen illustrated in the proportions of the parts of speech, the advance of civilization is ever at an increasing pace. As we penetrate back, change is slower and slower, and we can be certain that, in the earliest days of man, progress in technology and thought and language was infinitesimal as the millennia succeeded one another. Civilization is only some 7,000 years old, and then only in the Near East; and even agriculture is only a few thousand years old anywhere; and although language has advanced to something so vastly different from its origins, the bulk of that advance must have occurred within the last few tens of thousands of years. The stage at which words were still mainly of the type which we have inferred, with meanings of maximum human effort and little else, must have endured for a hundred or hundreds of millennia and left its unmistakable traces during long ages thereafter. It is true that phonetic decay and change, within the available limits, must have occurred from early times, so that even the languages of primitive peoples are changing, though they may be making little advance in material culture. Yet if we can only find languages resistant to phonetic decay, it would seem that the search need not be hopeless. If only their words survived unchanged their meanings might still be traced. And nothing is more striking in language than the differences in the rate of change between one language and another – and even between peoples of the same economic grade, and even between peoples speaking tongues descended from the same origin. While, for example, French would not be known as an Indo-European language but for its written record, Lithuanian and Greek, on the other hand, retain innumerable features of their parent. Of the families of languages, two are known to us over a period of three or four thousand years, the Indo-European for the lesser period and the Semitic for the longer. The first has, in most places, experienced innumerable changes; the second, as spoken in the present and the past, hardly any change in its radicals. There are hardly more differences between Semitic languages of today than between those of three or four thousand years ago. And if so little change is shown in four millennia, we are encouraged to think that it was slow indeed before that time. Probably there is little hope of finding visible traces of the earliest meanings in most of the tongues of men, but there may be great hope in others. And if we cannot find them in Semitic we shall not find them anywhere. If the survival, for which we look, would be a miracle, equally, Semitic, in its unique constancy, is a miracle.

In fact, the Semitic languages show unmistakable evidence of this origin of language. The phenomena which we shall detail have often been noticed, but it is submitted that their extent and their true significance have never been realized.

It might seem likely – we cannot tell – that we should find the clearest evidences of the origin of speech near the areas where man arose. Perhaps in that region any violent changes in language might be held in check by the example of neighbouring tongues. To the present author the evidence seems to indicate as the birth-place of man the areas around the great lakes of East Africa. There, as long as we know it, the earth has been most fertile and life exceptionally prolific. However that may be, two families of speech have chiefly originated in that region – one, the Semitic-Hamitic, which was spoken to the north-east in Egypt and Arabia and up to the borders of Asia Minor and the foot-hills of Persia; the other, the Bantu, which stretches to the south and covers the southern third of Africa.[1] Of the Semitic-Hamitic family, the Semitic has changed far less in historic times, and (to judge from the close resemblance of its various tongues at the beginning of history) far less in prehistoric times, than any other languages known to us. Let us take as our example the Hebrew of the Old Testament, though any other Semitic tongue would suffice. The Hebrews were economically somewhat less advanced than the Babylonians and Assyrians, and their language was spoken at a much earlier date than the Arabic that we know. They had been in closer touch with Egypt and Africa than the inhabitants of Central Arabia, where the Semitic tongues have developed to the furthest their characteristic features. The Bantu tongues, on the other hand, have spread themselves over Southern Africa within the last two millennia, but they are still close together and give no evidence of rapid change. The Zulu language, which we shall choose as another example, is one of the most conservative of these, and shows clear traces of the original speech-sounds and their original meanings. We shall draw comparison from the Indo-European tongues, in which English speakers must feel a special interest, but they have travelled too far and changed too much to serve for more than illustration.

Again and again in this book, as we inferred (if we were right) each characteristic of the earliest language, we were compelled to notice its survival in Semitic, and particularly in our example, Hebrew. We noted, first, the increase of vocabularies in the advance of civilization, and we noted the small Semitic vocabularies. We noted the diminution in the proportion of verbs – or rather the increase in the other parts of speech – during the advance of material culture, and in Semitic we found little but verbs and nouns. We noticed in languages 'roots' or radical words, bearing the meanings of verbs, out of which much of each vocabulary seemed to have issued; and in Semitic we noted that practically all radical words are verbs, and practically all verbs radical words, out of which the vocabulary seemed to have expanded. We inferred that the earliest functions of words were as imperatives of the second person singular, infinitives and aorists of the third person singular; and in Semitic we noted that (subject to some change in

[1] The so-called Sudanic group collects together all other languages of Africa except those of the African Food Gatherers and the Hottentots.

vowel attributable to a varying accent) the verb-root bears these three meanings. We inferred from the many languages that we examined that the roots and the earliest words consisted in the main of a succession of consonant and the vowel A, and we saw the same phenomenon in the Semitic radicals.

But there is one feature that distinguishes the Semitic from all other tongues. There are many languages which still exhibit their roots, or the bulk of their verbs, in the type CVC or CVCV (as, for example, Indo-European and Bantu and the tongues of the Nilotes) though the vowels are not limited to A. There are languages whose roots are commonly of the form CV, and some who exhibit all these forms. Semitic has the longest radicals of all known languages, for they are practically all triconsonantal. They consist, in Hebrew and some forms of Arabic,[1] of the type CVCVC, and in Arabic generally of the type CVCVCV, and in each language practically all radicals are of these respective types. This uniqueness is as striking as its uniformity. We have seen some of the reasons why this is so, and why Semitic has resisted change. As a people advances in material culture and its vocabulary increases, it must produce new words, and, among others, new verbs which will function as new roots. Many languages, including Common Indo-European, developed and increased the vowels, and formed new verb-roots of the old CVC(V) type but with varied vowels. The Semitic – so conservative in all its aspects – lengthened its verbs while keeping the old type of succession of consonant and vowel A; and ultimately, in its passion for regularity, increased almost all its roots to three consonants. These continued to be separated by the vowel A, and the vowel was only varied to conjugate the verbs and form from them the nouns. How potent a factor in the resistance to change this triconsonantal character must have been! Vowels (except the vowel A) are more variable than consonants, and a language of roots of three single consonants separated by A would be in the highest degree resistant to phonetic change. Moreover, as the conjugation is by change of vowel, to the linguistic mind of the people the essence and meaning of the word is in the consonants, as it has always been.

For many years a number of scholars have searched in these languages for earlier biliteral roots and their meanings. In the second half of the 19th century they were searching for the common tongue that might have been the parent of Indo-European and Semitic, and the common roots of such a language could not have consisted of

[1] As that of Aden.

more than two consonants. The search for a parent of Indo-European and Semitic is now out of fashion, but many scholars have noted, perhaps especially in Hebrew, words of two consonants that cannot satisfactorily be made to conform to triliteral type by such weak expedients as doubling the last letter. Our present purpose is different – namely, to search for the shorter, mainly biliteral, roots which we find in the bulk of the world's languages and the speech of children, and which we have concluded to be the forms of man's earliest words. We find many roots of these forms in Semitic, and the meanings they bear are *cut, break*.

Let us examine the Hebrew vocabulary for this purpose, and start with radicals beginning with a voiced labial and a dental. Here is an example that cannot be misunderstood. The following are all the Hebrew radicals (that is, verbs) beginning with b and t:

BT

batal	(Ar. sever, separate).
bataq	cut, cut off, cut down.
batar	cut in two (Ar. cut off, exterminate).
batat	cut off.

These four examples suggest that in some past time, before this language of triliteral roots emerged, there was a language containing the verb-root *bata* signifying to *cut*. Let us, for the present, assume this to be the correct explanation: we shall consider later whether there could be any other. It must be borne in mind that such a form as *cut off, cut down* (consisting of a verb followed by an adverb) is impossible in Hebrew. Instead (if our explanation is correct) a third consonant has been suffixed to the word *cut*. But the meaning of the four roots remains practically unchanged – *to separate* is an easy use of the word '*to cut*' (as in the English expression *to cut the cards*) and *to cut off* is a familiar figure for *exterminate*.

Now let us compare a number of other groups of verb roots beginning with a voiced labial and a dental. The following are all the Hebrew roots beginning with

BD

bada'	devise, invent (in a bad sense; Ar. *begin*).
badad	be separated.
badal	be divided.
badaq	tear, break.

Equally all these four examples indicate an earlier *bada*, meaning to *cut*, *break*. The only new sense is *devise*, *invent* for *bada'*. We can see the same process of change of meaning in English – for example to *cut a figure*, *cut a suit* (meaning to *make*); and the Arabic *begin* is paralleled by the English *to have a cut at*, to *break*.

The following are all the Hebrew roots beginning with

BZ

baza'	divide, cut through.
bazah	despise.
bazaz	spoil, plunder.
bazar	scatter.
buz	despise.

All these examples similarly show an earlier root baza, to *cut*, *break*. There are some new metaphors, however. The meaning of *despise* for bazah and buz is illustrated by the English figure to *cut an acquaintance* and the word *contemn* (Latin = cut). To *scatter* (bazar) is simply to *separate* in a certain way; and to *spoil* or *plunder* is to *smash* and *destroy*, and still more to *tear away*[1] and *to divide* among the members of the marauding band.[2] Languages are full of such associations.

The following are all roots beginning with

BṢ

baṣal	strip, strip off.
baṣa'	cut off, break off, gain by violence or wrong, finish, accomplish.
baṣaṣ	(Ar. be impressible).
baṣeq	swell.
baṣar	cut off, enclose, fortify, make inaccessible (as noun, a secret, mystery).

This group speaks for itself. The origin of the meaning *swell* is obscure. The meanings of the verbs baṣa' and baṣar are instructive.

We see, then, in the above groups, unmistakable evidence of older roots bata, bada, baza and baṣa, all signifying nothing but *cut*, *break*.

Now let us set out all the radicals containing an unvoiced labial and a dental as the first two consonants.

[1] As Latin rapina from rapio. Cf. baṣa', post.
[2] Cf. Greek (from da = cut, divide) daiō (divide), daïos (hostile, destructive, burning), daio (burn).

PṢ

paṣah	part, open (Ar. separate, remove; Aram. set free).
paṣaḥ	break forth, burst forth (Ar. & Eth. break, crush, shatter).
paṣal	peel (other Sem. langs. split, divide).
paṣam	split open.
paṣa'	bruise, wound (Aram. split).
paṣaṣ	break, shatter.
paṣar	press, push.
puṣ	be dispersed, scattered, overflow.

Here is unambiguous evidence of an earlier root paṣa, meaning *cut, break, crush*. Hence comes to *part, open* (as in the Latin patior = I am cut, I suffer; pateo = I am opened) and to *peel* and *wound*. To *overflow* is but to *scatter* (from *cut, divide*), but used of a different substance. To *press, push* is but a weakened form of *crush, strike*.

PS

pasag	pass between (N.H. split).
pasaḥ	(1) pass over.
	(2) limp (Ar. dislocate).
pasal	hew.
pasas	(1) spread.
	(2) disappear (As. do away with, blot out).

As we move from a plosive second consonant to a fricative second consonant the sense and sound weaken together, and the instances are perhaps not quite so clear, but clear enough. To *pass between* is but to *cut, pierce, divide*, and the same may apply to the meaning *pass over*. The Arabic suggests that *to limp* signifies originally *to be broken*.[1] From *divide, scatter*, comes *to spread* and *disappear*; and the latter sense may also be reached by way of *cut off, destroy*.

PT

patah	be wide open, spacious.
pataḥ	(1) open.
	(2) engrave (As. bore, penetrate).
patal	twist (i.e. break; see, post, ḥatal).
patar	solve, interpret.
patat	break up, crumble (pat = a fragment, bit of bread).

[1] As in some African languages.

Here pataḫ, with its two meanings of *open* and *engrave*, clearly shows the origin in to *cut open*; and from *to be opened* comes *to be spacious*. To *open* is also to *solve, interpret*. How the meaning 'twist' comes about, must remain uncertain, but the change is frequent.

PŚ

paśah	spread (also of disease; and Ar. also of news).
paśaʻ	step, march.
paśaq	part, open (N.H. and Aram. cut, sever, cleave).

These examples speak for themselves. From to *open* comes to *spread* and to *stretch* and so *step out*.

PSh

pashaḫ	tear to pieces.
pashaṭ	strip off, raid (As. obliterate; N.H. and Aram. stretch out, make plain).
pashaʻ	rebel, transgress.
push	be scattered, jump about.

To raid a country is to *cut into it, cut it open, pierce it*. To *rebel* is to *break away*; to *transgress* is to *break* a law or custom (cf. post, ḫataḫ) or to *break in* or *break through*.

We may include here a few supporting groups which are not in themselves conclusive because the number of verbs containing these letters is too small.

PṬ

paṭar	separate, remove, set free (As. and Ar. split, break; Ar. and Eth. also create).[1]

PZ

pazaz	(1) be refined (cf. Eng. *break down*).
	(2) be agile, supple (cf. *push*, supra).
pazar	scatter (Ar. tear, slit, separate, disperse).

PD

padah	set free, ransom (cf. post, paraʻ, paraq, palaṭ).

---

[1] See *post*, baraʼ.

ORIGIN OF LANGUAGE IN SEMITIC AND BANTU

We may, then, sum up these groups of labials-and-dentals by saying that, in a language that preceded Semitic, bata, bada, baza, baṣa, paṣa, pasa, pata, paśa, pasha, and probably also paṭa, paza and pada all signified to cut, break, smash.

With this group we may compare the Indo-European group PAT, PAD, FAT or FAD, meaning originally to cut, break, strike – e.g. Latin pati (to be cut?), to suffer; $\pi\alpha\theta\epsilon\hat{\imath}\nu$, to suffer; $\pi\alpha\tau\epsilon\hat{\imath}\nu$, to break a path; $\pi\acute{\alpha}\tau os$, a path (cf. French *route*, from rumpere); putare, to prune; patēre and pandere, to be opened, spread out; $\pi\epsilon\tau\acute{\alpha}\nu\nu\upsilon\mu\iota$, spread out; fatēri, to open oneself, confess; fatescere, to crack open; fodere, dig; findere, split; fundere, scatter; fendere, cut, strike; font-, spring, i.e. bursting forth.

Now let us take a number of kindred groups of verbs, in which the first consonant is a labial and the second a liquid, beginning with the largest and most significant group of all.[1]

PR

parad	divide, separate.
parah	blossom, bear fruit.
paraz	(Ar. remove, separate).
paraḥ	(1) bud, shoot, sprout.
	(2) break out (of leprosy and other eruptions).
paraṭ	break off.
parak	(1) rub, chafe, crumble.
	(2) shut off.
param	tear.
paras	break, divide (As. divide, hinder).
para'	(1) sprout.
	(2) excel (cf. qadam, maḫar).
	(3) let loose.
paraṣ	break, break through, break down, break out, burst open. (Ar. cut, slit, strike).
paraq	tear apart, tear off, tear away, snatch from, rescue (Ar. split, divide).
parar	(1) break, frustrate, annul (As. destroy, shatter).
	(2) split, divide.
paraś	spread, spread out, scatter.

[1] Throughout this chapter, under each heading of two Hebrew consonants (e.g. PR) all the radicals are set out which contain those as their first two consonants, whatever be the meaning.

parash   (1) make distinct (other Sem. langs. separate, distinguish, explain).
(2) pierce, sting.
(3) cause to burst forth.

This set of 14 verbs speaks for itself, but we may notice in parah, paraḫ and para' how, from the sense *to break*, comes to *break into leaf* or *flower* and to *bear* (Eng. equivalent) fruit and offspring, and to *break out* (of eruptions). Parash is an important instance of a common process in language, in which, from verbs meaning to separate, comes to *distinguish, explain* and *make clear*. We saw something similar in patar. A vast number of the world's words meaning *to know* originally signified *to separate, distinguish, see*; and therefore many words meaning *to know* properly signify *to get to know* and are used in a past or aorist tense (I got to know) with a present meaning (I know), cf. Greek perfect woida (I know), Latin video (I see), from *cut, split* – Skt. vidhyati (to pierce); Latin dīvido (divide), vidua (cut off, separated), hence Eng. *widow*. See also Hebrew yada', Psalm 139, lines 1-5.

PL

pala'   separate, distinguish, be distinguished, be extraordinary, wonderful.
palag   cleave, divide.
palah   be separated, distinct, wonderful.
palaḫ   cleave, plough, till the ground.
palaṭ   escape, be rescued (i.e. separated, torn away).
palal   separate, intervene, mediate, arbitrate, judge, pray (i.e. of the early priest mediating between God and the community).
palaṣ   shudder.
palash   mourn (originally burrow into the dust. As. dig a hole, N.H. break open).

BR

bara'   (1) shape, create (Ar. make by cutting) – cf. I.E. root kar = cut, create.
(2) be fat (Ar. be free of a thing, healthy).
barad   hail, be cold (derivation?).
barah   (1) eat.
(2) bind (see also patal, katal).
baraz   (Aram. bore, pierce).
baraḫ   pass through (from *pierce*), flee.

barak	kneel, bless.
baraq	flash (of lightning, i.e. burst).
barar	purify, select, test, prove.
bur	explain, clear up.

This group is perhaps not so clear as some. The idea of cutting or breaking is present in bara', barah (eat), baraz, baraḥ, baraq and barar. With bur compare parash, *supra*. Kneeling (barak) is a metaphorical 'breaking' of the legs.

Summing up this group, we see that para, pala and bara betray the same origin, *break*, *cut*.

Indo-European has similarly PAR or PER, meaning cut, divide, pierce, whose examples are numerous (e.g. per, par, pars, experior, περάω, πείρω, πόρος, πορεῖν, πειράω, foro, ferio, ford).

Let us, next, similarly examine a large number of groups of Hebrew verbs commencing with a velar (or palatal) and a dental:

GZ

gazah	cut, cut off.
gazaz	shear.
gazal	tear way, rob (Ar. cut off).
gazam	cut off.
gaza'	cut off.
gazar	cut, divide, cut off, destroy, decree (Ar. and N.H. cut, determine – see *post*, ḥatak).

GD

gadad	cut, penetrate, attack.
gadah	(cut, cut away).
gadal	become great, become strong (i.e. able to break things?).
gada'	cut off, hew down.
gadap	revile (Ar. cut, cut off, deny a favour, be ungrateful – cf. Eng. *cut* a friend).
gadar	shut off (i.e. cut off) wall off.
gadash	heap (i.e. separate off).
gud	invade (i.e. cut into), attack.

QṢ

qaṣab	cut off (N.H. decide).
qaṣah	(1) cut off.
	(2) decide, decree.

qaṣa'	(1) scrape, scape off.
	(2) cut off.
qaṣap	(1) be angry (i.e. break things?).
	(2) snap, break off.
qaṣaṣ	cut off (qeṣ = end).
qaṣar	(1) be short (i.e. be cut – cf. to *cut a play* – so Latin *curtus* and Eng. *short* both signify *cut*).
	(2) (from cut) reap, harvest.
quṣ	(1) feel a loathing (i.e. separate oneself from).
	(2) N.H. cut off.

QṬ

qaṭab	cut off, destroy.
qaṭal	slay.
qaṭon	be small (i.e. be 'cut').
qaṭap	pluck off, pluck out.
qaṭar	(1) smoke (destroy?).
	(2) shut off, enclose.
quṭ	loathe (see quṣ, *supra*).

QS

qasam	divide, distribute.
qasas	cut off, pluck off.

QD

qadad	bow down (cf. barak, *supra*).
qadaḥ	kindle (originally bore – the older method of making a fire – as in Aram, N.H.).
qadam	be in front (Eng. *beat*, cf. maḥar).
qadar	be dark.[1]
qadash	be separate, be holy.[2]

ḤT

ḥatah	tear away, snatch up (As. destroy).
ḥatak	determine (Aram. and N.H., cut, cut off, determine).
ḥatal	enfold, wrap up (see *ante*, patal).
ḥatam	seal (i.e. engrave).

---

[1] The etymology is obscure.
[2] Separateness is an important element in holiness in many of the world's languages and its religions and systems of magic (cf. Latin seco, sacer).

ḥatan   circumcise.
ḥatap   tear away, seize.
ḥatar   dig into, row (cf. Eng. to *ear*, i.e. plough, and *oar* – N.H. bore).
ḥatat   be shattered (Eth. be examined).

ḤṢ

ḥaṣab   hew, hew out.
ḥaṣah   divide.
ḥaṣaṣ   divide (As. cut in two, Eth. cut short, shorten).
ḥaṣar   shut off (i.e. divide), enclose, surround.

ḤṬ

ḥaṭa'   go astray, miss the mark, sin (i.e. break away, separate?).
ḥaṭab   cut wood, gather firewood.
ḥaṭaṭ   cut lines (Aram. dig, trench).
ḥaṭam   hold in, restrain (i.e. separate?).
ḥaṭap   seize, tear away.

ḤD

ḥadad   be sharp (i.e. cutting).
ḥadah   (1) be or become sharp.
            (2) rejoice (be keen, break out?)
ḥadal   cease (cf. Eng. *break off*).
ḥadaq   pierce.
ḥadar   shut off, surround, enclose (Eng. *cut off*).
ḥadash   repair, renew (cut?).
ḥud   avoid, turn aside (Eng. *cut, separate from*).

KT

katab   write (originally cut lines, scratch).
katal   bind (see *ante*, patal, barah).
katam   be stained (?).
katar   (cut off) surround.
katash   break small, pound.
katat   beat, crush.

KS

kasah   (1) hide (i.e. separate), cover – (see *post*, galah).
            (2) bind (see *ante*, katal).

kasaḥ   cut off, cut away, destroy.
kasal   be stupid (?).
kasam   shear.
kasas   compute (originally divide in the process of counting – Aram. break small, Ar. pulverize, As. cut up).
kasap   long for (?).

Accordingly there is clear evidence in this group that at some earlier time gaza, gada, qaṣa, qaṭa, qasa, qada, ḫata, ḫaṣa, ḥata, ḥada, kata and kasa all signified cut, break.

We are thereby reminded of the parallels in the Indo-European roots CD and CT, to cut (e.g. caedo, strike; scindo, tear; cudo, strike; catus, sharp; σκεδάννυμι, κίδναμαι, scatter, spread out).

Next, the kindred Hebrew groups of velar and liquid show:

GR

garab   scratch, itch.
garad   scratch, scrape (Ar. peel, shave).
garah   attack, stir up strife.
garaz   cut, cut off, exterminate.
garal   stones (as Latin saxum from sac, root of seco, cut).
garam   (1) lay aside, save (Ar. cut off).
            (2) break.
garan   grind, thresh (cf. Ar. grind, wear smooth, become accustomed).
garaʻ   lessen, restrain, withdraw (Aram. shave the head).
garap   scoop away, sweep away.
garar   cut, tear away, drag away.
garash   (cut off), cast out, drive out.
gur   turn aside (i.e. separate), sojourn.

GL

galab   shave, cut hair.
galah   uncover, reveal (cf. *ante*, kasah).
galaḥ   shave, be bald.
galal   roll away.
galam   fold, wrap up (see *ante*, patal, barah, katal, kasah).
galaʻ   uncover, lay bare, expose, reveal.

The whole of this group (except perhaps galam) is derived from gala, to shear, shave, uncover, reveal.

ḤR

ḥareb	(1) be dried up (destroyed?).
ḥarab	(2) be laid waste (destroyed?).
	(3) attack (Ar. plunder – from destroy?).
ḥarag	quake (derivation?).
ḥarad	tremble, be afraid (derivation?).
ḥarah	burn (destroy?), used of anger.
ḥaraz	to string (pierce), used of beads, etc.
ḥaraṭ	cut.
ḥarak	set in motion (Eng. *break*).
ḥaram	(1) exterminate, ban.
	(2) slit.
ḥaraʻ	(Ar. split, invent).
ḥarap	(1) reproach (Aram. sharpen – cf. Eng. 'cut').
	(2) pluck (at harvest).
	(3) acquire.
ḥaraṣ	cut, sharpen, decide (As. also dig).
ḥaraq	grind the teeth.
ḥarar	(1) be scorched, burn.
	(2) set free.
	(3) (As. pierce).
ḥaraś	(Ar. scratch, tear).
ḥarash	(1) cut, engrave, plough, devise (in bad sense – cf. bada').
	(2) be dumb, deaf (i.e. deprived, separated, broken).
ḥarat	engrave (Ar. pierce, bore, slit).

HR

harag	slay.
harah	conceive, be pregnant.
haras	break down, tear down.

These groups, then, show clear evidence that gara, gala, ḥara and hara formerly meant cut, break, destroy, and with them may be compared the ḥala and qara groups, which contain abundant further evidence.

With them, too, may be compared copious Indo-European parallels from the root KAR, cut – e.g. κείρω, cut; curtus, cut short; creo, create by cutting; κρίνω and cerno, separate; cornu, horn, i.e. piercing implement: Heb. qeren.

Now let us turn to the groups beginning with a nasal:

MN

myn	a kind, sect (i.e. cut off, separated – as Eng. sect, from Latin seco).
min	separation (hence, as preposition, *from*).
manah	count, number, assign (i.e. divide – Ar. divide).
manaḫ	make a gift (i.e. share, divide).
manan	divide.
manaʿ	withhold (i.e. separate).

MD

madad	measure (i.e. separate).
madah	ditto.

ML

malaʾ	fill (derivation?).
malaḫ	tear away, scatter.
malaṭ	slip away, escape.
malal	(1) speak.
	(2) scrape, rub.
	(3) fade away.
	(4) circumcise.
malaṣ	be smooth (i.e. worn down).
malaq	nip, nip off.
mul	circumcise.
mahal	circumcise.

MḤ

maḥa,	strike, clap.
maḥah	(1) wipe out.
	(2) strike.
maḥaṣ	shatter, wound.
maḥaq	destroy, annihilate.
maḥar	be in front (cf. qadam, nakaḥ).

NQ

naqab	(1) pierce, bore, mark off, designate.
	(2) curse (destroy?).
naqad	point, mark.

naqah	(be hollowed out) be emptied out, cleaned.
naqam	avenge (i.e. kill or wound).
naqaʻ	be cut off (Ar. and Eth. split, tear).
naqap	(1) break away, strike off.
	(2) shut off, surround, go round.
naqaq	cleave (of a cleft in rock).
naqar	bore, dig.
naqash	strike.

NK

nakaʼ	smite, scourge.
nakah	smite, kill, wound, attack.
nakaḫ	be in front (cf. qadam, maḫar).
nakal	be cunning (from cut, be sharp?).
nakar	(1) (separate) distinguish, recognize.
	(2) (separate) foreign.

NG

nagad	declare, make known.
nagah	enlighten, cause to shine.
nagaḫ	strike, gore.
nagal	(Ar. strike, split, pierce).
nagan	strike (a stringed instrument).
nagaʻ	strike, touch.
nagap	strike.
nagar	pour, flow, stretch out.
nagaś	drive, oppress (As. overthrow).
nagash	approach (from strike, touch?).

NT

nataḫ	cut up.
natak	pour out (divide, scatter?).
natan	give, put.
natas	tear, break down.
nataʻ	break, break down, break out
nataṣ	break down, pull down.
nataq	tear away, tear apart, pull away.
natar	(1) start up (Eng. *break*).
	(2) unfasten, set free.
natash	pluck up.

ND

nada'	drive away, thrust aside.
nadab	drive, incite.
nadad	flee (be driven away, separate?)
nadah	put away (As. overthrow, destroy).
nadaḫ	drive, impel, thrust away, banish.
nadap	drive, drive away, scatter (Ar. strike).
nadar	vow.

NS

nasah	test, try (i.e. cut open, separate).
nasaḫ	tear away.
nasak	(1) pour out (i.e. scatter).
	(2) weave (i.e. pierce?).
	(3) instal.
nasas	be sick, waste away.

These groups show mana, mada, mala, maḫa, naqa, naka, naga, nata, nada and nasa, all betraying the same origin.

Indo-European shows the following parallels: NEM and MEN, separate, distinguish, e.g. νέμω, memini; MAK and NAK, as macēre, beat, hack; macēre, be beaten, thin; necare, kill; nocēre, wound; νέκυς, νεκρός, corpse. MET, cut, separate, as meto, reap, mow; metior, μέτρον, measure; μαθεῖν, distinguish, learn. MAR, smash, kill, as mori, be killed; μέρος, division, etc.[1]

Next come the groups beginning with a labial and a velar.

BQ

baqah	test, prove (from *cut open*).
baqa'	break open, break through, break down, break into, cut open, tear to pieces, burst open.
baqaq	(1) be luxuriant (i.e. burst forth).
	(2) empty, lay waste (i.e. break, destroy).
baqar	seek, enquire (originally divide, cut open – so Ar. slit, rip).
baqash	seek (cf. baqar).

---

[1] Max Müller lists the enormous number of words derived from the root MAR in the Indo-European languages – see his *Lectures on the Science of Language*, vol. 2, Lecture VII.

BK

bakah   weep.[1]
bakar   bear the first child (i.e. break, burst).

BḪ

baḫan   examine, test, prove (from *cut open*).
baḫar   pick out, choose (i.e. separate).

These groups show baqa, baka and baha coming from the same origin and progressively weakening in sound and sense.

There are similar roots in Indo-European.[2]

Now let us turn to the groups commencing with a dental and velar:

DQ

daqaq   crush, pulverize (As. break in pieces).
daq   small, fine, thin (i.e. broken down).
daqar   pierce.

DK

daka'   crush.
dakah   crush, break.
dakak   crush, oppress.
duk   pound, beat.

DḪ

daḫah   thrust, push.
daḫaḫ   thrust down.
daḫap   drive, hasten.
daḫaq   thrust, oppress (Ar. drive away, remove).

SḪ

saḫab   drag away.
saḫah   scrape off, scour, clear away.

---

[1] From *burst* (into weeping). So Greek dak (=cut); dakno, bite; dakru, a tear (weeping). Latin lac (=rend); lacer, torn; lacrima=a tear (weeping). English tear=to rend and weep.

[2] Cf. φαγεῖν, πικρός, pingere, pungere, pugna.

saḥap   prostrate (As. overwhelm).
saḥar   go around, peddle, trade (from some unknown noun?).

With these biliteral roots, daqa, daka, daḥa and saḥa, (successively weakening in the second letter from plosive to fricative, and at the same time weakening in force), compare a number of Indo-European roots, DA, DAK, SAC (e.g. δάω, separate, distinguish, learn; δαίω, divide; δάκνω, bite; δείκνυμι, separate, single out, point to; docēre, point out, teach; digitus, finger (pointer); secare, cut; sagio, be sharp; sacer, separate, holy; scio, separate, distinguish, learn.

Here is a Hebrew group of two velars, and of two dentals:

ḤQ (cf. Eng. *hack*)

ḥaqah   cut in, carve.
ḥaqaq   cut in, decree.
ḥaqar   search, explore (from *cut in*).

ShS

shasah   plunder, spoil.
shasas   plunder, spoil.
shasaʿ   cleave, divide.
shasap   hew to pieces.

And with a dental and liquid:

ZR

zarah   scatter, winnow.
zaraḥ   break forth (of the sun).
zaram   pour forth (i.e. scatter).
zaraʿ   (1) scatter (seed).
               (2) stretch out.
zarap   drip.
zaraq   scatter, throw.
zarar   sneeze.

With this last group, compare the Indo-European sero, sow (seed); sors, share (division); tero, grind; τείρω, τρύω, rub away; τερέω and τράω, bore; δέρω, flay.

There is only one group in Hebrew beginning with the vowel A and an initial smooth breathing:

AK

akal   eat.
akap   press, urge.
akar   (Ar. dig.).

Similarly, in Indo-European, there is only one group beginning with a vowel, namely the same group, AK – e.g. ἄγνυμι, break; ὀξύς, sharp; ὠκύς, sharp, fast; and Latin acu, acuo, acer, aceo, acies, oculus, all signifying cutting, piercing.

CHAPTER NINETEEN

The Origin of Language as displayed in Semitic and Bantu (continued)

Let us now examine as a whole the Semitic phenomena set out in the previous chapter. We leapt to the conclusion that they could only be explained by supposing that the triconsonantal radicals with the vowel A had been biconsonantal verbs in an earlier state of language; that they had all borne the meanings of *cut, break, strike, crush*, and the like; and that their present form had been shaped by adding a suffixed consonant. In many cases, perhaps, the addition was merely to enable a biliteral verb to harmonize with the triliteral character that the language was assuming, but the extension, we thought, was in the normal course of the expansion of a vocabulary. At the same time, we concluded, the meanings of the verbs were undergoing a regular development through metaphor to diverse, physically weaker meanings. This was our opinion; but – forgetting for a moment all the supporting facts contained in the rest of this book – let us consider whether any other explanation could be offered for these circumstances.

Sayce, a distinguished linguist and Semitic scholar, discussing the alleged resemblances between Aryan and Semitic roots, said that they 'are in almost all cases easily accounted for by the imitation of natural sounds. The number of parallel roots that exist in Semitic of similar sound and meaning, such as katsats, ka'sa's, gazaz, gazah, gazam, gaza', gazal, gazar, khadad, gadad, kadad, gadah, guz, khatsats, khatsah, katsa', katsar, ca'sakh, ca'sam, khatsah, all containing the idea of "cutting", can only be explained, not by a theory of addition and subtraction, but by looking on particular sounds as so many phonetic types which presented themselves before the unconscious mind as symbols of the conceptions attached to them.'[1] Let us consider if this explanation explains.

He accounts for these parallel roots by the imitation of natural

[1] Sayce, vol. 2, p. 175.

sounds,[1] and he illustrates his remark by a list of 20 verbs containing 8 common biliteral elements. This is not the extent of the phenomenon. We set out in the previous chapter 300 verb-roots containing over 50 different biliteral elements of the most diverse phonetic types, all expressing similar meanings; and these are by no means all. If the imitation of natural sound be the cause and origin, the sound of cutting and breaking is infinitely varied. But in truth there is nothing in common between sounds of cutting and breaking and the sounds of speech.

It is right, however, always to remember that words are not to be found in a dictionary alone, but that they are, in some measure at least, associated in the mind with the concepts they are employed to symbolize. Men are not automats. But the meaning of words is got from their previous use, and if a particular speech-sound presents itself before the unconscious mind as a symbol of a conception to which it is felt to be attached, it is almost always because it has long been used in the same connexion. And though man is no automat, his speech-sounds must conform to phonetic types, and be used with symbolic references, approved and readily understood by a whole community. Hence one of the most striking features of language – the regularity of the forms which it evolves. Could anything in speech be imagined, of more regular and artificial form, than a language whose verbs all contain three single consonants, each separated by one vowel? Compared with such a phenomenon, is it more or less remarkable if the same language was preceded by another in which the bulk of the verbs contained two consonants separated by a vowel? It would, indeed, be almost remarkable if it were not so, for a vast number, and perhaps the majority, of the world's tongues have the bulk of their verb-roots of this form, and there is no other family of languages whose verbs are all of triliteral or longer form.[2] And if a community goes through the process of changing its verbs from biconsonantal to triconsonantal, it cannot, during a temporary age, jettison its verb-roots and abandon the use of speech until it is disposed to adopt a new language. The process of extension cannot affect all verbs at the same sudden moment, and the biliterals, during the process of expansion, must necessarily continue to be used with the same meanings. And if the language is capable of such conservative regularity as Semitic, it is not in the least surprising if

---

[1] See as to the onomatopoeic theory of the origin of language, *post*, p. 259.
[2] In ancient Egyptian the biliterals were extended to verbs of two, three and four consonants.

the biliterals and their meanings can still be discerned in the new words.

And why are these phonetic symbols, these common biliteral elements of these meanings, always at the beginning of the Semitic radical and not at the end? This is equally a feature of extreme regularity of form. In the 300 examples given in the last chapter, the two common consonants were in each case the first and second consonants of the Semitic verb. Minutely examining the Hebrew vocabulary I am unable to find any examples where the common consonants are the second and third except one or two doubtful cases,[1] and none where they are the first and third, except (if it be an exception) where a semi-vowel, instead of a vowel, is interposed.[2] Why, then, are these common 'phonetic types' at the beginning of the Semitic radical? The answer is, again, that they were originally the verbs of the language, subsequently extended by a suffixed consonant. This is a matter of significance. As we have often noticed, man, as a rule, makes no more effort in speech than is necessary to make himself understood. What can be inferred by the hearer is slurred or omitted. Language has evolved in so far as it is n essary for communication, and nothing else exists in speech. If the essence of a word or sentence is at its beginning rather than its end, an economy of effort is possible, for if the beginning gives the meaning, the rest can be slurred or omitted. When, therefore, details and refinements are added, development and differentiation of meaning and morphology, the basic idea being in the root the additions tend to be made more commonly by suffix than by prefix or infix. The meaning will thus be most quickly conveyed; but if the basic idea comes last, the hearer's attention must remain fixed till the end. So in the majority of languages the extension is by suffix, and the Indo-European, in its almost exclusive use of suffixes, is no exception.[3]

[1] 'AB (da'ab, da'eb, ya'ab, ka'ab, ta'ab, ta'eb), BḤ (zabaḥ, ṭabaḥ) BṬ (ḥabaṭ, labaṭ), DP (nadap, hadap, radap).
[2] Eg. buẓ, puṣ, quṣ, etc. (for which see previous chapter).
[3] There are, of course, languages in which the root is developed by prefixes and infixes. The following example from Khmer has often been quoted, but is particularly appropriate here:

kăt	to cut.
k'năt	to measure.
kŏmnăt	a piece.
t'kăt	pain, suffering.
dămkăt	pain, suffering.
skăt	to cut, cut off, fence off, bar off.
sankăt	a division.
bankăt	to cut, decide.

See Meillet and Cohen, p. 392. The version in Schmidt, *Die Sprachen der Sakei und Semang*, p. 568, differs in immaterial respects.

But even if we were to regard these common biliteral elements in the semitic verb as mere phonetic types, symbolizing the concepts to which they are attached, it is plain that they must have borne these meanings in the public mind at a time before some, at least, of the triliterals, in which they figure, came into use. It is impossible to imagine a group of anything up to 14[1] triliteral verb-roots as coming into existence at one swoop, all containing a common biliteral element with its common meaning. There must have been a time when the group contained a smaller number, one or two or three; and if so – whatever be the true explanation and origin – these biliteral elements, bearing these meanings, are older than the present state of the language – that is to say, older than Semitic as we know it. It is no small achievement to penetrate behind Semitic even to this extent.

And how are we to account for the existence of several of these biliterals, in the Semitic as we know it, alone and without a third consonant? In the imperative and infinitive, by reason of stress, there is a semi-vowel between the two consonants – buz, puṣ, push, bur, gud, quṣ, quṭ, ḫud, gur, duk – but in the third person of the aorist (or perfective) there is only the vowel A: baz, paṣ, pash,[2] etc. They can hardly have changed from a triliteral to a biliteral form, contrary to the whole spirit of the language. Moreover there are signs, throughout the Hebrew language, of earlier biliteral radicals, and a number of scholars, on quite other grounds, consider Hebrew to have originated with biliteral roots.

But there are other compelling reasons to regard the explanation of these phenomena as historical. One is the enormous extent of these common elements and meanings, showing their great age by the degree in which the vocabulary of the language embodies them – the degree in which they have extended themselves into new words. Allowing for all the natural change and decay in language and absorption of foreign words, we have set out 300 verb roots containing over 50 of these biliteral elements. These are the easiest to see, but there is strong evidence of another 30 of these elements, and some evidence of 30 more. But we need not stop here: it is difficult to look at them without inferring that these pairs of consonants have been arrived at by variation and differentiation of a smaller number bearing even more plainly

---

[1] As in the group PR.
[2] They have probably dropped the final a of Arabic, as in Hebrew generally and some other Semitic dialects.

the same wide set of meanings. For example our first list of labials and dentals – bata, bada, baza, baṣa, paṣa, pasa, pata, paśa, pasha, paṭa, paza and pada, all signifying cut and break – almost compel the inference of an earlier pair of labial and dental, less clearly enunciated, less clearly differentiated in meaning, with the same middle, nondescript vowel, and with similar meaning.

Still more significant – why, of all meanings, do these pairs of consonants all evidence the same group of meanings – *cut*, *break*, *strike*, *crush*? Why, if they are merely phonetic types, presenting themselves to the unconscious mind as symbols of certain concepts, do they not symbolize other concepts also? Why do we never find among them, for example, common phonetic elements meaning *sing*, *drink*, *love*, *woman* and a hundred others? Why *cut* and *break*, of all the meanings of the vocabulary? How unimportant was this meaning, in the daily life of the Hebrew of the Old Testament, compared with these and other conceptions that they might have symbolized?

In fact, in a very small number of cases, common biliterals express other meanings, and this adds further cogency to the argument. Examining the Hebrew vocabulary for this purpose with minute care I have only been able to find the three following groups.

The first contains a small number of words, signifying *join*, *bind*, *make strong*, which comprise the common biliterals ASh and ḤB. This is not to be wondered at, for although, at the beginning of things, man manufactures by cutting and breaking and crushing, there must be a trifling number of cases, in early times, of binding and joining: and indeed we have seen these meanings in isolated words in our groups, born out of *cut* and *break*. It is to be doubted whether these biliterals, used in this sense, are of the highest antiquity.

The second cluster signifies *moaning*, and contains the common biliterals AN, NH and (possibly) NA. It is therefore especially interesting, because the sounds N and A are of the first antiquity and the least prone to change, and we have seen in the language of children how the nasal consonant predominates in states of pain and strain. Still more important, these phonetic types have entered the language by the same process (if we are right) as the oldest words meaning *cut* and *break* – namely, by imitating the sounds made by a man in the course of the action they symbolize. In the one case, the oral sounds he made in an action of maximum physical force were imitated and came to be used as words expressing such action. In the other case the sounds he made in the course of moaning were imitated and used to express that action. It is onomatopoeia of the true kind, and the English *moan* is of the same type.

The third group was arrived at in the same way. It consists of the consonants LQ, LḤ and LSh, and signifies to *lick* – similar sounds to the Indo-European, bearing a similar meaning. In other words these biliterals repeat the sound made by the tongue in the course of the action referred to.

But perhaps the most convincing matter of all is not argument, but to watch the meanings of these biliteral words changing to express the conceptions of the Hebrew civilization, and to watch the same meanings undergoing similar changes in other tongues. 'L'étymologie', said Voltaire in a celebrated passage, 'est une science où les voyelles ne font rien, et les consonnes fort peu de chose.' Often, alas, it seems to be little more, but it is not with such an etymology that we are here concerned. In this history of meanings, primitive man has left behind him an unmistakable diary, setting out the thoughts that progressively occurred to him over the half-million years that have passed since first he appeared on earth. Its entries repay unending study. It is the joint diary of a community, and each meaning is usually reached by a number of paths from its predecessor. Often the detection of the paths demands an appreciation of material conditions and ways of thought that passed away long ago; always it implies the workings of an unchanging human nature. Often the best parallel is the homely figures of the slang of the people of today that becomes the language of the scholar of tomorrow. Always it is easily understood, and always it fascinates. There is no relic of the life of man half so precious or so significant. There is no aspect of language of equal importance. Whichever way we look at these phenomena we cannot fail to see in them the history of mind and language.

But our view that the Semitic languages were preceded by these biliteral roots can be better and more helpfully criticized and tested in quite another way. Sayce remarks, in the same passage, that 'words are changed rather by the action of phonetic decay than by the addition of new letters'. Is it not possible, it may be asked, that the Semitic triliteral radicals containing a common biliteral element – for example, the radicals batal, bataq, batar, batat – were preceded by an earlier triliteral root consisting of bata and some final consonant, and signifying *cut*, *break* and the like, and that from it these four forms emerged through a varying pronunciation of the final consonant? Is it not possible – as so often happens in language – that, upon these four forms of pronunciation arising, each came to be used in a separate, somewhat specialized sense, so that each achieved a meaning slightly varied from *cut* and *break*? Nothing is more likely. Such a thought is not sufficient to displace the arguments for an earlier, biliteral language, but it serves to remind us that, during the normal process of lengthening of the roots, a separate process was occurring of the creation of words by phonetic change and decay. Let us consider how this latter process would operate.

It was said earlier that the end of a word is more prone to weaken and change than the beginning. Firstly, words and sentences are expressed by a puff of outgoing breath, and generally the outflow of breath is weaker at the end than the beginning. Hence, in particular, plosives change to fricatives. Secondly, man does not generally make more effort in speech than is necessary to be understood, and if the beginning of a word is heard the rest is apt to be inferred by the listener, and, for that reason, slurred or omitted by the speaker. Hence a final consonant is apt to be pronounced carelessly and differently by different individuals, and as these varied forms become familiar each will tend to be used by the community in a slightly different sense, being distributed among its growing number of ideas. Accordingly the process of phonetic change that we are considering would be apt to produce the result that the first consonant of the triliteral verb would suffer the least change, and the last of the three the most. If such a process were long continued, but left its evidence in the regularly developed Semitic language, we would find that in a group of triliteral verbs, bearing variations of the meaning *cut*, *break*, the first letter would be comparatively constant, the second letter would vary and the third still more. In the result, in so far as such a group contained a common pair of consonants, it would be the first and second.[1] And this is what we have found.

We should also find, on this hypothesis, another result. We were convinced, in previous chapters, that language originated in single plosive consonants separated by the vowel A, with a large extent of reduplication. In the Semitic radicals there still survive two of these features – namely, that the consonants are always single, and separated by the vowel A. If the Semitic radicals emerged from earlier triliteral verbs of these meanings (whether more or less composed of reduplications such as bababa and tatata and the like) by phonetic decay and

[1] A common first consonant would not be noticed: the words are too numerous and varied.

change the second and third consonants would easily become differentiated, in the way we have mentioned, and the reduplication would disappear. And we should find, as the plosives were replaced by fricatives, that in the Semitic verbs, of such meanings as *cut* and *break*, the largest proportion of plosives would be in the first consonants, a lesser proportion among the second, and the least in the third. This is in fact what we find. There would remain the rest of the Semitic vocabulary – additions accruing over the ages – bearing no traces of the old meanings, and with no common introductory biliterals. In these we should find, in the first and second consonants, a smaller proportion of plosives and a greater of fricatives than in groups containing the older sounds and the older meanings. And this we in fact find. Indeed, it is not too much to say that the finer points of the pronunciation of the Hebrew consonants could be largely inferred merely from the proportion of words, of the original meanings, in which they appear.

This phenomenon can perhaps be best displayed in the following way. Let us separate from the rest of the Hebrew vocabulary three categories: the first consisting of verbs in which the origin from biliterals meaning *cut, break* is clearest; the second of verbs in which the origin is not so clear, though there is yet substantial evidence of it; the third of verbs containing a trace of such origin and no more. The first group, of clear cases, contains 27 biliterals[1] (included in those set out in the previous chapter); the second contains 52 biliterals,[2] half of which are listed in the previous chapter, and half not: and the third contains a further 31 biliterals.[3] In the first group, of 27 different biliterals which we have called *clear*, the first letter is a plosive in 21 cases (78%) and a fricative in only 6 (22%). In the second group (of 52 biliterals) the first letter is a plosive in only 29 cases (56%) and a fricative in 23 (44%). In the third group (of 31 biliterals) the first letter is a plosive in 13 cases only (42%) and a fricative in 18 (58%). Similarly in the *second* letter of each biliteral. In the first group (called *clear*) the plosives are fewer than in the first letters of that group, but there are still 12 plosives (44%) as against 15 fricatives (56%). In the second group the plosives are only 17 (33%) as against 35 fricatives

---

[1] 'Ak, bd, bz, bt, bq, gd, gz, gr, dq, dk, ḫt, ḥṣ, ḥq, ḥr, mn, nq, nt, pl, pṣ, ps, pt, psh, pr, qṭ, qs, qṣ, shs.

[2] Bḫ, bk, bṣ, br, bl, gl, gm, hr, hb, zr, ḫl, ḫṭ, tb, ta', tr, yg, ks, kr, kt, ml, mr, mḫ, ng, nk, ns, nd, sa', sp, sq, sḫ, pa, pz, pḫ, pṭ, pa', ṣl, ṣr, qd, qr, ql, qm, rṣ, rd, rs, rsh, śr, št, shb, shḫ, shṭ, shl, sha'.

[3] 'Az, dm, hg, zb, ḥś, ḥsh, ḥs, ḥp, tḫ, ksh, kp, lṭ, nz, nsh, nṣ, na', np, ny, sl, a'd, a'r, a'z, a's, a'ṣ, qb, qś, ql, rt, ra', śk, shm.

(67%), and the proportions in the third group are substantially the same. In the rest of the vocabulary fricatives predominate in the first letter as well as the second and third.[1]

Accordingly if we reject the belief in an origin of Semitic from biliterals, and suppose a differentiation of earlier triliterals, we still reach the same result – namely an origin in words of single plosives separated by the vowel A and bearing the meanings of maximum human effort – except that triliterals take the place of biliterals. But, as we have said, we would be wiser to regard the two processes as contemporary – a general process of extension of words from two to three consonants, and a general process of weakening and change of the ends of words.[2] As we have seen, it is not by one path, or impelled by one force, that language has advanced to its present condition. The course it has taken results from innumerable, diverse forces acting upon it, and variations in the speech of every member of each community.

One question remains. Assuming that the cause of the presence in Semitic of these common biliterals is historical, may not this process of development have occurred at any time? Is not language for ever undergoing the same processes? We saw in an earlier chapter that the nouns and other parts of speech developed from verbs in a set order in the beginnings of language, and that ever since they have continued, in the main, to be born out of verbs in the some order. Similarly, may not these innumerable meanings have continued to be born out of the arch-verbs, the verbs of maximum human effort? Indeed, we have given, as our best illustration of the process, usages of Modern English under which, for example, that mysterious word *cut* – of unknown and much-debated origin, and in form so like the Hebrew kat(a) and ḥat(a) and other biliterals that we have mentioned – gives rise to similar meanings in popular speech. Certainly it is true that the process is for ever repeating itself, for the channels of the mind were cut in this fashion in the earliest days of man, and thought has continued to pour along them ever since. But we cannot attribute to recent development the bulk of the enormous spread of this phenomenon in Semitic. Indeed, it is so wide as to suggest that, but for phonetic change and decay and the great addition of fricatives, these biliteral, plosive origins and their meanings might have been discerned throughout the

---

[1] We see the same situation in Indo-European. In the examples given in the previous chapter the predominance of plosives will be noticed, and especially in the first letter of each pair.

[2] Indeed this last test may be said to corroborate the view of a biliteral origin, for the proportion of plosives diminishes not only in the third radical but also in the second.

vocabulary. There is also one great difference between the old and the new. In Semitic these biliterals (in the clear cases) consist of two, mainly plosive, consonants with a separating A. In Modern English (apart from the word *cut*) the phonemes used are of many forms. But if we go back far enough – if we look in English for the words descended from similar ancient plosive biliteral roots of the same meanings – we can see them still in enormous profusion.

The examples given from Greek and Latin in the previous chapter are significant. If we are right in our reconstruction of the origin and history of language, it is, as we have said, easy to envisage the two divergent paths that Semitic and Indo-European took in the early days of language. The Semitic, whilst lengthening its radicals, kept with unique and characteristic regularity the pattern of the earliest words, retaining the vowel A and extending the alternation of CVCV to CVCVC or CVCVCV. It may have retained that vowel for the further reason that this process took place in its very early history when the other vowels were not yet pronounced with regularity and precision, and that it was only later that the vowel was varied for the purposes of accidence. On the other hand the Indo-European, like the bulk of other languages, increased its vocabulary by variation of the vowel in the biliteral root, as well as by irregular addition of consonants, sometimes making a consecutive pair of consonants – as in *scar* from *kar*, and *mergo* from *mar*, and so forth. The Bantu underwent a similar development, but generally its roots are still of the form CVCV.

It is not to be expected that tongues such as these will generally yield such palpable evidence of the origins of language. The forms of the biliteral roots have been altered to give all the necessary meanings of a developed language – in Africa by violent, if regular, mutation of consonants, and everywhere by change of vowels, and in many places by changing or dropping a final consonant, so much exposed to wear and decay. The regular mutation of consonants need not trouble us. In Bantu the decay of the final consonant is less than elsewhere, for the final vowel A survives (bona! see; tema! cut; geza! wash). The only way to check here our theory of the history of language is to collect together the roots containing the same two consonants, and to disregard the easily changing vowels.

If, then, we take the conservative Zulu language as our example, and gather together the radical verbs of the same two consonants, we shall see everywhere, as clearly as in Hebrew, the evidences of the same origin of language. We content ourselves with a few examples,[1] giving a few references to the Hebrew where necessary to illustrate the train of thought.

AB, AP

aba	distribute, divide (iz-abulo, secret affairs – cf. Heb. baṣar).[2]
apuca	take away by force, tear away.
apuka	get broken, sprained (regarded by the Zulu as a fracture – see Heb. and Ar. pasaḫ[1]), die suddenly.
apula	break, fracture, dislocate.[3]
eba	steal anything away.
ebula	peel off, strip off.
epa	thin out, pull up (of plants).
epula	save from danger, deliver.
opa	shed blood, bleed, pour out.

BC

băca, ukuti	lie open, splash out, sprawl.
baca	hide oneself, go elsewhere for refuge, stick to a person (cf. the two Eng. uses of *cleave*).
boca	beat a person, beat the life out of him.
buca	fall to pieces from rottenness.

BZ

baza	shave, pare, carve.

CB

caba	chop, break, cut, slay.
căba, ukuti	be flat, level, smooth.
coba	(1) chop up, rob of strength.
	(2) crack or kill lice.
comba	to mark.
cuba	squash or break up.
ciba	fling an assegai.
cibi, ukuti	squash, crush.

[1] Taken from Bryant's Zulu-English Dictionary (1905).
[2] *Ante*, p. 224.
[3] *Ante*, p. 225.

CS, CSh, CZ

casa	smash, break.
cosu, ukuti	tear off.
cosha	pick up.
cushe, ukuti	pierce, pass through.
cisha	extinguish, die.
caza	(1) separate, divide.
	(2) make incisions.
ceza	chip off.
cezu, ukuti	tear off.
cezula	(1) break, strike, cut off.
	(2) make turn off, or go off, or away.

DB

daba	(root) *cut*, as in:
dabula	tear, make to break forth into life, create (as God did the earth, see Heb. bara'[1]), split off, cut.
i-n-daba	matter, affair.
um-dabuli	surveyor (divider, measurer of land).
isi-dabuko	original source (i.e. place of breaking forth), original or ancient custom.
děbe, ukuti	cut, break.
duba	break up, ill-treat.

DRr[2]

dŏrro ukuti, dorroza, durruza	smash.
děrre, ukuti	squat sprawled out (i.e. 'do the splits').

DHl[3]

dhla	eat, cut, break.
dhle	(root) = tear (cf. dhlela, dhlebula, etc.).
dhli	(root) = tear (cf. dhlikiza, etc.).
u-dhli	contemptuous disregard (= cutting a person).
dhlo	(root) = cut, stab.
dhlu, ukuti	pierce, tear.

---

[1] *Ante*, p. 228.
[2] Rr is a strong guttural.
[3] Dhl represents a deep throat lisp resembling the sound of *thl* in Eng. *smoothly*.

FA

fa — die.
fa, ukuti — sprinkle (scatter).
u(lu)fa — a crack, chink, cleft.

FL

fala — scatter (cf. falakahla).
fela — die for.
fola — stoop, be bent (i.e. broken, cf. Hebrew barak), pierce.

GB

gaba — mark out with holes in a row the boundary of a field, or when planting potatoes (i.e. pierce, divide), rely on, take advantage.
isi-gaba — a piece divided off, a troop, regiment.
gaba — empty out (the stomach with an emetic).
gabe, ukuti — cut, cut open with a gash or slit, do anything in a big or thorough way.
guba — scoop out, 'pump' a person of secrets, do in a big way, toss wildly about.
geba — bend down (i.e. break).
gĕbe, ukuti — bend down, cut a big open wound.
i(li)-gebe — a deep pit or hole.
gebeza — cut a person a big, open wound.
gĕbu, ukuti — cut deeply into.
goba — bend, relax, retire from view (cf. gebe, ukuti).
goba — take a large piece from, relate a matter partially.

GM

gămu, ukuti — cut through, cut off, cut short.
i(li)-gamu — single item of speech (name, letter, word, statement).
isi-gamu — piece chopped off.
um-gamu — interval of space or time.
gamuka — cut off, cease, come to a stop.
gema — point out, aim at.
gămpu, ukuti — divided, cut, mark.

GZ

gazu, ukuti — cut, open, split, go bounding along.
i-ngozi — a wound, harm, danger, scar.
geza — wash (i.e. graze, scrape?).

HB

hăbu, ukuti   gape open, yawn open.
hĕbe, ukuti   give a gash to a person or animal, split a scalp.
hebeza   scare away.
hoba   grind grain, be in an alarmed state.

LM

lima   dig, cut up land with the hoe, grow a crop.
lamu!   break off! separate! (to persons fighting).
luma   bite, cause sharp pain.
lŭmu, ukuti   break, snap, pluck off.

PQ

păqa, ukuti   be in the open, pour out a bit, patter.
pĕqe, ukuti   cut, fold, bend.
pĭqi, ukuti   burst forth.
poqa   force, ravish.
pŏqo, ukuti   snap, break.
pŭqu, ukuti   throw off, discharge.

PRr

pŏrro, ukuti   smash, break, strike.
pŭrru, ukuti   smash, break, blurt out.

PHl[1]

pahla   shut off, encircle, surround, stow away.
păhla, ukuti   let out suddenly, blurt out (i.e. burst).
pahlaza   smash, break.
pehla   bore, work up anything.
pĕhle, ukuti   break in two with a gradual crashing sound.
pĭhli, ukuti   smash to bits, pour out in a heavy scattering.
pŏhlo, ukuti   smash with a crash, smash a person a crushing blow, crush up in the mouth.

QB

qăba, ukuti   patter (as drops of rain – i.e. scatter), give a person a mere drop or small quantity of something (cf. caba, chop).

---

[1] Hl has the sound of *thl* in *deathly*.

qăbu, ukuti   catch first sight of something, come to one's senses.
qib   = break (so qibula, qibuka, qibukana, qifuza = break).
qoba   cut up, chop up, break up, into small pieces (cf. coba).
qŏbo, ukuti strike a hard thing with stick or stone.
qĕbe, qĕbe ukuti   chatter about everything under the sun (i.e. scatter?).
quba   drive away, run along.
qŭbu, ukuti break out on all sides at once (of plants, affairs).

QD

qanda   be cutting (of cold, head-splitting), speak a decisive word, strike down, cleave, separate.
qonda   understand, grasp (i.e. distinguish).
qunda   blunt (a knife, by wear, chipping or turning the edges).
qeda   make an end of, kill, be the death of.
quda   be kept separate.

QP

qĕpu, ukuti break off, divide.
qopa   cut slits into, notch, derisively name a person (i.e. 'cut') begin to produce small fruit (i.e. burst, break).
qupula   pick out (i.e. separate).

QT

qata   break (cf. qota and quta).

QSh

qasha   fly off, spring off.
qashula   break, tear.
qesha }
queshe ukuti } notch, make jagged, growl or snarl, show the teeth.
qosha   put on airs.
qŭshu, ukuti   pierce, prick, give an exploding puff, munch.

QZ

qaza   (1) examine, inspect (i.e. cut open), seek, look for.
             (2) bind, grasp, catch suddenly hold of.
qĕzu, ukuti break, snap off, chip off, turn off the path.
qŏza   beat, get the better of, make a dull, knocking noise, do thoroughly, finish completely.

quza   make a person turn back on his way, pour out, fly at.
qŭzu, ukuti   tear, wrench off, knock off, strike against.

RrB

rraba   stand scattered about feeding (as cattle).
rrabe ukuti   give a glance at.
rrabu ukuti   cut by a single sharp slitting cut, take away from.
rrabela   cut up lengthwise.
rrĕbu, ukuti   tear, rend.
rrŏbo, ukuti   yield abundantly (i.e. burst forth).
rruba   fling a missile at.

RrW

rrăwu, ukuti   cut small slits in the skin.
rrĕwu, ukuti   tear, rend.
rrwĕ, ukuti } scratch, make a scratching sound.
rrweba
rrwi, ukuti   (1) tear, break.
              (2) be full, be angry.

SK

săka, ukuti   scatter, drop down broken in pieces, die suddenly, fall to pieces.
seka   support, prop up.
sekehla   crush, calumniate.
i(li)-seko   a stone on the hearth for propping up cooking pots.
isi-seko   a stone for roughing a grindstone or supporting it. (cf. Lat. saxum, from seco).
sika   cut, divide off, make an insinuation against a person, nearly reach to, approach to (cf. Heb. naga').
sĭki, ukuti   make a slight movement, aim at.
sikihli, ukuti   cut, fill, finish off.
soka   cut (foreskin).
suka   start off, get up, go off, fly off, originate from.

TB

tăba, ukuti   chop, cut, break (cf. caba).
taba   delight.

teba	(1) show wilful disregard or indifference for a person (i.e. 'cut' him).
	(2) waver, sway to and fro.
tĕbe, ukuti	chop, cut, break.
tĭbi, ukuti	yield to pressure of hand or foot.
toba	(1) bend.
	(2) soften.
tŏbo, ukuti	yield to pressure.
tuba	(1) break, smash, thump at, knock up, exhaust (a person).
	(2) become darkened.

TP

tapa	take away by a clutching of the hands, take in, look at, smite.
tĕpu, ukuti	snap, break.
topa	be polished, smooth, soft.

C

zaca	be or become thin, languish.
zăcu, ukuti	take out deeply, or largely.
zeca	⎫
zĕce, ukuti	⎬ sever, break.
zucu, ukuti	⎭

The above groups, from the Zulu vocabulary, are given merely by way of illustration. In Zulu, as in Semitic, the clearer cases contain a greater proportion of plosives than in the rest of the language, and the first letters of the biliterals contain a greater proportion than the second letters. The vowel A predominates among the clearest examples of radicals surviving in the old form with something near the old meaning – aba, ata, baca, caba, casa, caza, daba, and the rest – verb-roots that we inferred from the Hebrew vocabulary to have preceded Semitic in the ancient past. The number of groups of biliterals in Zulu that contain biliterals of the old meaning, or strong evidence of them, is very large. The impression is given even more clearly than in Hebrew that practically the whole vocabulary may have descended from them. The beginnings of language, that we inferred, seem to be nearer to hand. The total list of such biliterals, numbering over 150, is as follows. The clearer cases are printed in italics. There are a number of other biliterals, which show traces of the same origin but are not contained in this list.

ZULU

Ab, *ap*, *at*, al, *ahl*.
Ba, *be*, bq, bb, *bd*, *bl*, br, bj, bng, *bz̧*, bx, bdhl.
Cb, *cc*, *cd*, *cf*, *ck*, cm, cp, *cs*, *csh*, ct, *cz̧*.
Db, dng, *dl*, dm, *drr*, dw, dz.
Dhl.
Fa, fc, fd, fhl, fk, *fl*, ft, fx, fz.
Ga, *gb*, gqb, gc, *gd*, gj, *gl*, *gm*, gn, gq, *grr*, *gdhl*, gx, gz.
Ha, *hb*, *hl*, *hn*, *hp*, hq, hsh, hv, hw, hy, hz.
Jd, *jq*, jj, jw.
Kb, kd, kk, *kl*, km, *kt*, *khl*, kv, *kw*, kz.
Lm, lb, ll, lp.
Mn, mt, mh, mk, mrr, mb, mf, nb, nc, nq.
Pc, *pq*, *pk*, pd, *phl*, *pt*, *prr*, pl.
Qb, *qp*, *qm*, *qd*, *qt*, *qsh*, *qz̧*, *qk*.
Rrb, *rrm*, *rrw*, rrv, rrn, *rrl*, rry.
Sb, sp, *sv*, sm, sn, *sk*, sz.
Shy (shaya).
Tb, *tp*, tw, tc, *tn*, ts, *thl* (tahla, tuhlu).
Vc, vk, *vrr*, *vt*, *vv*.
Xv, xb, xp, xz.
Yc, *yl*, yp.
Zc, *z̧k*, zt, *z̧v*, *z̧w*, zf.

R

CHAPTER TWENTY

Theories of the Origin of Language

This, then, is the conclusion at which we have arrived as to the manner in which speech began, Its first sounds were of much the same phonetic type as the first articulate utterances of human babes – gasps of the form dă, bă, mă and the like – and they were uttered involuntarily in the course of a strenuous effort of the arm. Being phonetically different from other human cries, and normally accompanying such effort, they were associated with it in the mind, and were uttered by a man seeking such assistance from his fellow, together with a gesture mimicking the desired action. Soon these sounds, in each developing language, tended to take on a constant form – CV or CVC or CVCV – and to be differentiated and increased in number by a growing variation and precision of consonants and, later, of vowels; and at the same time the meanings were differentiated and increased and made more precise, so that they signified different types of effort of the arm. *Cut* and *break*, *crush*, *strike* were the commonest, for these are the commonest forms of maximum arm effort; and these are the earliest meanings of which we find traces in language. We need not repeat the story of their varying later development.

And now, before we bring this essay to a close, let us look at some of the best-known theories of the origin of speech, and consider whether, and to what extent, they, too, fit the circumstances which we have imagined, and how much of the truth they also contain.

Perhaps we should mention first the theory of the origin of language (if such it can be called) which is contained in the second account of the Creation, in the second chapter of the book of Genesis. According to this account 'the Lord God formed man of the dust of the ground and breathed into his nostrils the breath of life', and afterwards he created the trees and the rivers. And then 'out of the ground the Lord God formed every beast of the field, and every fowl of the air; and brought them unto the man to see what he would call them; and whatsoever the man called every living creature, that was the name thereof.

And the man gave names to all cattle, and to the fowl of the air and to every beast of the field'.

This simple story places man – God's first creature, created with all the mature mental attributes of man – at the centre and upon the pinnacle of the world. It is an account of the birth of language in man that seems to be derived from the birth of language in the human child. The child, the cynosure of his parents' eyes, as man is of God's eyes, utters towards his animal friends and playfellows some spontaneous, first, articulate sound, and the admiring parent notes it as the name of the animal, as God notes it in the story. So the child is first familiarized with names of animals and objects.

Alas, man is no longer thought of as the first creature but the last, gradually achieving since the beginning of the world his mature, mental equipment. He is no longer the centre of the universe except in his own eyes. But it can hardly be doubted that this picture of language as originating in the names of things – and especially of the animals, with which the child and the primitive man are so closely in sympathy – constitutes a theory which men are prone to conceive and prone to accept. But what should possess the speechless anthropoid to begin his career as a man by giving names to the animal kingdom, or to the few objects around him? and by what mental process did he come to do so? He must already have acquired speech in order to conceive the idea of naming them. Let us leave the Bible and turn to the more sophisticated theories of the Greeks and the modern world.

Perhaps the most familiar of these is the onomatopoeic, irreverently called by Max Müller the bow-wow theory. It sees the origin of speech in the imitation of natural sounds. This is certainly the source of the names of a number of birds – for example, the cuckoo, upupa (hoopoe), peewit and curlew – but of how many other words? Language did not commence, we thought, with a process of naming the animal kingdom.

There has in the past been a wide division of opinion between linguists as to the extent to which speech so began. It is to be doubted whether any consider this the sole source of language, or any deny that some words have had such a source: the difference is as to whether such an origin is negligible or important. The writers of greatest insight into the nature of language seem to me to be found in the former camp. Aristotle will have nothing to do with the theory of earlier Greek philosophers, including Plato, of the natural fitness of words to signify their meaning. He foreshadows the doctrine, referred to in this book, that the meaning of words is derived from their use.

Max Müller and Dwight Whitney have nothing to say for the theory. Sayce,[1] on the other hand, who accepted all the new notions that came from Germany in the 1870s and 1880s, goes so far as to refer to the 'probable onomatopoeic origin of the greater part of our vocabulary'. The German writers on the metaphysics of language, and modern writers who, having despaired of any progress towards a history of language, take their main interest in the study of the sounds of words and phonetic laws, have written much on this topic. With them, as with Plato and earlier Greek philosophers, it is a part of the larger subject of 'sound symbolism'. But whereas those Greek philosophers taught that words received their meaning from their natural fitness to symbolize it, the moderns only aver that many words do so.

There can be no doubt, firstly, that some English words are shaped by imitation of natural sound. There are, for example, the names of the birds referred to above, which are but the imitation of their songs or calls. And on the other hand many words, commonly regarded as deriving their meaning from their phonetic fitness, have no such origin. Max Müller gives the example of the English word 'thunder' – apparently onomatopoeic, if ever a word was – and yet, as he points out, it is derived from the Indo-European root *tan* or *ten*, meaning *stretch*, and so, from the stretching of the strings of a musical instrument, comes to signify sound. Another example is *sneeze* – a likely example if ever there was one – but in O.E. it was fneosan, and it has the same origin as the Greek pněo (to breathe) where there is no sound of sneezing and no sound-symbolism, notwithstanding Jespersen's view to the contrary.[1] Nor does *bow-wow* originate by way of imitation of a dog's bark, as Jespersen thought. It is one of the nursery sounds (papa, mama, baba, wawa) the last and least frequent of which is taken by English parents to mean the dog, and the consonants are improved and diversified on the model of the rhymed couplets pell-mell, roly-poly, helter-skelter, higgledy-piggledy, and the like.

But undoubtedly in modern Germanic languages are a number of words which seem to attempt the imitation of natural sound, and some writers have sought to arrange them in groups containing a common phonetic element in which some common meaning of this kind can be traced. Such, for example, are bump, thump, dump, crump, slump. A large proportion are sibilant words representing watery sounds – splash (and plash), sizzle, slop, sludge, slush, slosh; but one cannot be sure even of the origin of these. For example the same *sl* appears in

[1] Sayce, vol. 1, p. 149.   [1] Jespersen, p. 398.

groups of words of quite different meanings – slight, slender, slim; slash, slice, slit, slot, sliver; slip, slope, slide, slew; sleep, slumber; slack, slouch, slur, slink, slut, slattern, sloven, sluggard, sluggish. More convincing are the imitations of human vocal sound – for example the Greek *gru*, *gruzo*, English *grunt*, *grumble*, *grumpy* and *disgruntled*; and also *moan* and *mumble*. But there is no *gr* in the human grunt, and no *bl* in the human grumble and mumble. Accordingly the bulk of these double consonants cannot be regarded as earlier roots originating in imitation of natural sound.

In truth because language is so closely entwined with the growth and working of our mental processes, and so closely bound up with all our memories and feelings and cultural traditions, and so vital to our social life and progress; and because the use of each speech-sound is so familiar as to be almost instinctive, and the proper use of each word essential to all our social purposes – each word seems utterly appropriate to its use, whatever its origin. Consequently we are forever deceiving ourselves in searching for reasons why sound and sense seem to fit so well together. Many of the speech-sounds now indicating 'sound symbolism' seem to have been arrived at originally by quite other means.

Jespersen ends his discussion of this topic with the significant observation that 'though some echo words may be very old, the great majority are not; at any rate, in looking up the earliest ascertained date of a goodly number of such words in the N.E.D., I have been struck by the fact of so many of them being quite recent, not more than a few centuries old, and some not even that. . . . There is every probability that this class of words is really more frequent in the spoken language of recent times than it was formerly.'[1] This can hardly be doubted; and there is little of the phenomenon in the languages of the simpler peoples. We have found one reason in this book why it is so. These fricatives and pairs of successive consonants, which make up the bulk of these 'echo-words', are the recent parts of speech-sound. The roots – the early words of language – are not of these phonetic types. Nor were their meanings such, nor are such the principles of the change of meaning. Words change their meaning by a species of metaphor, not because of their symbolism of sound. As Dwight Whitney says: 'No account of the origin of language is scientific which does not join directly on to the later history of language without a break, being of

---

[1] Jespersen, p. 411. Similarly Dwight Whitney, L. G. at p. 297 refers to 'the undeniable presence of a considerable onomatopoeic element in later speech'.

one piece with that history.'[1] and the later history of language is an increase, not decrease, in the sway of sound-symbolism; or, as Jespersen has it, there was in history a slow, progressive development towards more adequate expressions, in which sound and sense are united in a marriage-union closer than was ever known to our remote ancestors.[2]

But we shall be nearer the truth of the matter if we take a broader view than this. The fundamental requisite of language is a faculty for hearing and imitating sound. Vocal sound may be uttered involuntarily; but there can be no language without a faculty to hear and imitate it. It is, as we said, the best opinion that the reason why the chimpanzee cannot speak is that he has little or no tendency to imitate sounds. Actions and gestures of human beings he readily and forever imitates, but he cannot be induced to imitate their speech sounds.[3] Language is in the widest sense onomatopoeic, but the sounds imitated are those that most interest man, namely the natural sounds of man. So, the range of frequencies to which the human ear is sensitive corresponds to the range of frequencies of the human voice in conversation. So each man learns the language of his community, and so language was born. And so, apart from the meanings of *cut* and *break* and the like, we only found in the Hebrew biliterals the meanings of *moan* and *lick*, both being groups of speech sounds which (like their similar English equivalents) imitate the sounds made by man in those two actions. Language arose from the need and purpose of communication between man; and above all it arose from the communication of requests for assistance. It does not follow from this that early man cannot have imitated some other natural sound – for example the conspicuous cry of another animal. But this is so much a subsidiary feature of the imitation of sound that it is unlikely in the extreme that it played a substantial part in the birth of language. However, we have concluded that language originated in the imitation of human sound made in cutting, breaking, piercing, crushing, striking. Those who believe that language originated in the purpose of imitating sound generally may have observed one common characteristic of these actions – they produce, above all other human actions, a loud and sudden noise. It is conceivable that that noise, as well as the accompanying gasp of the actor, served to render these actions distinct from other actions, and that the purpose to imitate both types of sound

---

[1] Ibid.
[2] Jespersen, p. 411.
[3] R. M. and A. W. Yerkes, *The Great Apes* (1929), p. 306; Yerkes and Learned, pp. 53-6, Köhler, p. 75, and T. S. Traill.

created language. To the present author it seems that this non-human sound may have been more significant as a means of impressing the mind of the imitator than of shaping the sound that he produced.

The second familiar theory of the origin of language is that which was named by Max Müller the pooh-pooh theory. This is the theory that speech originated in the cries or interjections of the human animal.

This is an unhelpful doctrine. Certainly before the emergence of speech there can have been no vocal sound but animal cries, just as before man there were only anthropoid apes; but as Max Müller observed, language begins where interjections end. In fact, man still utters cries and interjections, but their significance is always affective – expressing fear, surprise, despair, misery, pain or joy. On the other hand, each phonetic element in language has an intellectual significance. And it is not only the meaning but also the phonetic character of language that differs as the poles from cries and interjections. The latter are inarticulate; there are neither consonants nor vowels in the sense in which language consists of consonants and vowels. Lastly, there is no border-territory between language and cries. How then did the change occur? In particular, how does a feeling become an intellectual conception?

Darwin's contribution to this aspect of human history[1] has been much criticized. He was concerned to point to the continuity in body and mind between man and the other animals. He refers to the continued use by man of inarticulate cries to express his meaning, aided by gestures and movements of the muscles of the face. 'Our cries of pain', he says, 'fear, surprise, anger, together with their appropriate actions, are more expressive than any words.' That which distinguishes man from the lower animals is not, he says, the understanding of articulate sounds, for dogs understand many words and sentences. It is not the mere articulation of such sounds, for parrots and other birds possess this power. Nor is it the mere capacity to connect definite sounds with definite ideas, for some parrots connect unerringly words with things and persons with events. Man, he concludes, differs from the lower animals solely in his almost infinitely larger power of associating together the most diversified sounds and ideas; and this obviously depends on the high development of his mental powers.

But this is to fail to do justice to the difference, which is a difference in kind, not degree, if ever there was one. Before language appeared there were inarticulate cries with solely affective meaning: now there

[1] *Descent of Man*, chap. 3.

are inarticulate cries with solely affective meaning, and also articulate words with solely intellectual meaning. Accordingly the latter, it would seem, had a distinct origin. If we are right we have suggested the origin in this book.

But man is not a machine, and language is a resultant of innumerable forces and factors, and a mean of innumerable speech habits. It is conceivable that some cries – other than the interjections involuntarily emitted in the course of effort of the arms – have gone to the building up of speech and language. We have noticed one root in Semitic and one in Indo-European, bearing the meaning of *cut* and *break* and beginning with a vowel – namely, the same root agh, ag, ak or akh (Greek ag-numi, break; Latin ac-u, needle; Hebrew 'akal, eat, 'akar, dig). It is conceivable that sudden interjections of pain (like the German *ach*, English *ah*, Greek *achos*, pain, English *ache*) uttered when a man received a cut or wound, might reinforce the process, described in this book, whereby vocal sounds, concomitants of strenuous arm effort, came to indicate *cut, break, pierce, strike*. It is easy to imagine that if a highly vocal and excitable animal of few inhibitions received a serious cut or wound, such an ejaculation would be common. Accordingly those who incline to the pooh-pooh theory may see in it evidence of the origin of language which we have suggested. Certainly it has often been suggested that the Indo-European root agh, cut, originated in a cry of pain. Nevertheless the bulk of these biliterals commence with a consonant and are not of the forms of interjections, and this factor in the origin of speech is probably negligible.

A third theory of the origin of language was at one time enunciated by Max Müller, and called the ding-dong theory. It sought to explain the correspondence, of which we are often conscious, between sound and sense, by a law of nature, a mysterious law of harmony, that 'everything which is struck rings. Each substance has its peculiar ring.' So the sight of a dog strikes the observer as a gong is struck, and he utters the words 'dog runs' as a sound natural to the event. This takes us no further, whatever it may mean.

A fourth theory of origin, sometimes known as the yo-he-ho theory, is that of Noiré, referred to earlier in this book. He saw the source of speech in acts of joint or common work, in which, during intense physical effort, cries or sounds partly consonantal might be emitted, the product of a common impulse; and such sounds might come to be associated with the work performed and so become a symbol for it. To an extent the origin suggested in the present book marches with it – as indeed it marches with most of the theories referred to in this chapter. Language, we said, originated in exclamations uttered in work. But we pointed out that an origin of language in joint work posits a process of mind too precise for speechless anthropoids, a social sense too far developed, and even an economy too complex. In brief it pictures a group of men pulling on a rope, or dragging by joint effort a tree or rock too heavy for one to move. But there is no trace in the languages we have examined of even one original root signifying to pull, to drag.

A fifth theory, commonly advocated, is that language originated in gesture. Sayce, for example, justly refers to 'the way in which gestures precede spoken language, and lead on to the latter'. Several writers instance, as illustrating some such thesis, the sign languages of North America and other parts,[1] but such examples are misleading. Sign languages are commonly used for communication at great distances to which speech cannot carry, or between communities speaking different tongues. They are, of course, all used by persons who have a language of their own as old as ours, and are as familiar as we are with speech and its uses. They have mental processes built up with the assistance of language over a hundred millennia, and are familiar with movements and objects as separate items of experience, rendered distinct with the use of separate speech-terms. The question is (in the words of Dean Farrar): How did words first come to be accepted as signs at all? Or (to put the matter differently) how did various modulations of the human voice acquire any significance by being connected with outward or inward phenomena?[2] A gesture cannot become a word or sentence, though it may influence them.

Communication by gesture and communication by speech both belong to the latest stages of the evolution of the animals and man. Broadly speaking, one age witnessed the development of both, and both have continued in use ever since. But the age of gesture is somewhat earlier than that of speech, for gesture is the earlier to appear, and its use and importance decrease with the maturity of language.

But gesture cannot develop to its full variety and extent until, with the attainment of prehensile fore-limbs, manual gesture becomes possible, reaching its peak of elaboration in man.[3] The same circumstances witness the growth and development of speech, and we have suggested in this book that speech originated with interjections in-

---

[1] For examples among Food Gatherers (Australia), see e.g. Spencer and Gillen, *The Arunta* (1927), vol. 2, pp. 600 *et seq.*; and *Across Australia* (1912), vol. 2, p. 390.
[2] F. W. Farrar, *An Essay on the Origin of Language* (1860), pp. 36-7.
[3] See Macdonald Critchley, *The Language of Gesture* (1939).

voluntarily and automatically accompanying the forcible use of the fore-limbs. These sounds, being, as we said, of a phonetic character distinct and separate from man's other vocal sounds, and always (because involuntary) accompanying actions of this kind, came easily to indicate such action, and were imitated and repeated to indicate a request for it, but only together with a violent gesture mimicking the desired effort of the arm. In this way the gesture itself helped to shape the utterance of the precise sound which accompanied arm-effort and which constituted the oral part of the request. So, we concluded, speech began.

It must also be noted that, up to the point where speech began, gesture had a superiority over vocal sound for purposes of communication. Up to this point vocal sound had only an affective value. It could register, according to the condition of the animal, the anger, fear, hunger, comfort and the like, by which its cries were shaped, though this value might be increased by the surrounding circumstances – as, for example, a cry of alarm might help to call the attention of the group to a visible prowling enemy. Gesture was far more capable of objective reference. We have seen this among the chimpanzees. For example Köhler (in a passage cited earlier) says of them that 'it may be taken as positively proved that their gamut of *phonetics* is entirely subjective'. In regard to their gestures, on the other hand, he points out that chimpanzees understand 'between themselves' not merely subjective moods and emotional states but also definite desires and urges, and 'a considerable proportion of all desires is naturally shown by direct imitation of the actions which are desired. Thus, one chimpanzee who wishes to be accompanied by another, gives the latter a nudge, or pulls his hand, looking at him and making the movements of "walking" in the direction desired. One who wishes to receive bananas from another imitates the movement of snatching or grasping, accompanied by intensely pleading glances and pouts. The summoning of another animal from a considerable distance is often accompanied by a beckoning very human in character. . . . Rana, when she wished to be petted, stretched her hand out towards us, and at the same time clumsily stroked and petted herself, while gazing with eager pleading.'[1] We can easily see, therefore, that the earliest speech sounds were likely to be subsidiary to action and gesture, as we have concluded that they were.

Why, then, did speech finally emerge as the chief means of com-

[1] Köhler, p. 319 f.

munication and expression? What were the advantages of speech over gesture that caused this result? Speech carries out of sight and is useful in the dark; it leaves the limbs and eyes free for other occupations; and it is capable of an infinitely greater variety of expression. It is plain, however, that during untold millennia most of these advantages of speech would not operate. Animal cries, as well as speech, carry out of sight, and speech would not be needed for that purpose. Speech needed the visible surroundings for its meanings. Man did not use speech in the dark: when day ended he slept. As gesture long continued in use, speech did not leave the hands or eyes free. But it grew in variety; and so, though it originated as a junior partner to gesture – and, in a sense, the offspring of gesture because it was incidental to the action that gesture mimicked – gradually it became the senior partner owing to this greater variety of expression. But it could only express this variety by disengaging itself from gesture. This has been a slow process. Gesture is still used in large measure to supplement speech,[1] to communicate with persons of a foreign tongue or at a distance, or to avoid noise; but the extent of its use to supplement speech varies much from people to people, and if it had remained necessary, written speech would be impossible.

So long have gesture and speech continued in partnership that until comparatively recent times in its history speech has retained many of the same characteristics as gesture, moulded by the same circumstances. We have concluded that, in its earliest days, language consisted of verbs, and though other parts of speech were gradually added, the verbs still constituted almost half of the vocabulary at the close of the Palaeolithic Age. They had still no tenses. The nouns had come next, formed out of the verbs, and then a few adjectives – in number varying much from people to people – at first formed out of the verbs and later from nouns. At the close of the Palaeolithic Age there was also a substantial number of adverbs, formed from verbs, but the proportion decreased later, and it was not till modern times that adverbs were formed in large number out of the adjectives. The pronoun *I* was common from early times, and somewhat later the pronoun *thou*, but pronouns of the third person were unknown. Up to this point, and before the formation of adverbs from the adjectives, it is likely that gesture continued important, for the parts of speech other than verbs and nouns and adverbs were insignificantly represented, especially prepositions and conjunctions. Language has in this respect – that

[1] For an example from the Andaman Islands, see *ante*, p. 57.

is to say, in its function – largely changed its character since, but gesture has remained subject to the same limitations.

For example, Charles Aubert, in his book *L'Art Mimique*,[1] tells of the difficulty of expressing some parts of speech by the silent drama. Personal pronouns of the first and second persons, he says, can be interpreted with ease (for the first and second person are always on the stage), but the personal pronouns of the third person can only be expressed when they apply to people actually present. Demonstrative pronouns can be expressed with even greater ease, but relative pronouns not at all. Verbs constitute 'the life and richness' of the mimetic language. The function of the verb being to represent 'actions, passions and situations', it is 'le mot par excellence et presque le mot unique du langage mimique, puisque la pantomime ne s'exprime que par du mouvement et de l'action' (p. 178). But it is impossible to conjugate the tenses. A gentleman, dressed for the ball, returns home to be greeted by his wife with the remark: 'While you were dancing there, I was weeping here alone.' The words must be enacted as follows: 'Down there – you dance – alone – here – I weep.' Nouns are always represented by actions. The gesture of fanning expresses a fan. 'Give me a key' is enacted by 'give!' and 'what is used for opening'. Adjectives are usually interpreted by verbs. They are divided for this purpose into four classes: adjectives derived from verbs are treated as verbs; adjectives of imitation as verbs of action; adjectives of sensation as verbs of feeling; and adjectives of description are represented by gesture. So, the adjective 'lazy' is represented by an action of indolent walking, and 'happy' by smiling. Colour is impossible to interpret (except by pointing out some visible object of the same hue). This manner of expressing adjectives, says Aubert, is a delicate art. On the other hand, adverbs are enacted without difficulty – being treated as verbs – except adverbs of time (such as *at present, tomorrow, henceforth, all at once*, etc.) which are impossible to represent. Prepositions and conjunctions are impossible to express – but then again they are unnecessary. 'En somme,' says Aubert, 'à part quelques exceptions relativement peu nombreuses, tous les mots que nous pouvous exprimer par la mimique, sont ou deviennent forcément des verbes.' The chapter almost reads as a description, by an eye-witness, of language as we have imagined it in a primitive stage of development during the Old Stone Age.

We may conclude by agreeing with Macdonald Critchley in query-

[1] (1901). English translation by E. Sears, *The Art of Pantomime* (1927).

ing the conclusion of some writers that the earliest human language was a language of gesture. Gesture was not a forerunner so much as an elder brother of speech. It still possesses a number of advantages over speech. Instinctive gestures are international and comprehensible to all. They can be executed more rapidly than speech, and can sometimes express shades of meaning which can only be described in language with elaboration. They can sometimes describe a physical fact (for example a spiral) when it would be difficult or impossible by means of language alone. It seems, therefore, as he says, that gesture should be regarded as an important modality of communication with origins at least as remote and with powers of enriching and enhancing speech.[1]

More recently Paget[2] advanced another theory of the origin of language, which might be called the mouth-gesture theory.

He begins by setting out (p. 126) what he calls 'the conclusions of the philologists' that 'the earliest human language may be said to have been a language of gesture signs'. He adds (p. 132) that 'gestures, which were previously made by hand, were unconsciously copied by movements or positions of the mouth, tongue or lips', and calls to aid the following observation of Darwin: 'There are other actions which are commonly performed under certain circumstances independently of habit, and which seem to be due to imitation or some kind of sympathy. Thus, persons cutting anything with a pair of scissors may be seen to move their jaws simultaneously with the blades of the scissors. Children learning to write often twist about their tongue as their fingers move, in a ridiculous fashion.'[3] Sir R. Paget's argument proceeds that 'originally man expressed his ideas by gesture, but as he gesticulated with his hands, his tongue, lips and jaw unconsciously followed in a ridiculous fashion, "understudying" the action of the hands. The consequence was that when, owing to pressure of other business, the principal actors (the hands) retired from the stage – as much as principal actors ever do – their understudies, the tongue, lips and jaw, were already proficient in the pantomime art. Then,' he suggests, 'the great discovery was made that if, while making a gesture with the tongue and lips, air was blown through the oral or nasal cavities, the gesture became audible as a whispered speech sound', and voiced speech resulted in a similar way. Then our ancestors discovered

[1] Ibid., p. 121.
[2] Sir Richard Paget, *Human Speech* (1930).
[3] Darwin, *The Expression of the Emotions*, p. 35.

that not all gestures of tongue and lips were equally suitable, and they 'limited mouth pantomime to up and down, and to and fro movements. In this way arose a new system of conventional gesture of the organs of articulation from which nearly all human speech took its origin.'[1] So, for example, if, in the course of eating, mouth, tongue and lips are moved, and while this gesture sign is made air is blown through the vocal cavities, we automatically produce *mnyum* or *mnya*, which would be understood everywhere as meaning *to eat*. Similarly the action of sucking produced *sip* or *sup*[2]; and the action of stabbing and spearing *peth*, *puth* or possibly *pul*.[3]

This, like the onomatopoeic, is a dangerous theory. It gives scope for unlimited self-deception, chiefly arising from a feeling of the utter fitness of a word of one's native language for its use. The theory cannot be accepted that mouth gestures were consciously made vocal as the result of a discovery that this could be done by blowing out air. But, like most theories of the origin of speech, it contains some truth. It has the great merit, in the first place, of deriving language from words signifying human actions. We have seen two relevant instances in the Hebrew biliterals: the first consisting of the pairs LQ, LḤ and LSh, all signifying the Indo-European *lick* (Latin lingo, Skt. liḥ, Greek leicho); and the second consisting of the pairs AN, NH and (possibly) NA, all signifying the English nasal expression *moan*. None of these are, properly speaking, instances of Sir R. Paget's process: they are not mouth gestures accompanying and mimicking arm-action; they are imitations of the sounds of licking and moaning.

But we have concluded, in this book, that speech originated in vocal sounds automatically accompanying effort of the arm, and those who wish to do so (adapting and altering to a slight degree Sir R. Paget's theory) may see, in the early biliterals, sounds that to some extent were shaped by gestures of tongue and lips accompanying, shadowing and understudying the action of the arm. Indeed it may be thought that the process which he describes would be likely to begin with the most violent physical action, for it is in such action – every nerve and muscle of the body being strained – that mouth gesture would be most certain, most audible and most distinctive.

A further theory of the origin of speech was proposed some years ago by the Danish linguist Jespersen.[4] So far as it goes it is the reverse

---

[1] Paget, pp. 133-4.
[2] Ibid., p. 137.   [3] Ibid., p. 141.
[4] Chap. 21 of his *Language, Its Nature Development and Origin* (1922); *Ency. Brit.*, art. 'Language'.

of what is suggested in the present book. According to him, 'we must imagine primitive language as consisting (chiefly, at least) of very long words, full of difficult sounds, and sung rather than spoken'. It is the strangest of all theories, but must be taken seriously because of the learning of the author.

Jespersen, unlike many other linguists of the present century, was not prepared to accept the proposition that the origins of speech are unknowable. He rightly maintained that, like other problems, it should be approached upon a broad examination of evidence, but he did not carry out this self-appointed task, and based his conclusions on a small part of the available materials. His theory stands or falls as a whole, but let us look at its parts separately.

He suggests that 'there once was a time when all speech was song, or rather when these two actions were not yet differentiated'.[1] 'Language', he said, 'was born in the courting days of mankind; the first utterances of speech I fancy to myself like something between the nightly love-lyrics of puss upon the tiles and melodious love-songs of the nightingale.'[2] These notions he probably obtained from Darwin. That great scientist, concerned to show the continuity in mind as well as body between man and the other animals, and the continuity between speech and animal cries, suggested that 'primeval man, or rather some progenitor of man, probably first used his voice in producing true musical cadences, that is in singing, as do some of the gibbon-apes at the present day; and we may conclude from a widespread analogy, that this power would have been especially exerted during the courtship of the sexes – would have expressed various emotions, such as love, jealousy, triumph – and would have served as a challenge to rivals. It is, therefore, probable that the imitation of musical cries by articulate [sic][3] sounds may have given rise to words expressive of various complex emotions.'[4] This suggestion occurs in the third chapter of his *Descent of Man*, and is part of a passage which has met with little approval. Everything said in the present book militates against this view. There is little that can be called singing among the gibbons and nothing among the other anthropoid apes.

[1] Ibid., p. 420.
[2] Ibid., p. 434.
[3] This begs the whole question. If primeval man possessed articulate sounds, why did he need to imitate musical cries? And how does one imitate musical cries by articulate sounds?
[4] He ends by saying 'May not some unusually wise ape-like animal have imitated the growl of a beast of prey, and thus told his fellow-monkeys the nature of the expected danger? This would have been a first step in the formation of a language.'

Every human being of normal mental powers can speak, but a vast number are incapable of song. As for courtship, if we are to judge from the habits of the bulk of mankind it has always been a singularly silent occupation. Sexual relations and processes are the last to change in any animal, and if primitive men won their wives by singing, the present situation would be incredible. But the whole conception is not only erroneous but irrelevant. It only adds another animal cry or shriek. By what process does a tone become a word? The two things are wholly disparate. The question, in its narrowest terms, is: How did the consonants come? In the tone languages of which we know, the number of tones employed has generally increased, not decreased, in the course of history. Man's capacity to sing is probably the slow product of his evolution since language appeared. That primitive man was more vocal than woman is possible – but that is another story. When we turn to consider meaning, the theory is even stranger. By what means did love or other emotion form a link in a chain of intellectual development? How did an emotion become a verb or noun? That is the problem that must be answered, and which we have sought to answer in this book.

In these 'singing tunes', says Jespersen, were uttered, at the birth of language, 'very long words full of difficult sounds'.[1] He is led to this conclusion from observing everywhere, as he says, firstly, the tendency to shorten words,[2] and secondly, 'the tendency to make pronunciation more easy, so as to lessen the muscular effort; difficult combinations of sounds are discarded, those only being retained which are pronounced with ease'. Let us consider the length of words first.

There are two tendencies in language – one to lengthen words, the other to shorten them. The latter is a phonetic process – a tendency to reduce the effort required on the part of the speaker, so long as the meaning is understood. So the old I.E. root *gen*, to be born (as in genus and γένος and kin), is reduced to gn (as in *gnatus*) and to *n* alone (as in *natus*). So, too, the initial consonants in the English *know*, *gnaw* and *wrong*, still sounded in the 15th century, have since been dropped. More extensive is the dropping of the endings or unaccented portions of words. But the tendency to *increase* the length of words is equally important, and extends throughout human history. It is wholly unscientific and misleading to separate words from sentences as though they were distinct entities of different characters. Language originated

---

[1] 'Long, conglomerations of sounds . . . long strings of syllables' (*Ency. Brit.*).
[2] Jespersen, p. 328.

in sentences, but sentences which were also single words. In the course of the advance to civilization, man's communications and conceptions have ever increased in number, and his vocabulary has increased. In terms of the sentence, this has meant a noticeable increase in its length. But what is expressed in one language by a solid sentence or phrase (as in Eskimo, Iroquois or Sumerian) is expressed by words in another language. By and large, this has meant an increase in the length of the words as well as the sentences. In English (notwithstanding a certain phonetic shortening) we can hardly fail to notice the contrast between the monosyllabic old Anglo-Saxon words and the sesquipedalian Romance additions to the vocabulary. So, while the old root gen and kin is reduced to a single n, it has expanded into *naturalization*. Jespersen harps upon the long Latin words – hominibus nobilibus, cantavisset[1] and other Latin quadrisyllables. But Latin is a modern language in the sense of this book. The difference is not a matter of date but of economic and mental advance. It is not true that the vocabularies of the Food Gatherers consist of 'long strings of sounds'. In North America and Australia there are some solid phrases; in Bushman and Andamanese there is nothing of the sort. But a consideration of the speech of children makes the theory even stranger. Nothing is plainer than the inability of a modern child, when speech commences, to pronounce a word of more than one syllable unless the syllables are identical. To change the 'set' of the vocal organs between one syllable and the next is at first impossible. We can see that, unless primitive man was born with mature vocal powers, as Pallas Athene sprang fully armed from the head of Zeus, the 'long words' or 'strings of syllables' that Jespersen imagines can only have been repetitions of one consonant and vowel.

As for the elimination of 'difficult sounds', this is part of the second process mentioned above, by which the effort of pronunciation is reduced to a minimum. So *gnatus* becomes *natus*, and the difficulty of the 'gn' is eliminated. But it cannot have been very difficult to those who spoke it; and even if it was, the difficulty was only created when the intermediate *e* was dropped. If this had created a difficulty, it would not have been dropped. But the whole theory is remarkable in the extreme. Does it require to be supported by argument, that when man was first producing consonants and articulate speech, he could only have done so by degrees, and that he must first have acquired the sounds easiest to him, whatever they were? Especially must they have

[1] Elaborated by grammatical apparatus from hŏmo, gno- and cano.

been the easiest sounds, when the existence of a language depended on the ability of the individual readily to pronounce and hear them. It is impossible to look at the world's languages without noticing the number of tongues in which the syllables are of the form CV, and it is impossible to resist the inference that this is because these are the easiest for man to pronounce, just as they are the earliest articulate sounds of human babes. And the commonest sounds in the world's languages – initial p, t, k, b, d, g, n, m and the vowel A – are also the easiest to pronounce, and they change the least in the history of words[1] and are also the sounds of the earliest words of human babes.

The last theory that we shall mention was adduced over a century ago, in the early days of modern linguistics. In 1823 was published in Edinburgh *The History of the European Languages*, by Alexander Murray, D.D. It was published from his papers after his death, and if he had lived, no doubt he would have made further progress. In this work[2] he sets out 9 words which he calls 'the foundations of language. ... They were uttered at first, and probably for several generations, in an insulated manner. The circumstances of the actions were communicated by gestures and the variable tunes of the voice; but the actions themselves were expressed by their suitable monosyllable.' They were as follows:

'I. To strike or move with swift equable penetrating or sharp effect was AG! AG!

If the motion was less sudden but of the same species, WAG.

If made with force, and a great effort, HWAG.

These are varieties of one word, originally used to mark the motion of fire, water, wind, darts.

II. To strike with a quick, vigorous, compelling force, BAG or BWAG, of which FAG and PAG are softer varieties.

III. To strike with a harsh, violent, strong blow, DWAG of which THWAG and TWAG are varieties.

IV. To move or strike with a quick, tottering, unequal impulse, GWAG or CWAG.

V. To strike with a pliant slap, LAG and HLAG.

VI. To press by strong force or impulse, so as to condense, bruise or compel, MAG.

VII. To strike with a crushing, destroying power, NAG and HNAG.

---

[1] See Jespersen himself at p. 199, quoting Meillet.   [2] Vol. 1, p. 312.

VIII. To strike with a strong, rude, sharp, penetrating power, RAG or HRAG.

IX. To move with a weighty, strong impulse, SWAG.'

Dr Murray's theory was not known to me when the nucleus of the present book was arrived at, but it is widely known, and has been referred to ever since his day with amusement and ribaldry. It contains obvious errors; but it attributes the beginnings of articulate speech to a small number of monosyllables signifying various types of striking, the first of which, AG, signifies 'to strike ... with swift ... penetrating or sharp effect'. If the views contained in the present book are correct, Dr Murray had already achieved a portion of the truth.

FINIS

List of Abbreviated References

Adam.   Lucien Adam, *Grammaire de la langue Jâgane* (Paris, 1885).
Ar.   Arabic.
As.   Assyrian.
B.A.E.   *Bureau of American Ethnology, Annual Reports.*
Bentley.   W. H. Bentley, *Dictionary and Grammar of the Kongo Language* (1887).
Bleek, *Naron.*   D. F. Bleek, *The Naron* (1928).
Boas, *Chinook.   Chinook*, by Franz Boas, in *H.A.I.L.*, Part I, pp. 562 f.
Ellis.   Report of Researches into the language of the South Andaman Island, arranged by A. J. Ellis from the papers of E. H. Man and R. C. Temple – an appendix to *The Andaman Islanders* by E. H. Man (1932 ed.).
Eth.   Ethnology.
Evolution of Law and Order, by A. S. Diamond (1951).
Goddard.   P. E. Goddard, *Athapascan* (Hupa), in *H.A.I.L.*, Part I, p. 91 f.
H.A.I.L.   *Handbook of American Indian Languages*, ed. by Franz Boas, Bureau of American Ethnology, Bulletin 40.
Hobhouse.   *Mind in Evolution*, by L. T. Hobhouse.
Hollis, *Masai.* A. C. Hollis, *The Masai* (1905).
Homburger.   L. Homburger, *The Negro-African Languages* (London, 1949).
Jespersen.   O. Jespersen, *Language, Its Nature, Development and Origin* (1922).
Johnston.   Sir H. Johnston, *A Comparative Study of the Bantu and Semi-Bantu Languages* (1919).
J.R.A.I.   *Journal of the Royal Anthropological Institute.*
Köhler.   W. Köhler, *The Mentality of Apes* (1925).
Lewis.   M. M. Lewis, *Infant Speech* (1936).
Maingard.   L. F. Maingard, *The Khomani Dialect of Bushman*, in *Bushmen of the Southern Kalahari*, ed. by Jones and Doke (1937).
Max Müller.   *Lectures on the Science of Language*, 9th ed. (1877).

LIST OF ABBREVIATED REFERENCES

Meaning of Meaning, by C. K. Ogden and I. A. Richards, 6th ed. (1944).
Meillet.   A. Meillet, *Linguistique Historique et Linguistique Générale*.
Meillet & Cohen.   A. Meillet & M. Cohen   *Les Langues du Monde*.
Morrison.   W. M. Morrison, *Grammar and Dictionary of the Buluba-Lulua Language* (New York, 1906).
Negus.   V. E. Negus, *The Mechanism of the Larynx* (1929).
Paget.   Sir R. Paget, *Human Speech* (1890).
Primitive Law.   A. S. Diamond, *Primitive Law* (1935, 2nd ed. 1950).
Ray.   S. H. Ray, *A Comparative Study of the Melanesian Island Languages* (1926).
Sayce.   A. H. Sayce, *Introduction to the Science of Language* (4th ed. 1900).
Strehlow.   T. G. H. Strehlow, *Aranda Phonetics and Grammar* (1942).
Uhlenbeck.   C. C. Uhlenbeck, *A Concise Blackfoot Grammar* (Amsterdam, 1938).
Valentine.   C. W. Valentine, *The Psychology of Early Childhood* (3rd ed., 1946).
Westermann.   D. Westermann, *A Study of the Ewe Language* (trans. by A. L. Bickford-Smith, 1930).
Whitney, L. G.   W. Dwight-Whitney, *The Life and Growth of Language* (1896 ed.)
Wright.   W. Wright, *Comparative Grammar of the Semitic Languages* (1890)
Yerkes and Learned.   *Chimpanzee Intelligence*, by Yerkes and Learned (Baltimore, 1922).

Index

Acholi, 113, 135
Agriculture, primitive, 40-42
Ainu, 113, 135
America, North, 41, 49, 56, 102. *See* individual languages
Andaman, 40, 56-58, 85, 96, 99, 102, 113, 273
Anglo-Saxon, *See* English, Old
Animal behaviour, 142 *et seq.*
Animal cries, 16, 263
Aorist, 130 *et seq.*
Arabic, 52, 109, 116, 125, 184, 221-237, 250
Aramaic, 207, 225, 226, 230-233
Aranda, 56, 98, 107, 109, 110, 265
Armenian, 131, 141
Assyrian, 44, 116, 130, 164, 167, 206, 221, 225-238
Australians, 40, 52, 55, 91, 102, 113, 265, 273
Azande, 47, 50, 202

Babylonian. *See* Assyrian
Bantu, 44, 52, 53, 83, 89, 100, 113, 116, 127, 134, 137, 182, 198, 221, 249
Bari, 55, 135, 207
Beowulf, 30
Bini, 48, 51
Blackfoot, 41, 49, 56, 99, 102, 113, 135
Browning, 36
Bugotu, 43, 49
Buluba-Lulua, 47, 50, 100, 101, 127, 183, 206
Burns, 36

Bushman, 40, 55, 83, 85, 89, 90, 98, 99, 135, 187, 206, 273

Canara, 91, 102, 113
Chaucer, 24
Children's speech, 94, 95, 97, 169-172, 201-208
Chimpanzees, 147, 150, 152-161, 208, 262
Chinese, 91, 219
Chinook, 41, 49
Consonants, 17, 68-72, 76, 78, 82-86, 186-200, 202 *et seq.*, 213, 219-257
Coos, 136
Copula, 22, 181-185

Dante, 24
Description-statement, 19, 120
Dialect, 10, 191
Dinka, 45, 50, 84, 113
Duke of York Island, 43, 49
Dyola, 118

English, Middle, 29, 51
English, Old, 29-31, 50, 124, 132, 133, 163, 175, 216, 260

Fijian, 43, 49, 53, 79, 103, 113, 118
Finnish, 90, 113, 131
Finno-Ugrian, 90, 113, 119, 123, 131, 137, 141
Food gatherers, 40, 122, 142
French, 108, 168, 169, 183, 207, 216, 217, 227

Galla, 125
Ganda, 48, 51, 183

INDEX

Gender, 99
German, 124, 125, 133, 183, 184, 216, 217
Gesture, 151 et seq., 265 et seq.
Grammar, 93 et seq.
Greek, 48, 51, 111, 116, 124, 127, 129-135, 167, 176, 182, 183, 206, 207, 220, 224, 228, 237-239, 260, 264

Haida, 96
Hamitic, 44, 77, 89, 113, 123, 125, 133, 144, 221
Hausa, 48, 130, 187, 206
Hawaian, 43, 49, 118, 197
Hebrew, 24, 51-53, 76, 99, 103, 112, 119, 125, 130, 167, 176, 182-184, 206, 221-255, 264
Hittite, 99, 116
Homer, 24, 30, 52, 131, 137, 183
Hungarian, 90, 119, 123, 131, 141
Hupa, 101, 184

Ila, 134
Imperative. *See* Request for action
Indo-European, 103, 111, 116, 127, 137, 140, 183, 196, 206, 219, 222, 227, 229, 232-239, 249
Indonesian, 113, 206
Infinitive, 123 et seq.
Interjections, 263-269
Iroquois, 41, 273
Italian, 127

Johnson's dictionary, 29, 51

Kamba, 45, 50, 83
Keats, 36
Kikuyu, 45, 50, 83, 183
Kongo, 47, 50, 104

Lango, 45, 50, 55, 84, 89, 113, 135, 207-217
Language, 9-13

Larynx, 187, 209 et seq.
Latin, 48, 51, 66-69, 111, 114, 115, 132, 135, 167, 175, 182-184, 206, 207, 224-239, 264, 273

Malagasy, 118
Malay, 91, 96
Malayo-Polynesian, 42, 52, 102, 113, 135. *And see* Polynesian, Melanesian
Manchu, 91
Mangarevan, 118
Maori, 43, 49, 53, 85, 103, 113, 116, 118, 124, 197, 206
Masai, 108, 135, 184, 185, 206
Mayombe, 46, 50
Meaning, 9, 17, 84, 86, 129, 162-185, 214 et seq.
Melanesian, 42, 91, 99, 103, 113, 135, 206
Metaphor, 166, et seq.
Milton, 24, 34, 35
Mongolian, 90
Mon-Khmer, 91, 102, 242
Mordvin, 119
Mota, 43, 49, 113, 115, 206
Motu, 80, 118

Nandi, 89, 113, 116, 136, 141
Natick, 41, 49
Negative, 115, 200
Nuer, 89
Nupe, 113, 135

Onomatopoeia, 92-94, 241, 244, 245, 259-263
Ostyak, 119

Particular languages, 10, 37, 38
Parts of speech, 17, 18
Pastoralists, 44
Phonetics, 190 et seq.
Physiology of speech, 186 et seq., 209 et seq.

Plosive consonants, 190 et seq., 202-208, 213, 214, 246-248
Polynesian, 42, 43, 84, 103, 116, 118, 197, 219
Pope, 36
Pronouns, 88 et seq.

Quileute, 81

Reduplication, 203-206, 217
Request for action, 19-22, 111-122, 129, 143-145
Roots, 66-92, 111 et seq., 123 et seq., 130 et seq., 240 et seq.

Sa'a and Ulawa, 43, 49
Samoan, 43, 49, 53, 80, 197
Samoyed, 90, 113
Sanskrit, 68, 131, 141, 183, 228
Semitic, 44, 52, 71, 76, 88, 89, 101, 111, 115, 116, 123, 125, 130, 133, 137, 140, 141, 144
Sentences, 9, 16, 17, 18-22, 120, 121
Serer, 118
Shakespeare, 24-37, 51
Shelley, 36,
Shilluk, 45, 50, 84, 116, 118
Siamese, 135
Slavonic, 131, 141, 206

Somali, 109, 113, 125, 133
Speech, 9, 12, 186 et seq.
Spenser, 24, 35
Statement, 19-22, 130 et seq.
Suahili, 48, 51, 127
Sudanic, 89, 113, 133, 137
Sumerian, 44, 81, 88, 97, 101, 112, 116
Suslawan, 56, 81

Tahitian, 118, 197
Takelma, 56, 113
Tamil, 91, 102, 113
Telugu, 102, 113
Tennyson, 36
Theories of origin of language, 258-275
Tibertan, 113, 141
Tongan, 43, 49, 113, 197
Tonkawa, 56
Tsimshian, 100, 116, 118
Tungusian, 90
Turkish, 90, 113, 131, 133, 137, 141

Vowels, 68, 72, 186 et seq., 202 et seq., 213, 215

Wordsworth, 36
Writing, effect of, 10-12